I0819518

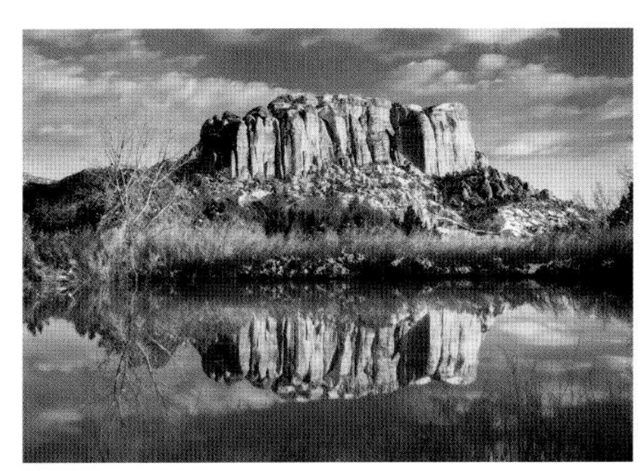

GHOST RANCH

and the Faraway Nearby

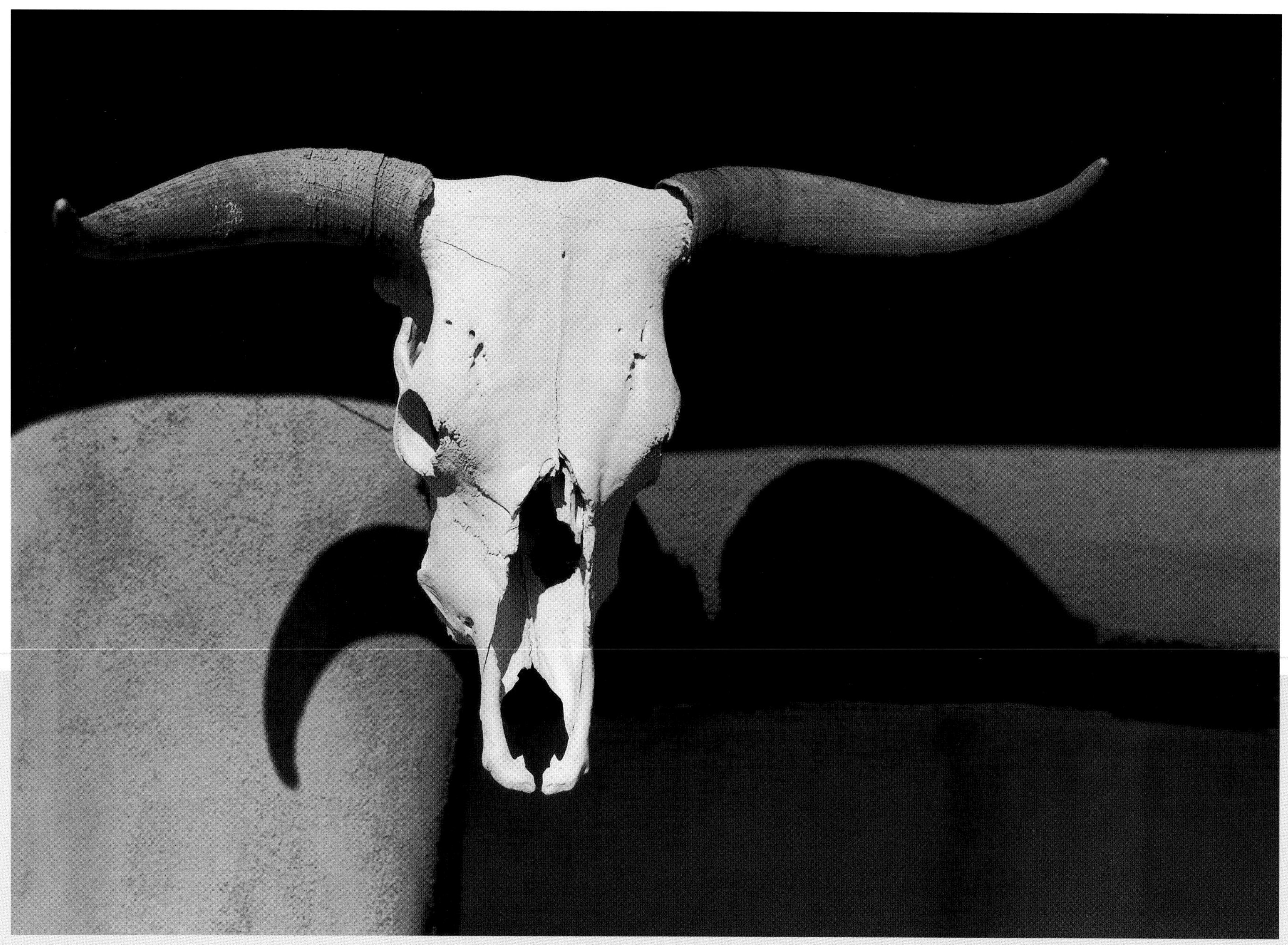

GHOST RANCH

and the Faraway Nearby

PHOTOGRAPHS BY

Craig Varjabedian

INTRODUCTION BY

Jay Packer

ESSAYS BY

Marin Sardy, Belden C. Lane,
Douglas A. Fairfield, AND Rob Craig

AFTERWORD BY

Georgia O'Keeffe

UNIVERSITY OF NEW MEXICO PRESS
ALBUQUERQUE

Presentation of the exhibition at the Albuquerque Museum of Art and History was funded with support from the National Endowment for the Humanities *We the People* Initiative and the New Mexico Humanities Council: Helping New Mexicans discover who we were, who we are and who we hope to be. Additional funding has been provided by the National Ghost Ranch Foundation.

(Frontispiece)
Plate 1: Cow Skull on Ghost House, Ghost Ranch, New Mexico, 2006

PRINTED AND BOUND in China by Everbest Printing Company Ltd. through Four Colour Imports, Ltd.
13 12 11 10 09 1 2 3 4 5

LIBRARY OF CONGRESS CATALOGING-IN-PUBLICATION DATA

Varjabedian, Craig, 1957–
Ghost Ranch and the faraway nearby / photographs by Craig Varjabedian ;
essays by Jay Packer . . . [et. al.]; afterword by Georgia O'Keeffe. — 1st ed.
p. cm.
Includes bibliographical references.
ISBN 978-0-8263-3621-7 (hardcover : alk. paper)
1. Abiquiu Region (N.M.)—Pictorial works. 2. Abiquiu Region (N.M.)—Description and travel.
3. Ghost Ranch (Abiquiu, N.M.)—Pictorial works. 4. Ghost Ranch (Abiquiu, N.M.)—Description and travel. I. Title.
F804.A23V37 2009
978.9'52—dc22
2008046273

MAP (*p. xv*) by Bette Brodsky
QUOTE (*p. 17*) Adams, Ansel. *Ansel Adams: Letters and Images 1916-1984*. Edited by Mary Street Alinder and Andrea Gray Stillman. First edition. (Boston: Little, Brown, 1988), 98.
BOOK DESIGN AND TYPE COMPOSITION by Melissa Tandysh

A NOTE ABOUT THE TYPE

The text in *Ghost Ranch and the Faraway Nearby* was set in Dante, a serif font with a subtle horizontal stress. It was collaboratively designed in the 1950s by Giovanni Mardersteig of the Officina Bodoni and Charles Malin of Monotype, who adapted it for letterpress use. Freed from the constraints of older typesetting technologies, Monotype designers again reworked the Dante type style in the 1990s to better capture the liveliness, elegance, and legibility of Mardersteig's original design. The display type was set in Cronos, designed by Robert Slimbach of Adobe Systems. Cronos is a sans serif font that still retains elements of old-style typefaces inspired by Italian Renaissance calligraphy. Cronos offers a warmth and fluidity of form suggestive of the handwritten word.

DEDICATION

TO

Arthur Newton Pack,

who discovered the real treasure of Ghost Ranch,

TO

Reverend David Rogge,

who planted the seeds that became this volume,

AND TO

the generations of individuals, past, present, and future,

who find inspiration, transformation, and renewal

in the beauty, awe and sanctuary of this unique place.

CONTENTS

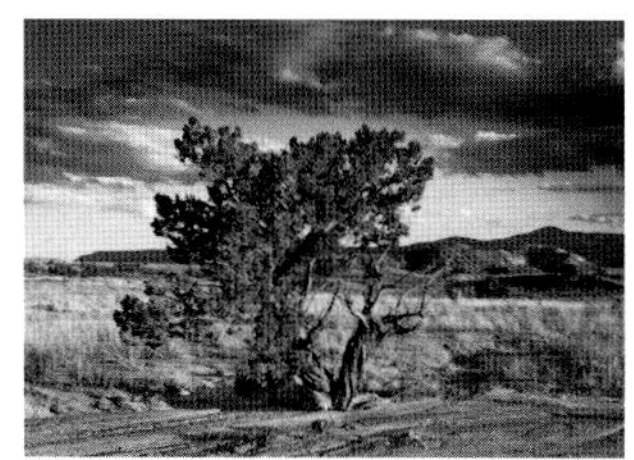

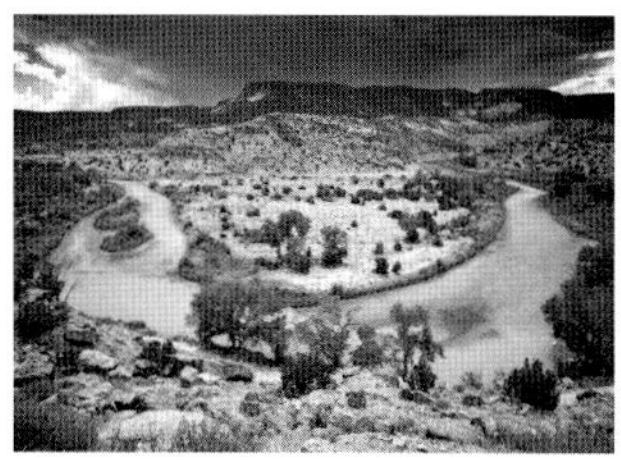

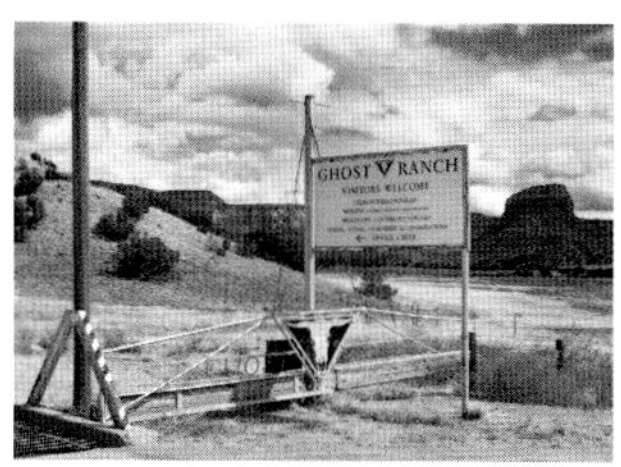

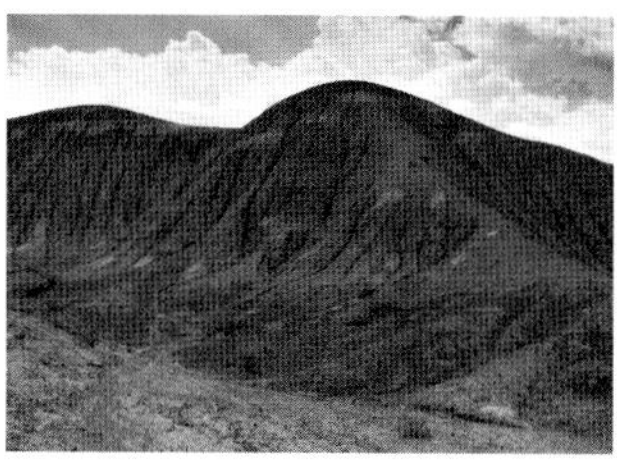

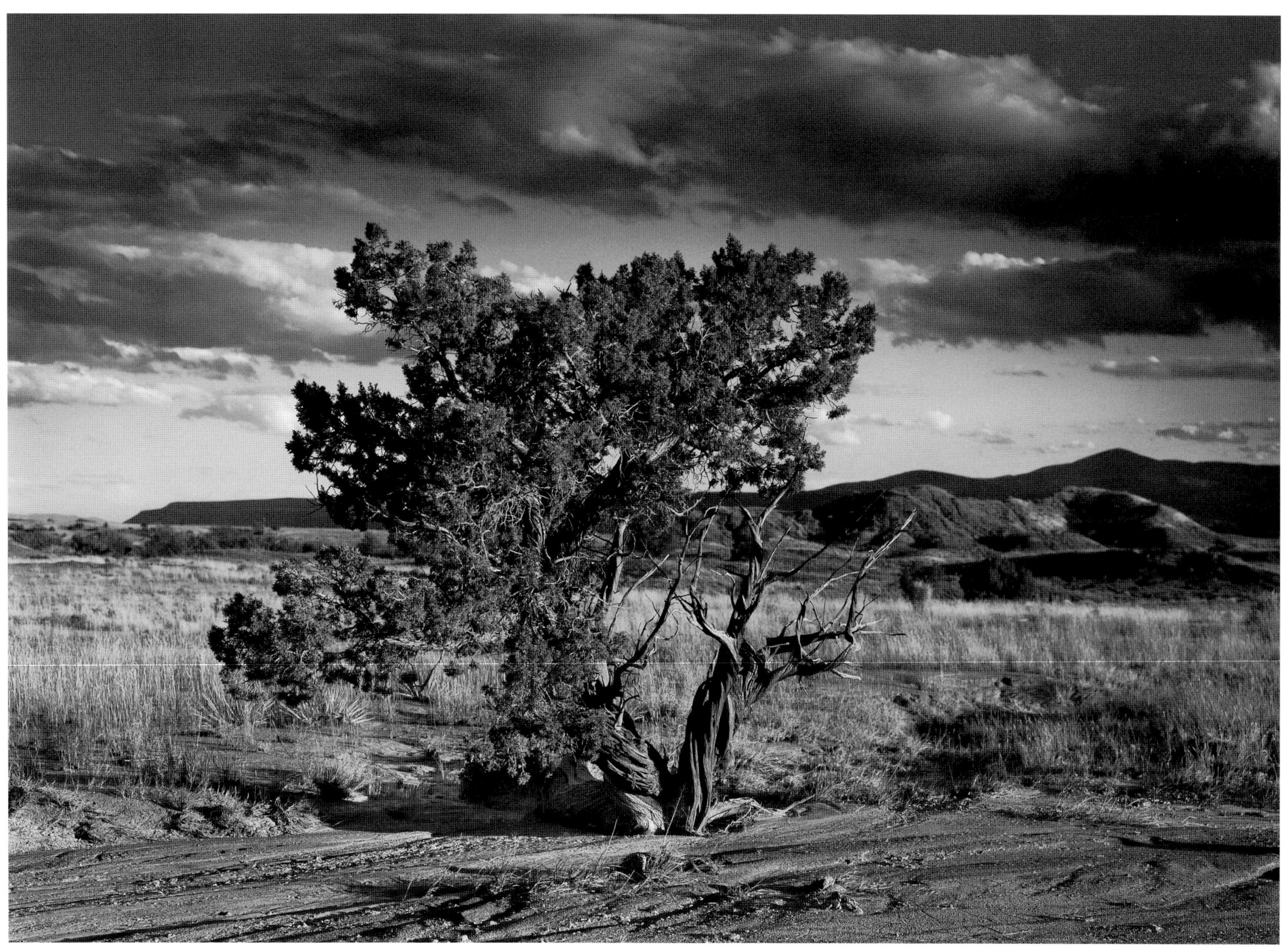

Plate 2: Old Juniper, Painted Desert (Arroyo Seco Pasture), Ghost Ranch, New Mexico, 2004

RANCH DIRECTOR'S FOREWORD | *Ghost Ranch: Transformation* | DEBRA HEPLER

IN OUR CULTURE, THE ELUSIVE WORD "TRANSFORM" HAS BEEN used to describe anything: a child's toy; a home renovation; a mountaintop experience. It is often heard at Ghost Ranch from the mouths of artists and theologians, first-time guests and life-timers, teens and elders, those seeking to find themselves and those thinking they've got life all figured out. Like you and me, all are ordinary people experiencing the serendipity that places us in this time and space.

Ghost Ranch is an enigma. Its history encompasses dinosaurs roaming millions of years before us, landscapes formed by oceans and seismic climate changes, and *gallinas* settled by common ancestors. Its present unfolds as a place of personal development, of awe in God and in our own awakened capabilities.

Native Americans, Spanish explorers, cattle rustlers, debutantes, artists: all shared this special place. This commonality of experience reminds us that Ghost Ranch does not "belong" to anyone, neither persons nor peoples, no matter how often either tries to capture it.

Ghost Ranch is a gift, by God and of God, for our pleasure and our transformation. Transformation from the artificial worlds we've created for ourselves into the real essence of our being. In us, "being" and "creating" have become lost arts; in Ghost Ranch, we can revel in them as they are revealed in us.

Mountains of flint and the dusty sage may appear as static desert, but the changing reflections of sun and moon against the rock speak otherwise, and release us from our incessant need to analyze and understand. These are proof that it is always a new moment, a new day, a new life at Ghost Ranch.

How do we portray this transformation? How do we tell of a personal, encompassing, spiritual experience?

Craig Varjabedian, as a vessel with a lens, conveys the wonder and splendor of Ghost Ranch, deftly releasing the landscape's revealed transcendence and cradling it for us who see less clearly. Listen as his photography calls us into that transcendence, and wait for the echoing transformation in our souls.

Debra Hepler is executive director of Ghost Ranch.

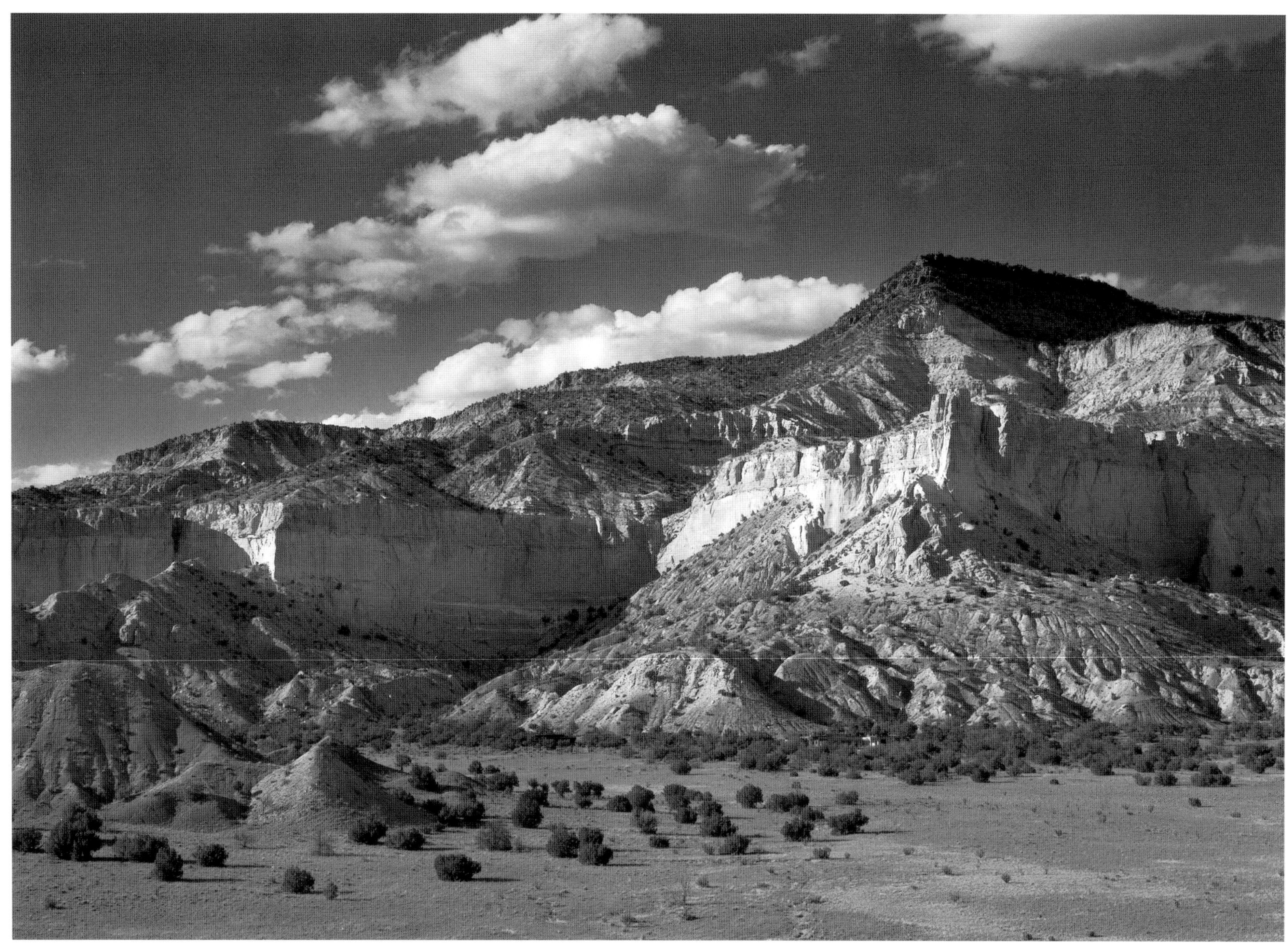

Plate 3: Cliff Face and Hills, Summer, Ghost Ranch, New Mexico, 2005

MUSEUM DIRECTOR'S FOREWORD | CATHY L. WRIGHT

THE ALBUQUERQUE MUSEUM OF ART AND HISTORY IS PLEASED to present a project that brings together Craig Varjabedian, one of New Mexico's best photographers, with one of the state's icons of history and culture, Ghost Ranch. The unique geologic wonders of this magical place near Abiquiu first came into public view after the artist Georgia O'Keeffe featured them in her paintings. O'Keeffe's pictures depicted her perceptions and feelings about the place she called home, and those of us who have experienced Ghost Ranch recognize in her work the extraordinary things that can be seen and sensed there.

In 1994 the Albuquerque Museum exhibited Craig's first major body of photographs, *En Divina Luz: The Penitente Moradas of New Mexico*. I've known Craig for twenty years, also working with him on his exhibition *By the Grace of Light*. With *Ghost Ranch and the Faraway Nearby* Craig now has produced three enduring projects that combine fine art and documentary photography, and establish him as an artist of consequence, one who is able to make the essence of New Mexico visible to us all.

We want to thank the City of Albuquerque and the Cultural Services Department, as well as the Albuquerque Museum Foundation, for their continuous support of our programs.

With great appreciation for Craig's expertise in his art and his evocation of this special place, Ghost Ranch, we are honored to present his latest body of work. It is an exhibition that captures a sense of place through the aesthetic of photography, and that invites the viewer to be transported and participate in its being. It is a visual journey into the heart, mind, and soul.

Cathy L. Wright is director of the Albuquerque Museum of Art and History.

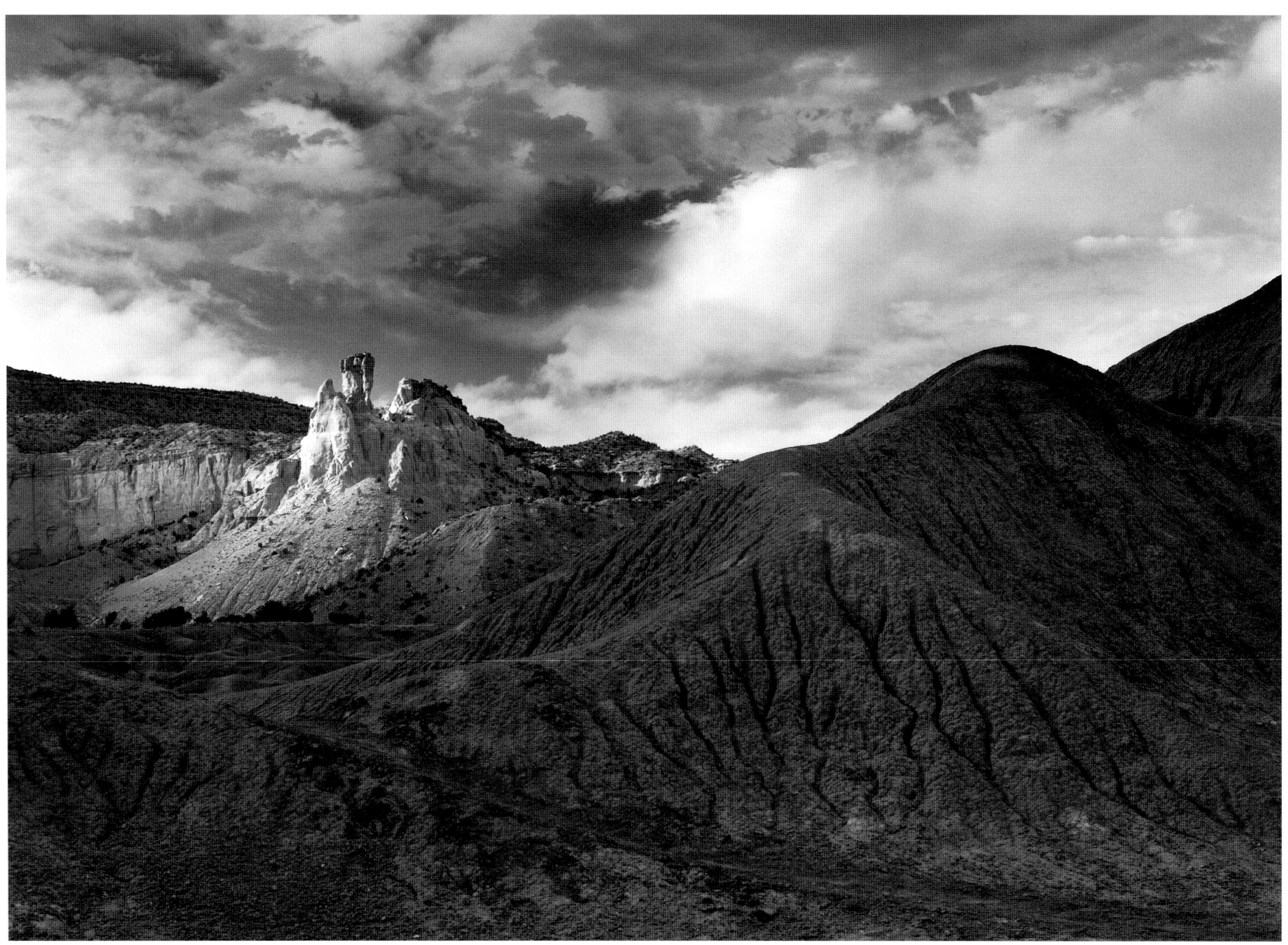

Plate 4: Chimney Rock and the Red Hills of Ghost Ranch, New Mexico, 2007

PREFACE | CRAIG VARJABEDIAN

Of all the things I wondered about on this land, I wondered the hardest about the seduction of certain geographies that feel like home—not by story or blood but merely by their forms and colors. How our perceptions are our only internal map of the world, how there are places that claim you and places that warn you away. How you can fall in love with the light.

—ELLEN MELOY[1]

WITH AN ALMOST CRYSTALLINE CLARITY I REMEMBER THE FIRST time I saw Chimney Rock and the red hills of Ghost Ranch. Shortly after I arrived in New Mexico in 1985 my friend Dan took me to Abiquiu, just northwest of Santa Fe, to see the place that so powerfully captured the heart of painter Georgia O'Keeffe. When I arrived, I knew I had come home: it was at Ghost Ranch that, on some profound level, I learned to make photographs.

I returned to Ghost Ranch whenever I could. I wandered its sandstone cliffs, ochre hills, pinnacles, and arroyos with my camera. Becoming quiet, I somehow matched my rhythms to those of the land, listened to its instruction, and waited for the light to unfold.

While working on my book *En Divina Luz: The Penitente Moradas of New Mexico*,[2] I went to Ghost Ranch to confer with David Rogge, then development director for the ranch, seeking his advice about grant writing to complete my photographic work. As we walked toward the dining hall from his office, David said, "You ought to do a book on Ghost Ranch," and the seeds were sown. I remember looking out across the alfalfa field, fixing my gaze on Pack's Point, and feeling absolutely overwhelmed by the idea of creating a body of work about this powerful and vast landscape. I was engulfed by a sense of inadequacy to make images that dared approach the awe I experienced in its presence.

Much to my regret, David was called home far too early to see the results of the seeds he planted.

For more than twenty years I have explored and photographed Ghost Ranch. As I look back, it seems that the land has been both my subject and my patient teacher. Here I have learned that light has moods: it comes to life, flourishes, and then dies. It can be fleeting and evanescent, disappearing before my camera and I have a chance to respond. And sometimes, like a benediction, the photographer and the camera become aligned with the unfolding moment and an exceptional photograph is made. But not always. More often than not photographers have experiences similar to those of fishermen, who speak with great enthusiasm about the big one that got away.

Photographing this landscape affirmed something too that I had learned from celebrated twentieth-century photographer Paul Caponigro. He explained to me over one long darkroom session that the earth has an intelligence and even a pulse all its own. When I finally learned to quiet myself and turn off the internal dialogue and the judgmental mind and allowed myself to truly be present in the moment, I discovered that I was exploring a place that was quite literally alive. Free to allow my eye to wander without preconception or expectation, I explored the land, receptive to impressions that would harmonize somewhere deep inside, unearthing moments of extreme clarity. Meaningful photographs would often materialize almost as if by magic on the ground glass of my camera.

This book is not an exhaustive catalogue of Ghost Ranch. I did not seek to photograph Ghost Ranch in its entirety: a wide and varied landscape representing almost 21,000 acres, much of it not easily accessed. And there were places on the ranch that simply did not call me to photograph them. Often an intimate arrangement of rocks and juniper trees is as eloquent as a large mesa bathed in the glow of afternoon sun light set against a dramatic sky.

The photographs in this book are sequenced to evoke a kinship with the wide range of experiences I had while contemplating and photographing this land. It is my hope through my work with a camera to discover and reveal hidden aspects of man's relationship with the land and possibly with something greater than himself.

Eckhart Tolle once wrote:

> You are not separate from nature. We are all part of the One Life that manifests itself in countless forms throughout the universe, forms that are all completely interconnected. When you recognize the sacredness, the beauty, the incredible stillness and dignity in which a flower or a tree exists, you add something to the flower and the tree. Through your recognition, your awareness, nature too comes to know itself. It comes to know its own beauty and sacredness through you.[3]

In the end, places like Ghost Ranch defy our explanations of them. While certainly a landscape can be explained in terms of the different strata of rock in a landform or the flora and fauna that occupy the space, for me the true meaning of a place transcends the words we use to describe it. Ghost Ranch, and places like it, exist simply to exist. In so doing they can inspire and instruct, they can transform and heal us and perhaps help us find our place and connection in the world.

Craig Varjabedian
Santa Fe, New Mexico

Notes

1. Ellen Meloy, *The Anthropology of Turquoise: Meditations on Landscape, Art, and Spirit* (New York: Pantheon Books, 2002), front inside cover.
2. Craig Varjabedian, *En Divina Luz: The Penitente Moradas of New Mexico* (Albuquerque: University of New Mexico Press, 1994).
3. Eckhart Tolle, *Stillness Speaks* (Novato, CA: New World Library, 2003), 84.

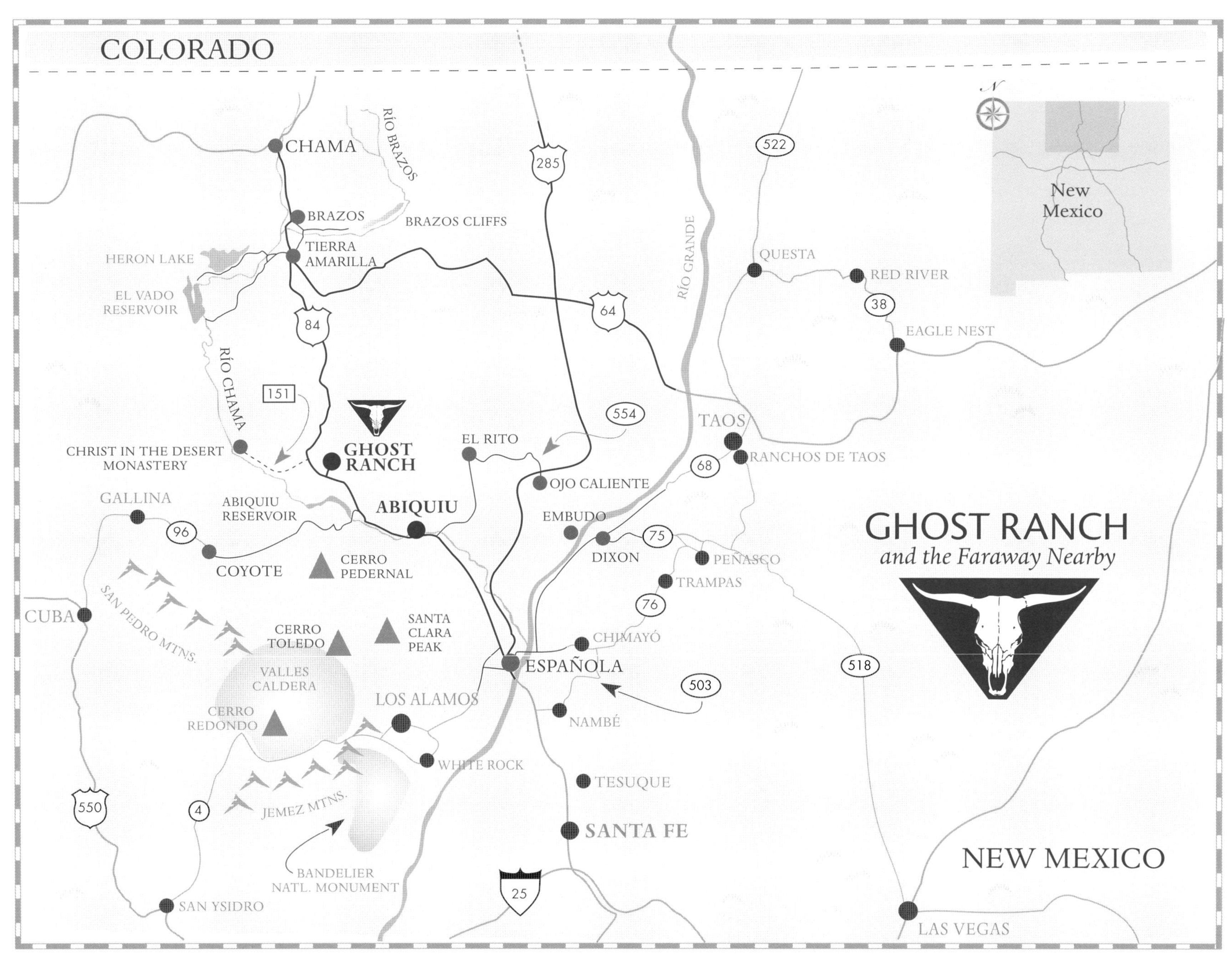

COLORADO
CHAMA
RÍO BRAZOS
285
522
BRAZOS
BRAZOS CLIFFS
New
Mexico
HERON LAKE
TIERRA
AMARILLA
RÍO GRANDE
QUESTA
RED RIVER
EL VADO
RESERVOIR
38
64
84
EAGLE NEST
RÍO CHAMA
151
554
TAOS
GHOST
RANCH
EL RITO
CHRIST IN THE DESERT
MONASTERY
RANCHOS DE TAOS
68
OJO CALIENTE
GALLINA
ABIQUIU
RESERVOIR
ABIQUIU
EMBUDO
GHOST RANCH
and the Faraway Nearby
96
75
DIXON
PEÑASCO
COYOTE
CERRO
PEDERNAL
TRAMPAS
76
SAN PEDRO MTNS.
CUBA
SANTA
CLARA
PEAK
CERRO
TOLEDO
CHIMAYÓ
518
ESPAÑOLA
VALLES
CALDERA
503
LOS ALAMOS
CERRO
REDONDO
NAMBÉ
WHITE ROCK
TESUQUE
550
4
JEMEZ MTNS.
SANTA FE
NEW MEXICO
BANDELIER
NATL. MONUMENT
25
SAN YSIDRO
LAS VEGAS

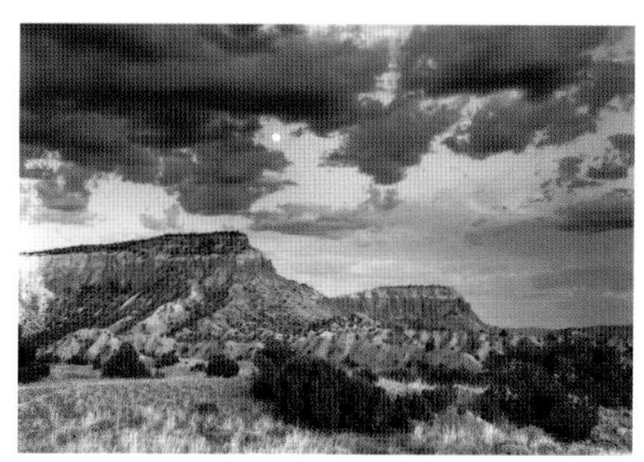

GHOST RANCH

and the Faraway Nearby

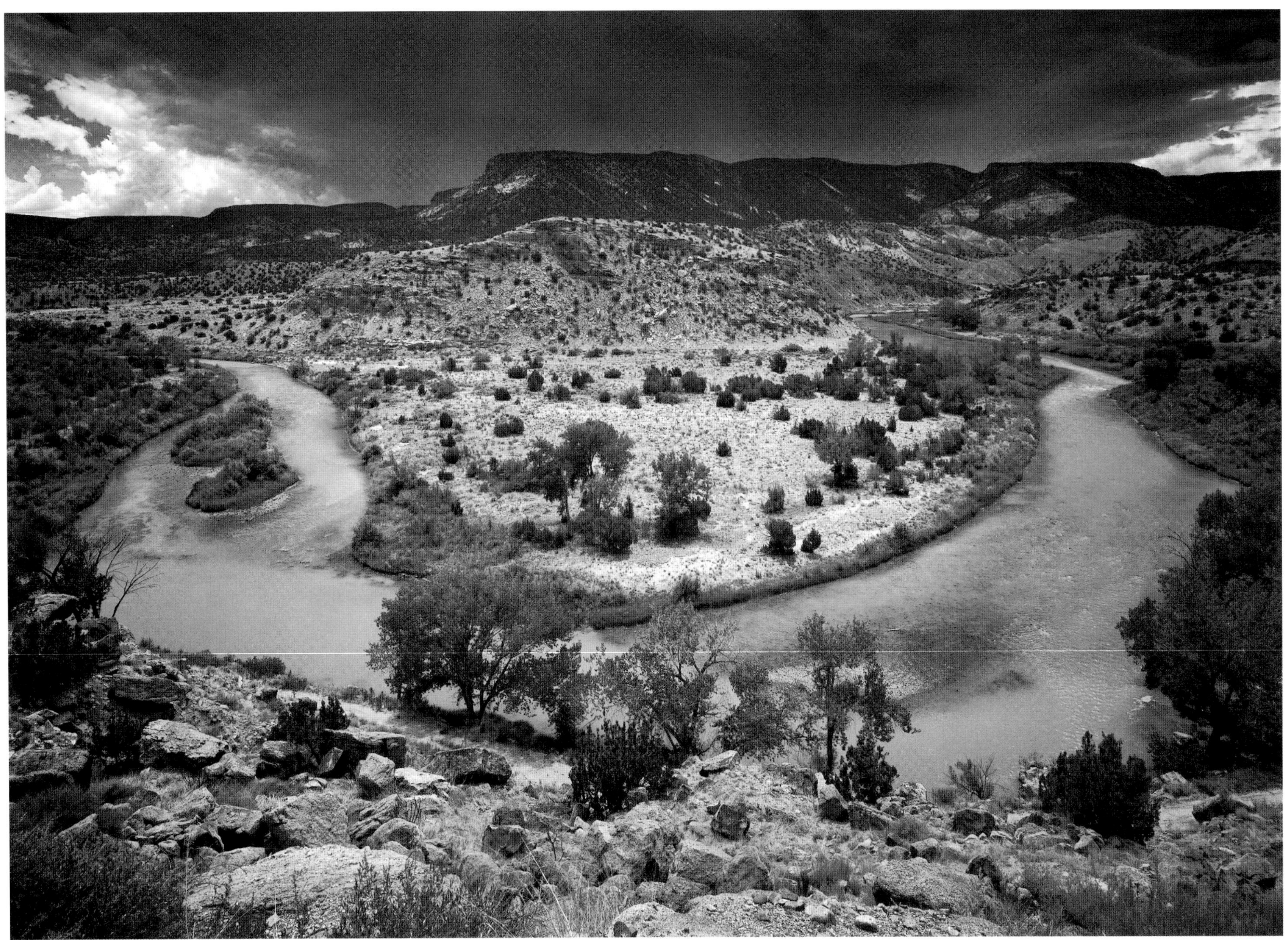

Plate 5: Bend of the Rio Chama and Approaching Storm, near Abiquiu, New Mexico, 2006

FARAWAY

Introduction

JAY PACKER

High in the San Juan Mountains of southern Colorado, the rivulets that will become the Rio Chama trickle from beneath an alpine snowfield. Sunshine and gravity drive meltwater on a long downhill run through northern New Mexico to join the residue of spring showers, the effluent of summer thunderstorms, and a smattering of smaller tributaries for eventual union with the storied Rio Grande just north of Española. In its course, the river winds though canyons, reservoirs, and pasturelands, past fertile fields, towering mesas, and silent mountains, toward the basin known as the Piedra Lumbre, the Land of Shining Stone.

On the southern edge of the basin just above the Abiquiu Dam, El Rito del Yeso, the "Little River of Gypsum," joins the Rio Chama. The angular canyons and mesas slowly sculpted by this small stream over the immensity of geologic time are currently known to us as Ghost Ranch.

Many come to the Ranch for a week or two of rest, reflection, and recreation. They hike beneath the silent stone walls in the cool of the morning, watch spreading cumulonimbus clouds coalesce in the immense blue dome of the afternoon sky, marvel at the sandstone spires and eroded ochre badlands shining in the warm rays of the setting sun. For these visitors, the light and land are generous and open: a respite from urban stress and sprawl.

A smaller number of visitors are drawn to live in this high desert landscape, responding to its heady mix of dramatic landform, saturated organic color, clarifying light, and enduring seasonal rhythm. Drawing both inspiration and sustenance from the land and light, they come to pursue various callings: drawing, weaving, painting, writing, sculpting, storytelling. Their journeys may require years and meander in unexpected directions, but in the fullness of time, they will ultimately be welcomed by the land, transformed by their passage through it, and re-created as its story is renewed in their work.

For a few, the country is both captivating and tantalizing but not so forthcoming. In addition to its other enchantments, they perceive a powerful, elusive mystery dwelling in the canyons, submerged in the arroyos, and woven into the mesas. Impassive buttes, rolling grasslands, silent juniper and piñon forests, and haunting sky hint

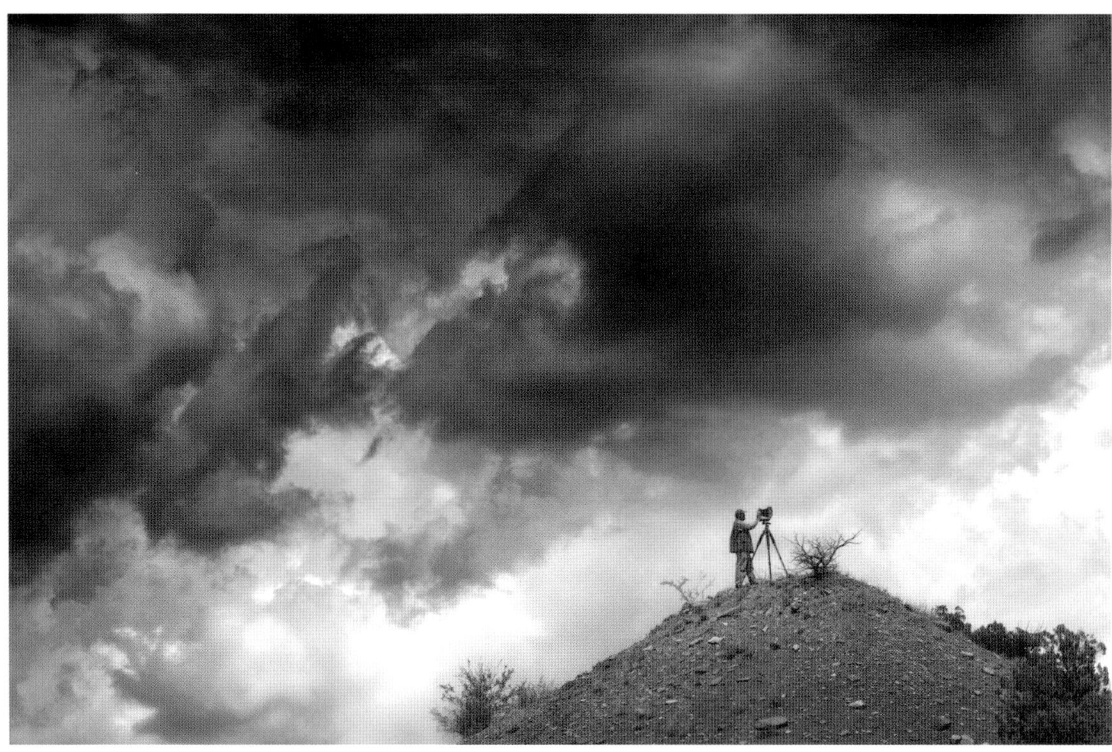

"Craig Varjabedian at Ghost Ranch, 2007," by Jay Packer.

at another only partially glimpsed dimension, a veiled "landscape behind the landscape."

> There is a landscape behind the landscape that we are
> always reaching for and seeking with our eyes and hearts.
> It is the landscape that is always there, and always receding.[1]

These seekers come to the Piedra Lumbre in search of this other landscape, and thus for its Architect.

They have come for centuries, building kivas, churches, monasteries, moradas, zendos, and mosques along the river and its tributaries. It would be difficult to find a comparable rural area in the United States with half the range of religious options as are available in the Chama Valley. The Presbyterians are the current stewards of Ghost Ranch, but the Christ in the Desert Benedictine Monastery is just across the highway, the Dar al Islam Mosque is down the road, the Church of Santo Tomas de Abiquiu stands at the center of its village, and the poignant adobe ruins of the Santa Rosa de Lima Church guard the riverbank to the south. Clearly, something inherent in this place suggests that a search for the Divine might here bear fruit.

> We live in two landscapes, as Augustine might have said,
> One that's eternal and divine,
> And one that's just the backyard.[2]

Some backyard! To this multidimensional landscape over twenty years ago came the young photographer Craig Varjabedian. Canadian by birth, Armenian by heritage, inquisitive and unconventional by nature, he first came to New Mexico at the suggestion of Ansel Adams. Although he arrived as an artist drawn to the landscape and culture, his remarkable project with the Penitente Brotherhood and their moradas (resulting in his book *En Divina Luz*) unexpectedly deepened his focus. In the decades that followed, he has diligently sought this "landscape behind the landscape" in the Rio Chama watershed. As with the pilgrims who preceded him, this quest led Craig to Ghost Ranch.

Energized by his early encounters with Adams, Craig was also powerfully influenced by the photography of Paul Caponigro. Caponigro, like Edward Weston before him, strove to see beyond the surface appearance of things to the "quintessence of the thing itself," the deeper reality behind and within a photographic subject.

In the landscape, such an approach requires time for the photographer to establish a relationship with the object of his attention; rather than arranging or orchestrating an image, he must instead cultivate meditative patience, receptive stillness, and the ability to be fully present for the subject to reveal itself. Ghost Ranch proved to be nothing if not coy; it was nearly twenty years before Craig felt ready for the daunting task of photographing this place.

But photograph it he did, and in your hands is the proof; I commend his images to your contemplation. The noted philosopher Yogi Berra astutely observed, "Sometimes you can see a lot just by looking."

True, yet both Ghost Ranch and the photographs of Craig Varjabedian may appear very different to you as the vantage points along your own journey change; I would recommend looking at both more than once. Look carefully into the shadows, around the corners, inside the canyons, behind the buttes, under the red hills, and deep into the sky; you may indeed see traces of another landscape, the one that earlier pilgrims sought through the holy places they built nearby:

> Or dreaming in old chapels where
> The dim aisles pulse with murmurings
> That part are music, part are prayer—
> Or rush of hidden wings.[3]

Within these images, I am confident you'll hear the murmurings, the music, and the prayers; listen carefully for the rustling of wings.

Jay Packer is a photographer and writer and practices medicine in California.

Notes

1. Nicolas Rothwell, "Mapping our Imagination," *The Australian*, Jan. 5, 2008.
2. Charles Wright, *Appalachia* (New York: Farrar, Straus and Giroux, 1998).
3. Don Marquis, "The Name," *Dreams and Dust* (New York: Harper & Bros., 1915).

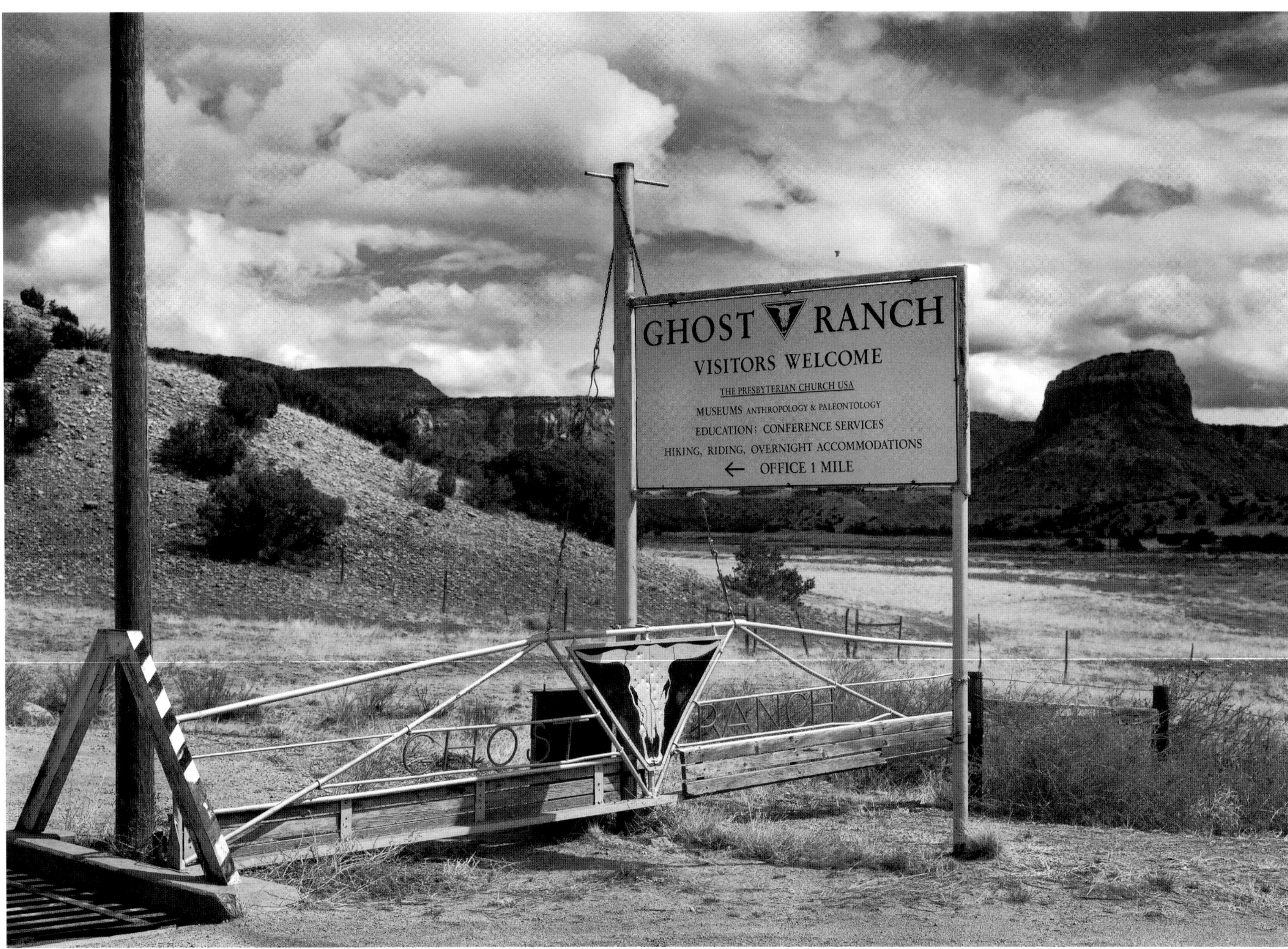

Plate 6: Ranch Entrance with Arthur Pack's Original Bumper Gate, Ghost Ranch, New Mexico, 2007

GHOST RANCH

A Place for Sojourns

MARIN SARDY

From the broad Colorado Plateau, sunset-red and carving the horizon into pieces, the cliffs of Ghost Ranch rise up suddenly. They are the Piedra Lumbre, the cliffs of Shining Stone, and at Ghost Ranch they divide the world in two: the earth and the sky, the vast and the miniscule. It's the graphic beauty of the cracked earth beneath your feet, and the impact of a huge high-altitude anvil cloud driving past. It's the interplay between the flash of blue when a migrating songbird swoops low, and the sudden shift in light when the sun hits a mesa top—a change so complete it's atmospheric in effect.

Kant proposed that the difference between that which we call beautiful and what we refer to as sublime is less an aesthetic distinction than an emotional one. The beautiful, he argued, is simply pleasing and brings about a sense of joy. But the sublime always includes an additional element—an extremity of size or simplicity that inspires feelings such as awe, melancholy, even fear. It is a composite quality of various elements in a scene, not the characteristic of any single object, and at Ghost Ranch, you may encounter it around every corner. It's in the way your eye somehow gets pulled upward—by the sheer pillars of stone, the cloud shadows playing on the high rocks, or the fingerlike tree branches reaching skyward—or alternatively, downward, into the elaborate wonder of white gypsum glinting among blades of dry grass.

This quality is what Craig Varjabedian feels the landscape is giving him when he takes photographs around Ghost Ranch's 32-square-mile spread, relying on a personal, idiosyncratic combination of equipment for the particular visual interpretation it renders. He uses a large-format camera that creates 5" × 7" negatives, and a set of handcrafted Carl Zeiss Protar convertible lenses that are nearly one hundred years old. Together these components capture an extraordinary amount of detail and somehow seem to magnify the mood of the scene. "Compared to today's lenses, the lenses I use tend to describe space very differently—almost the air and the light—in a way that makes it visible in the picture," he explains. "At least, that's what I see in my photographs, and it's perfect for what I do. They help create a more contemplative image."

Contemplation may be inevitable in desert landscapes: Two primary contributions to Western thought to come from desert cultures are, in fact, infinity and zero. Desert vistas hint at both. It's in the way the distant horizon is always visible, as is everything within the scene. Each tree is clearly individuated; every boulder stands tall above the empty ground; a bird's flight path can be traced in its entirety. And it is all encompassed in the open dome of sky. The reach of the eye is long here—limited in some places by only the curve of the earth—suggesting an endlessness in which all things exist at once,

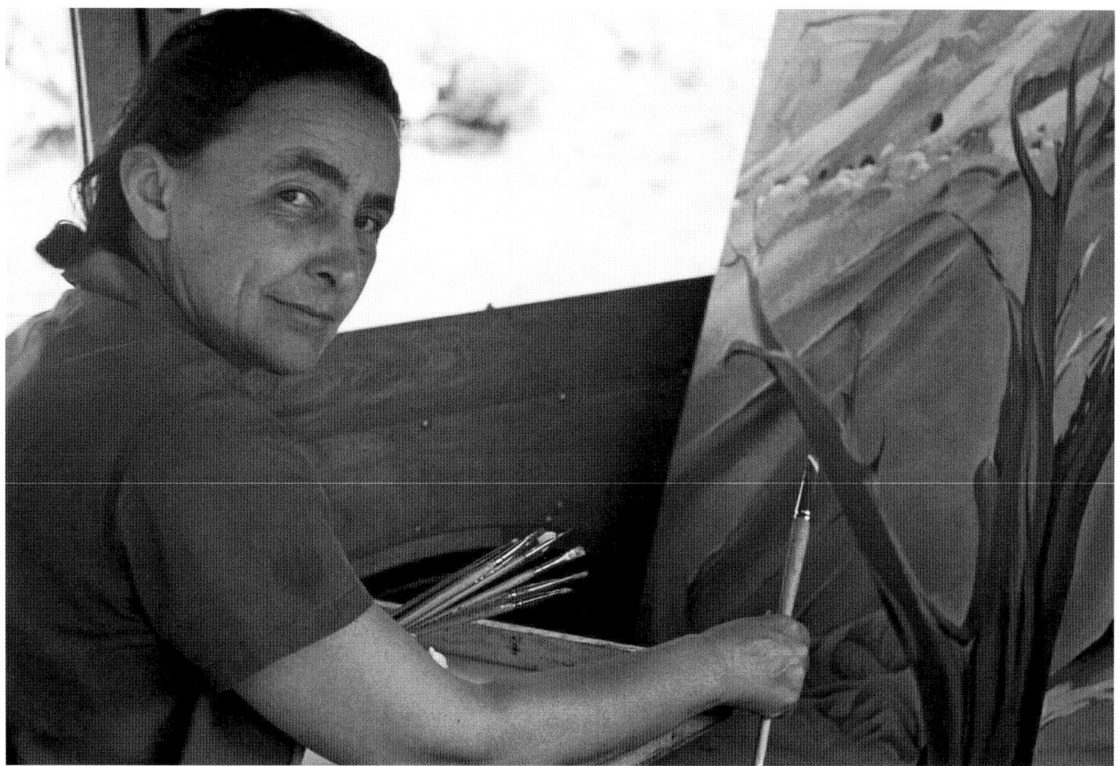

"O'Keeffe painting in her car, Ghost Ranch, New Mexico, 1937." Photograph by Ansel Adams. Collection Center for Creative Photography, University of Arizona © The Ansel Adams Publishing Right Trust.

and therefore also the opposite. If you stand near the main cluster of adobe buildings at Ghost Ranch and turn to face away from the embracing rock, that's where you find it.

And the rock does embrace. The form of the sandstone cliffs gives the place a hidden, protected feeling, almost like an ancient walled city—only this one comes in Technicolor: rust and russet fading to peach, yellow, and lavender, in bands narrow and wide. The easternmost cliffs of the broad, rough arc, including Kitchen Mesa and the pillars that rim the banks of the Rito del Yeso (Yeso Creek), are made of a hard, gleaming stone and solidly embody the grandeur for which the West is known. Farther west, however, the walls rise less abruptly, with hills of earth leading away to slightly more distant mesa tops to the north, behind the spires of Chimney Rock and the twin chimneys locals have long called Puerta del Cielo (Heaven's Gate). Here the scale of things diminishes—and the shapes grow stranger. Fields of porous boulders lie clustered beneath odd mounds of red-brown dirt, which squat before taller, more varied versions that in turn give way to knobby cliffs with wind-rounded stone shoulders perching on the mesa rim like pigeons, or goblins. The land in this part of the ranch has a fairyland quality to it, and one half expects those goblin stones to wake up, turn toward distant Pedernal, and bid it good morning. This is a rare quality in the desert. It's easy enough to feel as if you are walking among sprites in a hushed forest glen or at the banks of a woodland pond, but the hardness and vastness of the desert doesn't lend itself to such imaginings so easily.

Georgia O'Keeffe and the Faraway Nearby

Perhaps this fairyland quality is part of what Georgia O'Keeffe found so compelling about the place. Her former home—a U-shaped adobe on twelve acres—was strategically set by its first owner, Arthur Pack, among the red pygmy hills halfway between the stone centurions of Chimney Rock and Puerta del Cielo, with the cliff that spreads between them forming a natural amphitheater at the house's back. At its front lies the Piedra Lumbre basin, beyond which the Rio Chama (and now, Abiquiu Lake) divides the land briefly at the foot of broken-topped Cerro Pedernal's gentle ascent into the ever-moving sky. Never in all her years within that semicircular Shangri La did O'Keeffe ever paint a cliff to the east of Chimney Rock.

As the background, so the view: Pedernal is a soft-shouldered mountain, distinct but not overbearing. (O'Keeffe once said that Pedernal belonged to her—that God told her if she painted it enough, she could have it.)[1] It is no Grand Teton. It is not a subject Thomas Moran would have chosen to paint. Yet that huge vista, punctuated by Pedernal's suggestively up-tilted ledge top, rarely fails to suggest infinity. And that's the point. O'Keeffe's West was not a conqueror's West. The land was not a foe, so there was no need for her paintings to suggest that living in the West was akin to some sort of clash of the Titans. It was her front yard—a piece of daily life. And while it may have hinted at the awesome limitlessness of human imagination, it was also simply a place to stand and learn and grow. This it was from her first step onto Ghost Ranch in 1934 until her death in 1986.

O'Keeffe had spent almost every summer in New Mexico since 1929, staying at the Taos residence of Mabel Dodge Luhan, and had heard about the secret paradise but never could find it. The road to the ranch was, at that time, changeable and unreliably marked by cattle or horse skulls. When luck conspired to at last bring her to the hidden gem, she immediately made it her new home. She stayed in a casita she rented seasonally from owner Arthur Pack until 1936, the year she showed up unannounced and found her favorite cabin already occupied. After getting an earful of her indignation, Pack gave her his former home to rent—the house set between Chimney Rock and Puerta del Cielo, which he called Rancho de los Burros. Four years later O'Keeffe convinced him to sell her the house and a parcel of its surrounds.

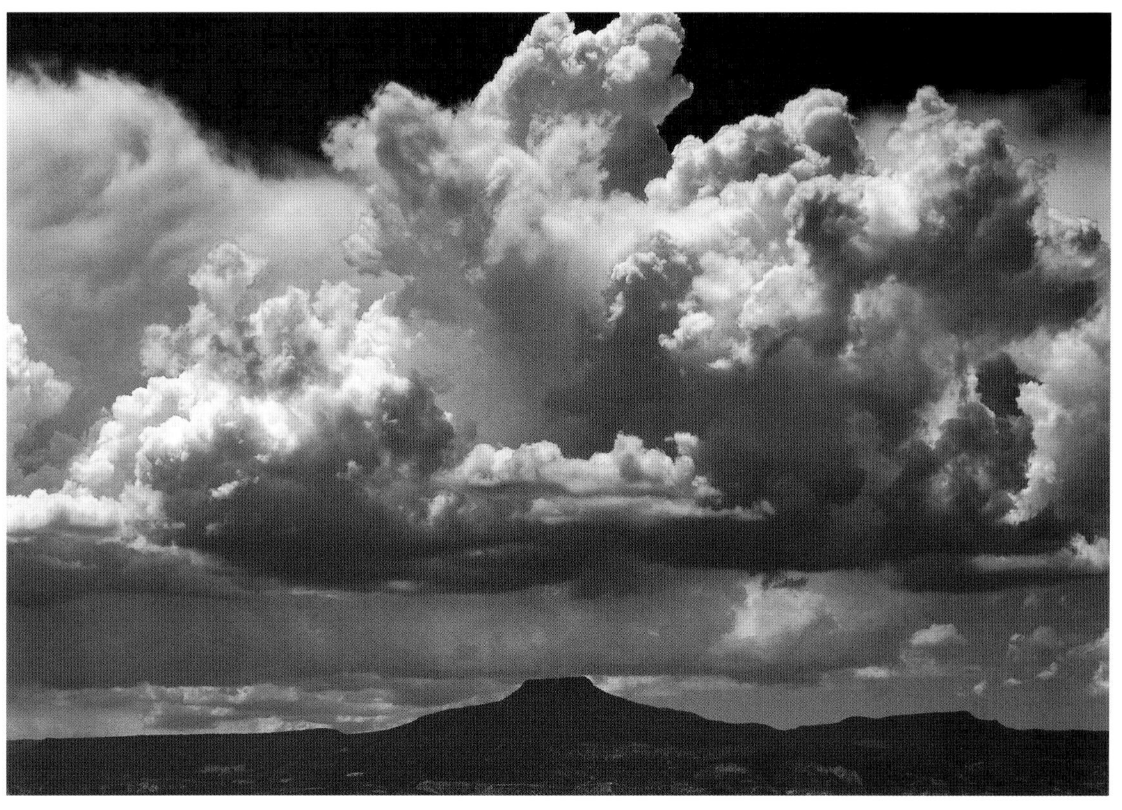

"Clouds over Cerro Pedernal, No. 3, Ghost Ranch, New Mexico 2006," by Craig Varjabedian.

It has been said that in her art and in her life, O'Keeffe reimagined the West. Perhaps in doing so, she also in some way reimagined beauty. Unlike her contemporary and fellow New Mexico artist Henriette Wyeth, whose lovely blooms and faces celebrated a traditional concept of beauty based in softness and delicacy, O'Keeffe took dry bones and skeletal ridges and gave the world a new way to look at them.

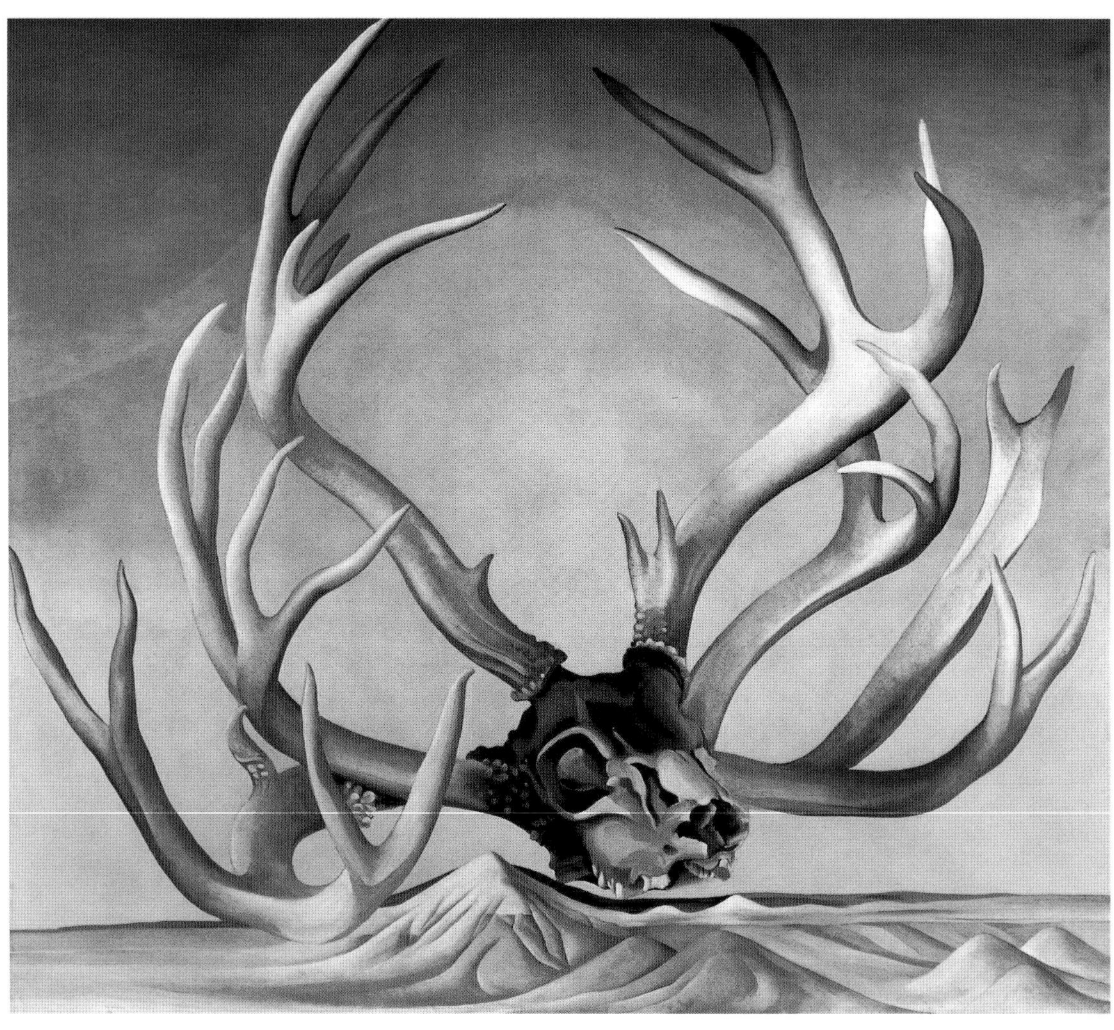

Georgia O'Keeffe, *From the Faraway, Nearby*, 1938, Oil on canvas. The Metropolitan Museum of Art, Alfred Steiglitz Collection, 1959 (59.204.2) Image © The Metropolitan Museum of Art.

"You say it is too bad that I don't always paint flowers," she once said. "A flower touches almost everyone's heart. A red hill doesn't touch everyone's heart as it touches mine and I suppose there is no reason why it should."[2] In her person as well as in her work—she generally dressed either in jeans or in long black skirts and shawls during her time at Ghost Ranch—she had, she explained, "used these things to say what is to me the wideness and wonder of the world as I live in it."[3] Here the bones and the distance came together in the same enveloping sensation echoed in her painting of an elk skull over Pedernal and its famously mysterious title: *From the Faraway, Nearby*. What she found in the West, and at Ghost Ranch, was a place where the open possibility of the landscape became one with what she felt inside herself, where depth and focus at once conflated the spatial orientation of the objects she painted, and pulled her nearer to her creative source. It is the place where O'Keeffe offered the world neither the beautiful nor the sublime, but something unique that borrowed from both and formed them anew.

Transition and Transformation

In New Mexico the constant motion of the clouds, with light breaking through in endlessly variant ways, may be thrilling but it is also commonplace. At Ghost Ranch, however, something additional happens. Here the atmosphere's processes do more than drive gigantic shadows across the plains and hilltops. That changing light gets captured by the colored cliffs, which act like prisms in the way they rearrange, magnify, and transmute the sun and air, so that the rock formations never look the same from one moment to the next. It is as if they wish to tell the world that Ghost Ranch always has been and will forever be a place of sojourns—a place of both transition and transformation, where visitors rarely stay long but invariably leave somehow changed. And the place, in turn, respects their passage through its spaces, keeping record of their time there in stone, bone, and story.

The ghosts of Ghost Ranch have, over the centuries, scattered across the wide landscape, unmoved to abandon the place that shaped them. Now they still roam among the fabled rocks and around the many buildings, some of which are many decades old and made from real adobe bricks, of the very earth beneath them. In Spanish colonial days, there were whisperings of a monstrous beast that lived at the foot of Mesa Huerfano (Orphan Mesa)—a thirty-foot-long serpent *brujo* known as Vivaron. The dragonlike creature had bones made of stone, was known to devour men and cattle, and could kill with its breath or even a sidelong glance. In the creek bottom beneath Mesa Huerfano, the spirits of the dead called to unsuspecting visitors, whispering warnings into the wind.

Vivaron may have still been watching while children swam in Ghost Ranch's first swimming pool. No longer in use, only the pool's concrete rim is visible now, flush with the earth that fills it in much like a skeleton embedded in rock. The spring-fed delight was placed by Arthur Pack at the banks of the Rito del Yeso near the mouth of Yeso Canyon, and was attended by both Pack's own clan and the children of ranch workers, including Floyd Trujillo, who learned to swim there as a child and then worked at the ranch for the next thirty-five years. Now in his seventies, Trujillo also remembers the only alternative: "We had to go in the river. We'd waddle in and a lot of times we came out dirtier than when we went in." Vivaron had reappeared by then. In 1934 Pack, who had heard of the creature in stories, directed a crew of paleontologists from the University of Chicago to Orphan Mesa for a dig. Within hours they unearthed a twenty-foot-long coiled skeleton of a prehistoric monster today known as a phytosaur. The crocodile-like 200-million-year-old beast had been waiting there since the Triassic Period, to become one among what would eventually amount to thousands of bones in a dozen species of vertebrate fossils (including Coelophysis, one of the earliest known dinosaurs) uncovered from the red rock of Ghost Ranch.

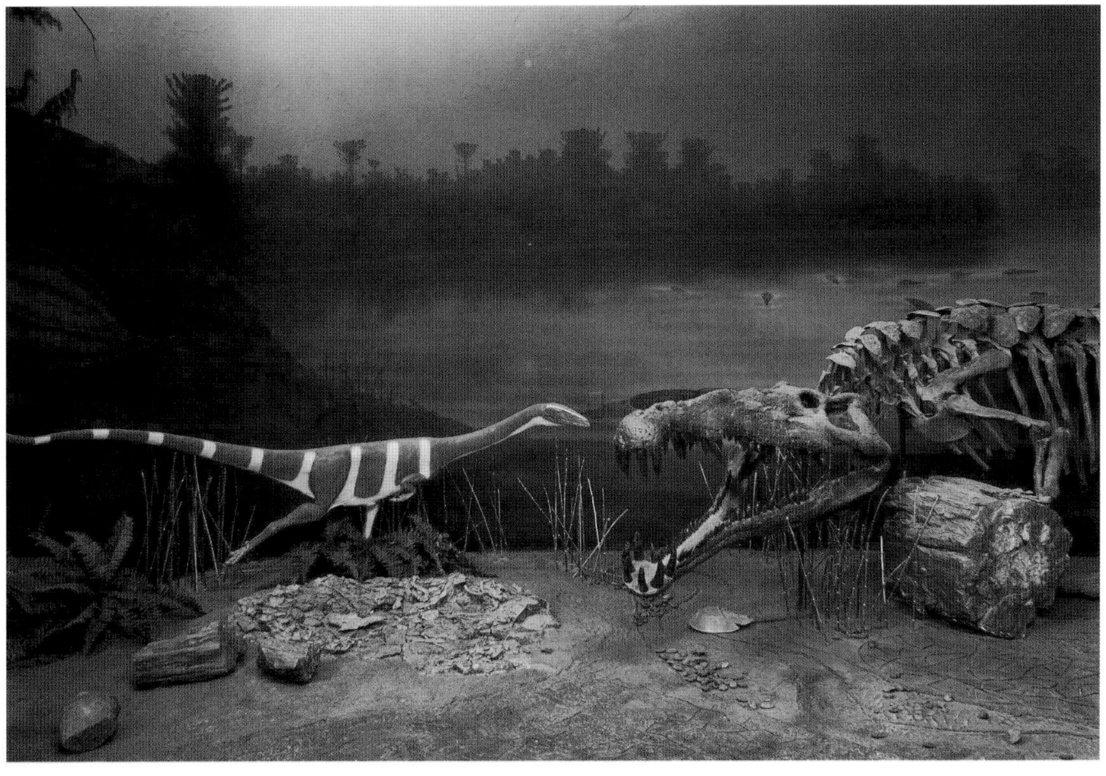

"Coelophysis model and phytosaur skeleton, The Ruth Hall Museum of Paleontology, Ghost Ranch, New Mexico, 2005." Coelophysis is the state fossil of New Mexico.

Like the bone, so the stone. East of Yeso Canyon, on the uninhabited side of the high cliffs that enclose the heart of Ghost Ranch like a ribcage, an abandoned homestead continues its slow return to the land. Two dugout jacal casitas and a root cellar constructed by David "Blackie" and Lottie Burnham, with their son, Bill, and daughter, Dorthy, still catch the wind that sweeps across the open plain. Warped planks and water-stained interior walls mark the decay, but

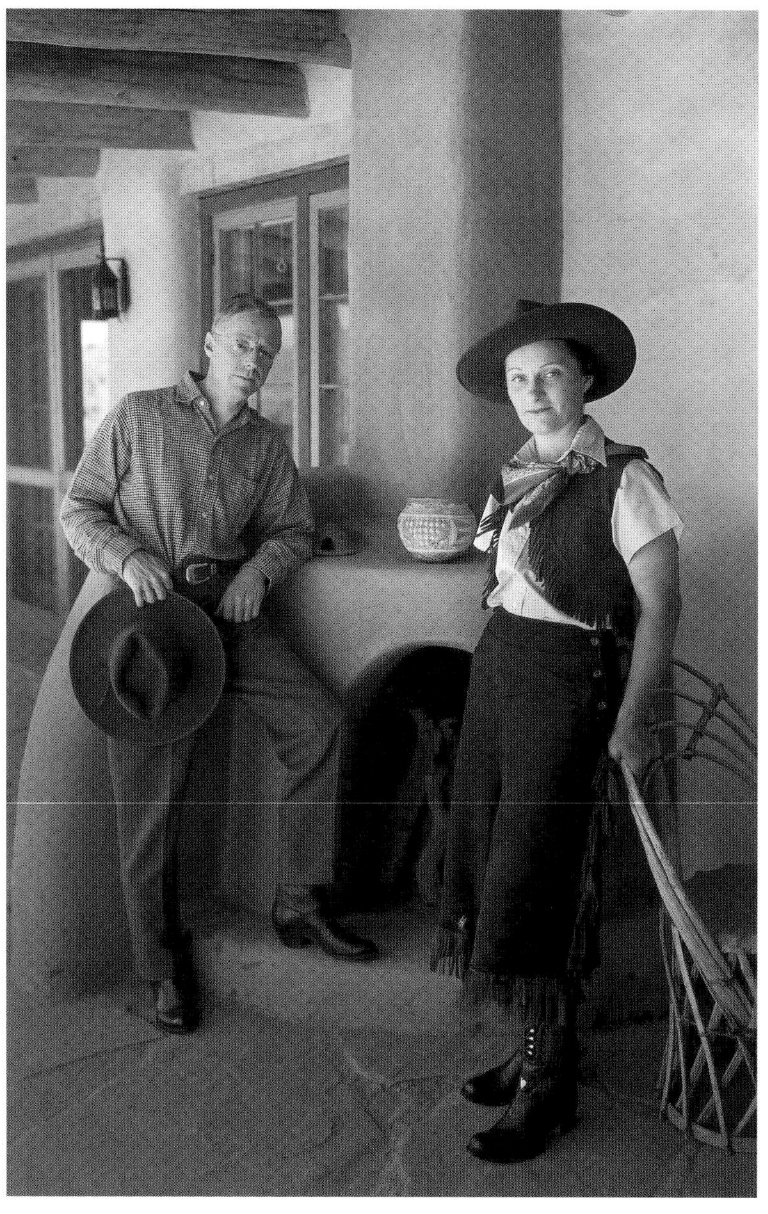

among the rough-hewn vigas and skewed window frames, touches of unexpected delicacy remain in the form of murals and detailing Lottie painted on the walls, including a peak that resembles Pedernal (apparently before God deeded it to O'Keeffe). Outside, a childish but careful carving of a horse has been etched nearly a half-inch deep into a flat stone nested in the ground—the lasting creative legacy of a young and lonely Dorthy Burnham.

History comes in micro and macro scales, too, and Ghost Ranch conflates world events just as it does feelings and images: Across the highway, overlooking Lake Abiquiu, a few red stone-slab walls still hold up a small piece of FDR's New Deal. Built in 1935 at the height of the Great Depression by northern New Mexican members of the Civilian Conservation Corps, the camp's half-dozen buildings headquartered a project to renew depleted rangeland. Now the single, meandering rear wall of an old motor port mimics the cliffs behind it, seeming to reach forward with stone arms as if to take hold of Pedernal. Among rusted cans scattered on the ground nearby, a piece of an old taillight with part of its Chevrolet emblem still visible attests to the structure's original purpose. A dozen yards away an adobe hut, its edges softened by rain and time, collapses inward while a strong wind rushes by. Whistling through the sagebrush, hitting the old buildings, a gust furls momentarily before going on across the rolling terrain. The wind, too, is another sojourner.

Caroline Stanley, Arthur Pack, and the Presbyterians

From its earliest human history, the Rito del Yeso, the life-giving heart of Ghost Ranch, was used as a stopover by the region's Native peoples.

"Arthur and Phoebe Pack, Ghost Ranch, New Mexico, ca. 1945," by T. Harmon Packhurst, Collection of the Palace of the Governors (MNM/DCA), negative no. 89653.

Tewa, Navajo, Ute, and Apache passed through on hunting expeditions, staying beneath the monolithic mesas in the piñon woods at the perpetually flowing creek, which could always be counted on for fresh water. In the 1800s, the Gallegos family founded Arroyo Seco Ranch in the same spot, but a few decades later abandoned the operation. After that, stories of Vivaron kept the area's Spanish settlers away.

The exception was a pair of brothers, the Archuletas, who moved in and built small jacal homes at the mouth of Yeso Canyon. The spot's haunted reputation served their purposes well: as leaders of a gang of cattle rustlers, they could easily hide their ill-begotten bounty. It was widely suspected that they were murderers—especially after travelers known to be passing through the area were never seen again (but their gear was spotted on the horses of crewmembers). Lacking the resources to take on an entire band of thieves, the neighbors did nothing until, one night, the Archuletas brought about their own end. An argument broke out between the two over an amount of gold. By morning, one brother was dead from axe wounds, and the other's wife and daughter had escaped to nearby San Juan Pueblo, where they told of the death and several others. A posse raided the hideout and hanged the remaining brother and his gang, it is said, from the cottonwood tree that still stands near the old casitas.

El Rancho de los Brujos (Ranch of the Witches), as it was now called, passed through the hands of three different Spanish families in the next twenty years, but no one wanted to actually live there. Its next resident owner would not move in until 1931, and by that time she, too, would have acquired it by nearly inexplicable means: Caroline Bishop Stanley was given the deed in 1929 by her husband, Roy Pfaffle, an Iowa-born New Mexico cowboy who won the property from a member of the Salazar clan in a high-stakes poker match. For her part, Stanley moved there two years later on the heels of their divorce and the collapse of the couple's San Gabriel dude ranch in Alcalde (both events stemming in no small part from Pfaffle's gambling problem). And although the undaunted Bostonite—along with her Steinway, her Navajo rug collection, and her English housekeeper—only owned the ranch for seven years, her stay marked a seminal turning point in the development of the place she officially called Ghost Ranch. Protected for a century by its own bad juju, it was as pristine a retreat as anyone could wish for. So Stanley would make it a well-known dude ranch where wealthy Easterners, in search of a ruggedness and freedom their lives sorely lacked, could test themselves against the elements and soak up the peace.

But Stanley didn't invent the sanctuary she called Ghost Ranch so much as she found the heart of what was already there—and of what she brought with her. She had first been sent out West in 1915 by family members who hoped she would forget the musician she wanted to marry. At thirty-five, she was no naïve child, but one must wonder what the family thought when she not only refused to return to Boston, but within a year had gotten hitched, during a long horse-packing trip, to one of her guides. By the time she set to work at her new property, she had already managed two guest ranches and traveled extensively in the Four Corners region. By 1935, Stanley's crew of cowboys, wranglers, mechanics, and guides had built, with local workers from nearby villages and thousands of handmade adobe bricks, facilities for up to twenty guests.

It was only two years later that she sold her project to Arthur Pack. The business couldn't sustain itself through the Great Depression, and Stanley herself was getting remarried and ready to move on. Pack, a transplant from Princeton, had the deep pockets required to keep the place going. He came from a logging dynasty dating back to the mid-1800s, and a father who was one of the first and most committed environmentalists in the New World. Inspired by Charles Pack's lifelong crusade for responsible timber harvesting, young Arthur cofounded the groundbreaking *Nature Magazine*, on which he worked as editor and writer in Princeton, and then from Ghost Ranch.

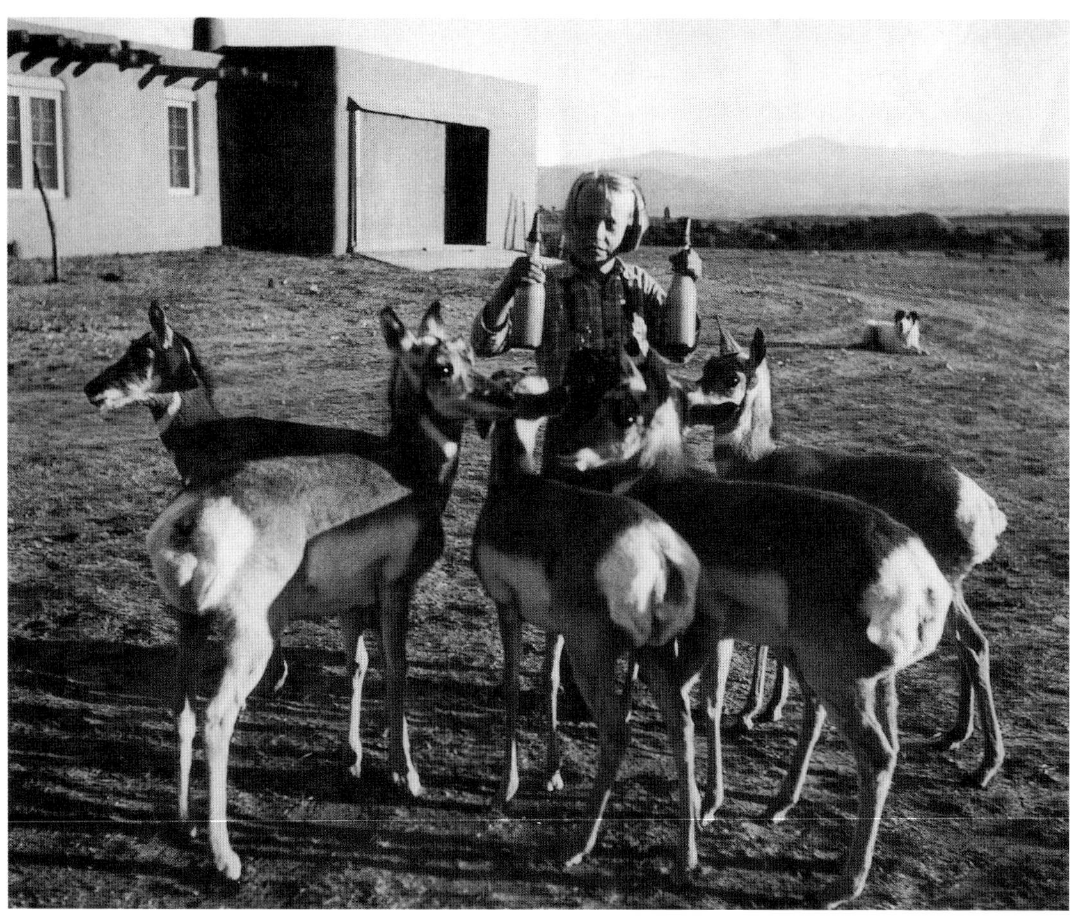

"Peggy Pack feeding antelope, Ghost Ranch, New Mexico, ca. 1930s," from the Pack family archive.

Adventurous and passionate about the outdoors, Arthur and his wife Brownie didn't hesitate to move to New Mexico when a doctor recommended taking their daughter Peggy, who battled recurrent pneumonia, to a dry climate for a couple of years. Their home, Rancho de los Burros, was the adobe in the Painted Desert that O'Keeffe—who discovered Ghost Ranch at about the same time—would later claim as her sanctuary and eventually purchase. Pack ran the place according to his personal ethic: more than a haven for "dudes," it was also a working ranch and additionally a stunning piece of earth that deserved protection. He even went as far as flying in pronghorn antelope calves in his single-engine plane to repopulate their historic range. "They fit in the seat behind the pilot," remembers his daughter, Peggy Pack McKinley. "We bottle-fed them, and they followed us all over, until they got big and went out onto the range."

It was in this same spirit that, through the hard years of World War II, Pack and his second wife Phoebe hosted servicemen at cut-rate prices at their new Ghost Ranch Lodge in Tucson, which they opened in 1941 in order to begin splitting their time between there and New Mexico. At the original Ghost Ranch, following an intensive interrogation, they also agreed to being designated an official R&R spot for men working in the secret city on the nearby Los Alamos Plateau. Although the men couldn't speak about their work, Pack recognized Robert Oppenheimer from a photo, and also noticed that in general their all-American names didn't match the distinctively foreign accents. After the war, when his dinner guests could speak more openly, Pack heard firsthand accounts, from the likes of Enrico Fermi, Niels Bohr, and Richard Feynman, of how they had harnessed nuclear fission and witnessed its devastating power. Now even suggestions of wisps of mushroom clouds could be counted among the ranch's ghosts.

Pack decided to relinquish ownership of Ghost Ranch in the mid-fifties, but he and Phoebe felt strongly that it shouldn't be sold.

As postwar hosts to not only stars like Cary Grant and John Wayne, but also the now-civilian servicemen who had learned about the place during stays at the Tucson lodge, the Packs didn't want the ranch to continue on as another elite playground for a chosen few. To sell it to another private owner would be, they felt, a breach of trust between themselves and the land. So although O'Keeffe was unsurprisingly livid when she found out he didn't plan to sell the place to her (and stormed Pack's living room to deliver a diatribe driving the point home), Ghost Ranch was given instead as a gift to the Presbyterian Church, based on the idea that it would be used as a center for outdoor education and a spiritual retreat.

The Magic Place

With a history that by mid-century included some of the continent's oldest dinosaur fossils, the country's foremost woman artist, a leading pioneer of the conservation movement, and the world-altering Manhattan Project, it was almost foretold that Ghost Ranch couldn't get through the 1960s untouched by the social upheaval that came to define that decade. Nicknames like the Magic Place, as well as stories of visiting college students sitting around the campfire planning the protests they would stage back home, attest to this. But out of that era also came what now stands as perhaps the single greatest example of the place's transformative power—an event whose architect, ranch director Jim Hall, considered to be the greatest accomplishment in Ghost Ranch history and in his own life as well.

A minister who grew up in New Mexico, Jim Hall was the college-educated son of the legendary itinerant cowboy preacher Ralph Hall. Jim Hall had first supported the Presbyterian Church's expansion project for Ghost Ranch as a volunteer from his home down in Hobbs. Why the Church later chose him to direct the ranch was obvious: he knew the inner workings of a real ranch, was intimately familiar with New Mexico and its people, and was adamantly egalitarian in his approach to his work, whether the practical or the spiritual sort. "Theology," he once said pointedly, "is what you *do*."[4]

Despite the striking scenery that made it famous, Hall knew Ghost Ranch was—and still is—in many ways a quintessential New Mexico *rancho*. Even today, thickets of cottonwood and scrub oak in the creek bottom skirt a fenced alfalfa field (and one very old horse). Sprawling trees dwarf the adobe buildings they shade. And in the undulating badlands that reach far to the south, pocked by scattered piñon and cholla, cow patties and hoof prints indicate the presence of cattle roaming freely. Hall knew the ranch had supported herds of cattle for most of the past century, beginning in the days of the open range, and with this in mind, he implemented several projects to specifically benefit local *rancheros*, such as the Winter Grazing Program, which provided the use of rangeland and free courses in animal husbandry to anyone with even a single cow. He also understood rural life well enough to know when to throw a party. "Hall would cook steaks for the whole staff at the end of the summer," recalls retired ranch hand Floyd Trujillo. "He did it to celebrate the good work that had been done. He knew the value of what went into the ranch."

The 1960s also marked the rich beginnings of the Hispanic pride movement, and its force in northern New Mexico went largely to the Alianza Federal de las Mercedes (Federal Alliance for Land Grants), an activist group that by 1967 was burning barns, cutting fences, and demanding the return of ancestral Hispanic lands from Anglo-American landowners. Led by the explosive and charismatic Reies López Tijerina, the group was most famous for its armed takeover of the Rio Arriba County Courthouse in the nearby village of Tierra Amarilla. Tijerina was a passionate and formidable leader: trained as a Pentecostal minister, he was also thoroughly versed in the systematic disenfranchisement of Hispanic New Mexicans and the dubious history by which the majority of their lands had been lost to English-speaking, and largely absentee, landowners. He was captured just a week after the courthouse assault (in the largest manhunt in state history), but by June of 1969, out of prison and back at the helm of Alianza, had placed Ghost Ranch at the top of his list of properties to reclaim.

So when Hall heard that Tijerina and a cavalcade of nearly a hundred cars were on their way to Ghost Ranch, ready to put him under citizen's arrest and occupy all 21,000 acres of ranch property, he greeted them in his Sunday best, among tables spread with coffee and cookies, and agreed to let Tijerina address the crowd. By the end of the speechmaking—by Tijerina, Hall, and Father Bob Kirsch, a Catholic priest who came up from his Abiquiu parish to speak in defense of the Presbyterians—the anger-primed crowd had instead been defused. Tijerina left politely and amicably.

The close call, however, spurred Hall to consider the needs of the community more seriously, and culminated in what would come to be called the Great Land Trade. In 1975, in an ingenious move that took advantage of a pending land trade between Ghost Ranch and the Forest Service, Hall showed up asking not for additional land for the ranch, but asked instead that the Forest Service cede 115 disputed holdings—Hispanic residencies going back generations, which now legally belonged to the U.S. government—to the people who still lived on the properties as squatters. In this single move, one Catholic chapel, two penitente moradas, one cemetery, and 111 family ranches returned to the private ownership of the people who had used them for centuries—and Ghost Ranch, at last, gave as much to the people of northern New Mexico as it had for a half a century given to the wealthy, famous, and gifted.

Ineffable Wonder

Today, looking up at the surging red stone walls surrounding Ghost Ranch, it seems they must have been frightening to European beholders who had never seen the earth take on such shades and forms. Yet it makes sense, too, that many found in the epic stone suggestions of something greater than terror: some ineffable wonder in the variety and vastness of the universe. O'Keeffe found the raw materials of a unique and revolutionary artistic vision. Others found transcendence in all its guises. Craig Varjabedian, despite avoiding immersing himself in O'Keeffe's paintings at the start of his photographic journey, discovered later that they had both been drawn to similar aspects of the landscape. "I think the place taught us," he explains. "I think she really tapped into something up here that was beyond her."

Long after Hall, Pack, O'Keeffe, and Stanley had all departed, Varjabedian spent five years living in Abiquiu, returning to Ghost Ranch day after day to watch, wait, and just be with the landscape. He refused to begin until he felt he truly understood what he was looking at. "I wanted the land to tell me how to photograph it," he explains. "Every time I went out there, I had these rapturous visions." Now, after twenty years of image-making pilgrimages he, too, has left the place—but not without absorbing some part of it that changed him in the very deepest sense. "I look at it from the perspective that I went there to learn something, and the camera became the vehicle to do that," he says. "I knew I was done when the place stopped revealing images to me."

Marin Sardy is a writer and editor in chief of Santa Fean *magazine.*

Notes

1. Laurie Lisle, *Portrait of an Artist: A Biography of Georgia O'Keeffe* (New York: Seaview Press, 1980; Washington Square Press printing, 1981), 299.
2. Georgia O'Keeffe, *Georgia O'Keeffe* (New York: Viking Press, 1976), quote accompanying Plate 25.
3. Georgia O'Keeffe, *Georgia O'Keeffe* (New York: Viking Press, 1976), quote accompanying Plate 71.
4. Leslie Poling-Kempes, *Ghost Ranch* (Tucson: University of Arizona Press, 2005), 247.

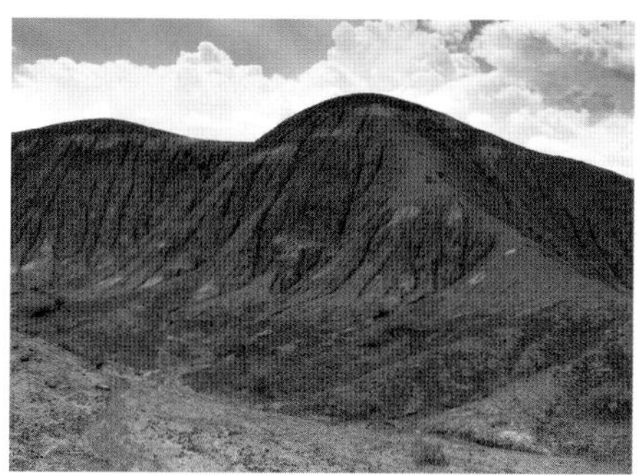

"It is all very beautiful and magical here—a quality which cannot be described. You have to live it and breathe it, let the sun bake it into you. The skies and land are so enormous, and the detail so precise and exquisite that wherever you are you are isolated in a glowing world between the macro and the micro, where everything is sidewise under you and over you, and the clocks stopped long ago."

ANSEL ADAMS IN A LETTER TO ALFRED STIEGLITZ

FROM GHOST RANCH, 1937

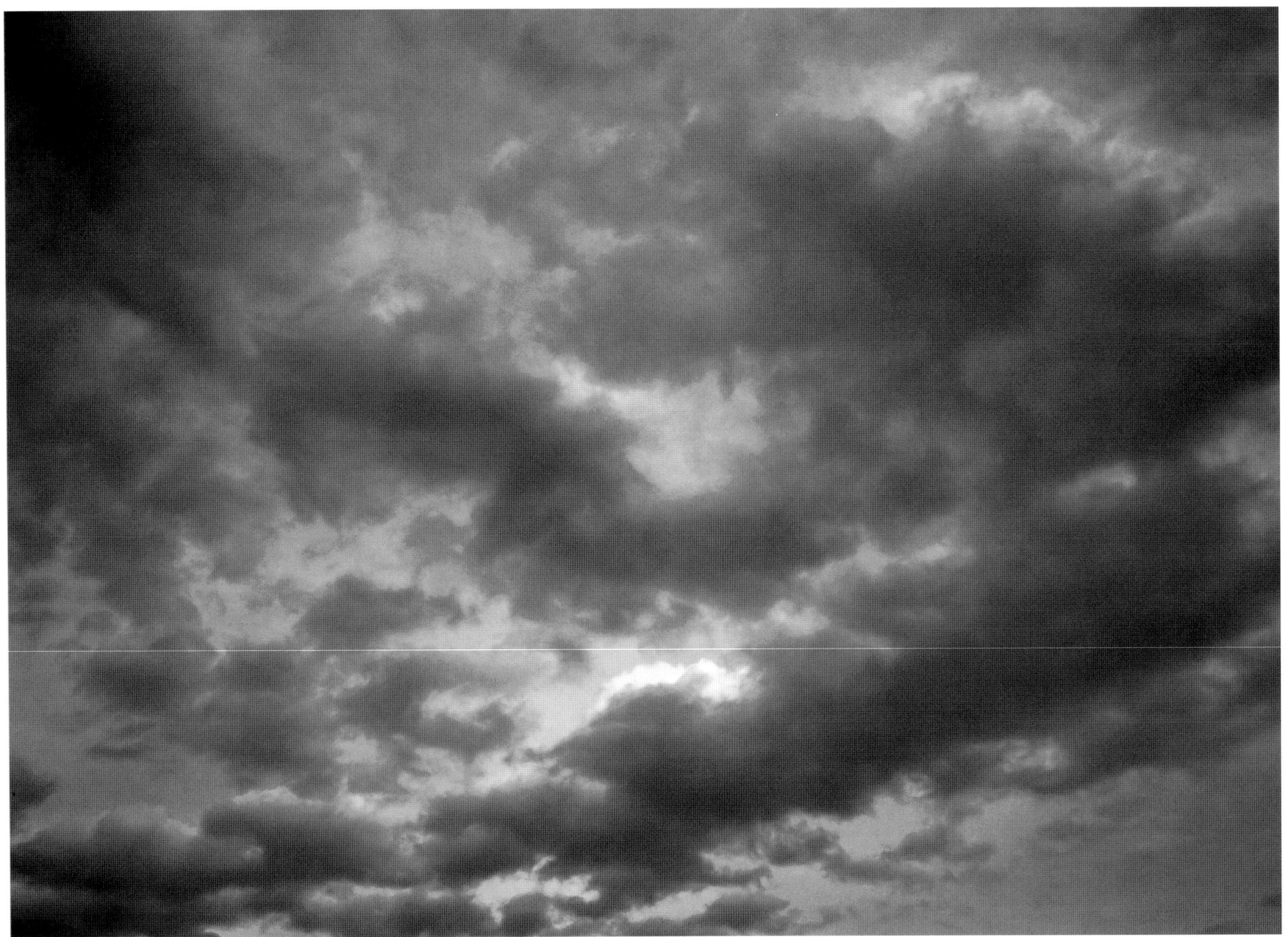

Plate 7: Clouds at Twilight, Ghost Ranch, New Mexico, 2007

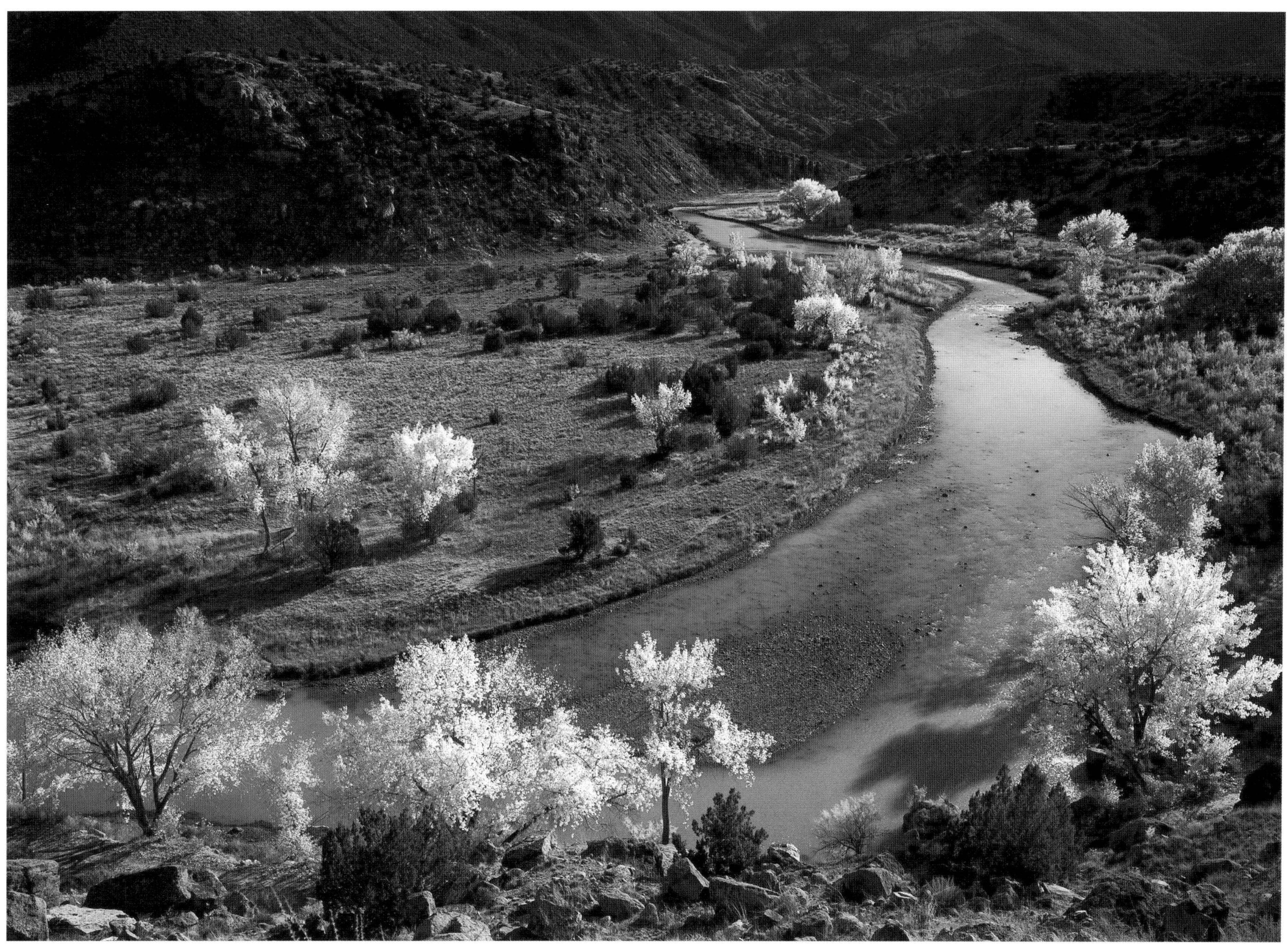

Plate 8: Rio Chama from the Overlook, Late Afternoon Light, near Abiquiu, New Mexico, 1997

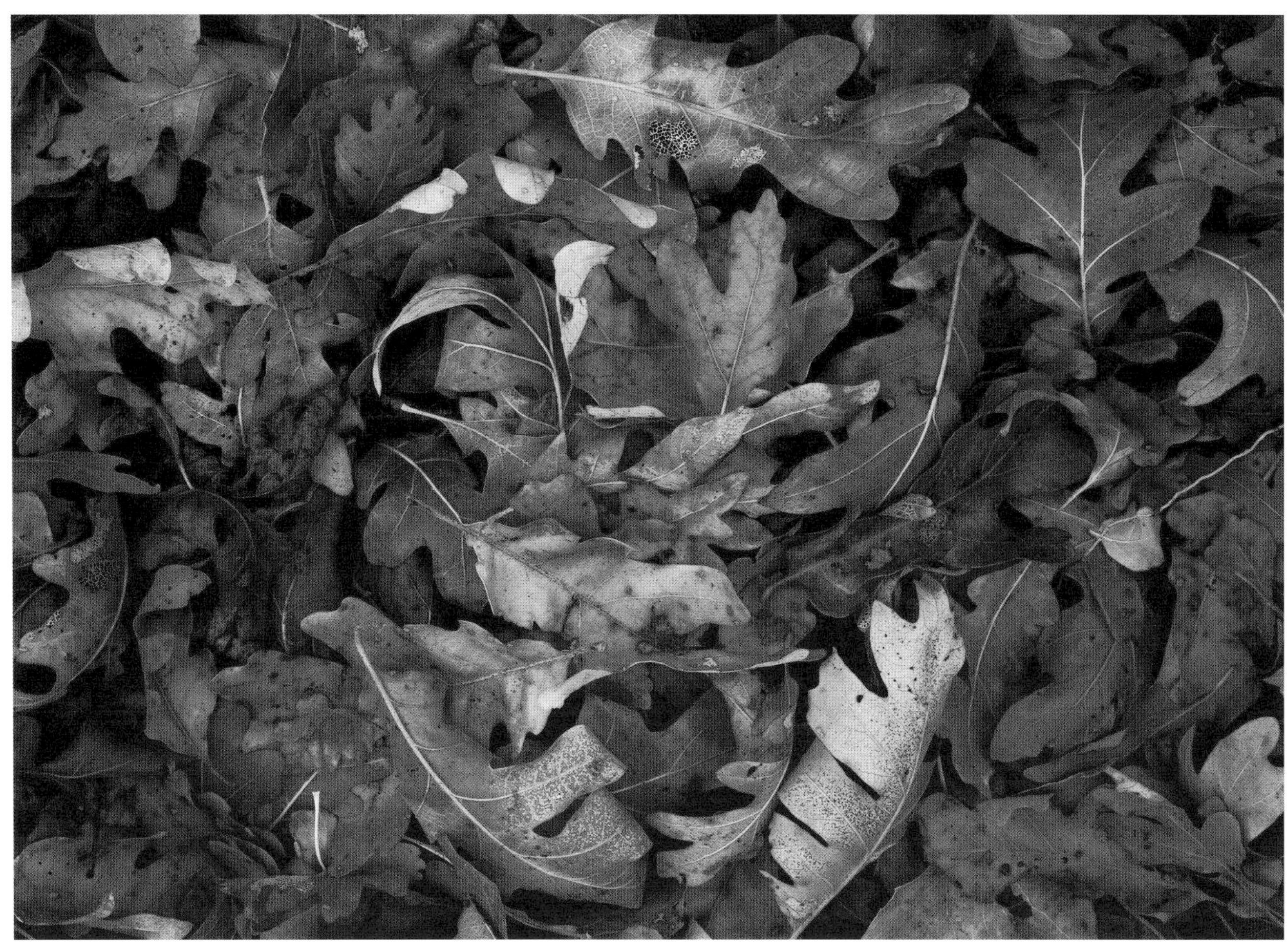

Plate 9: Oak Leaves along Box Canyon Trail, Winter, Ghost Ranch, New Mexico, 2005

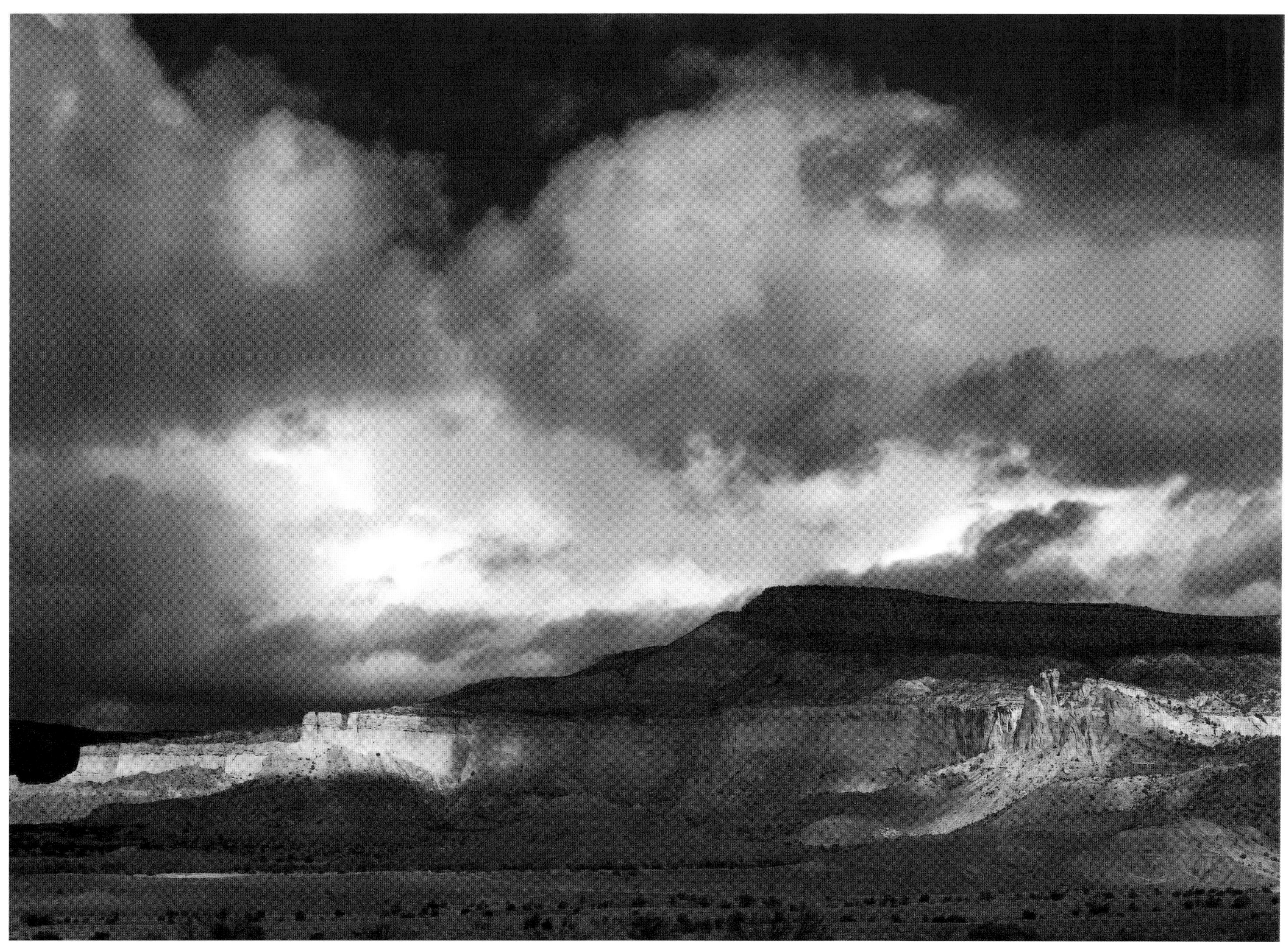

Plate 10: Storm Breaking over Painted Desert, Ghost Ranch, New Mexico, 2006

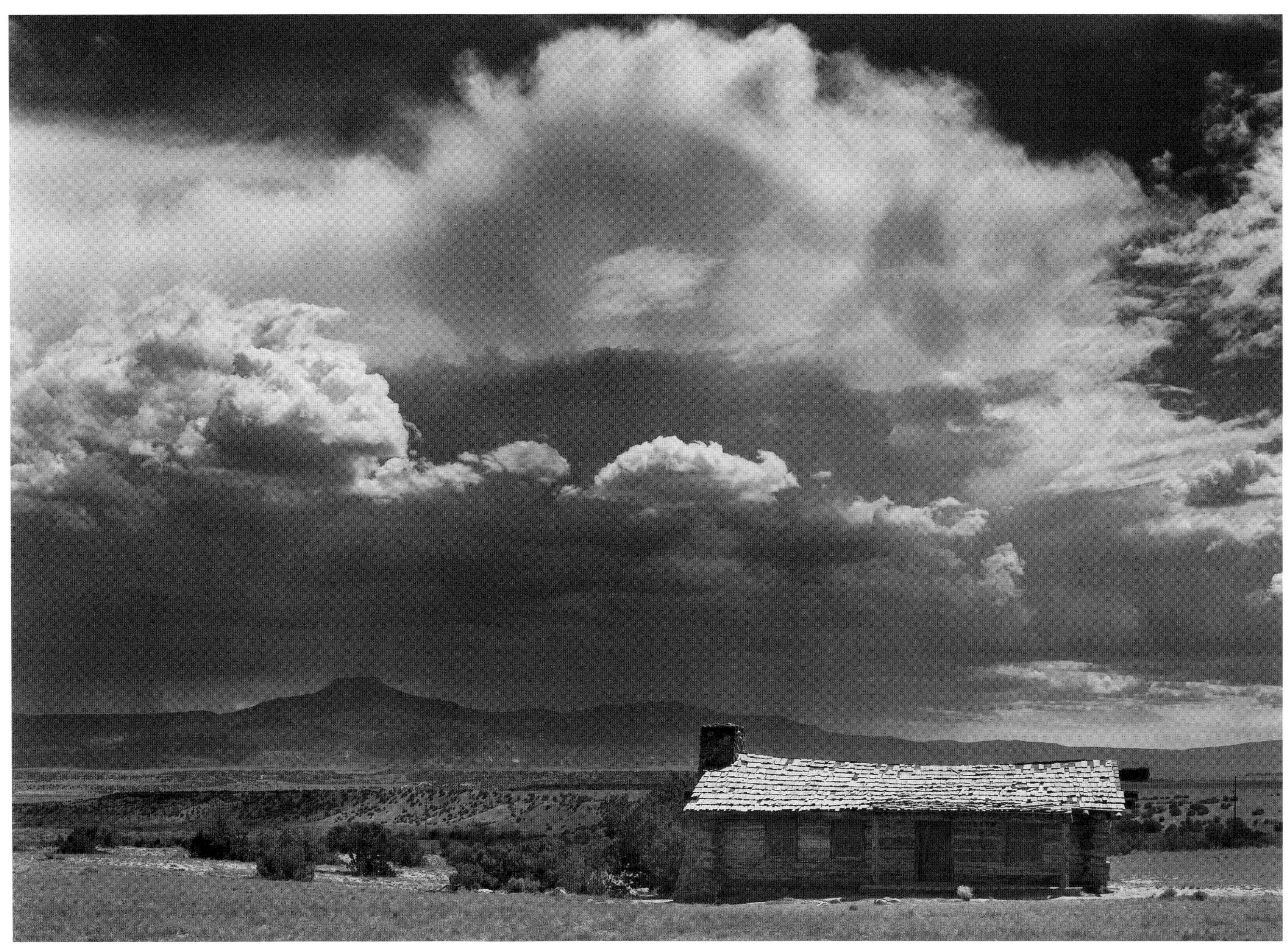

Plate 11: Approaching Storm over City Slickers Movie Cabin, Ghost Ranch, New Mexico, 2004

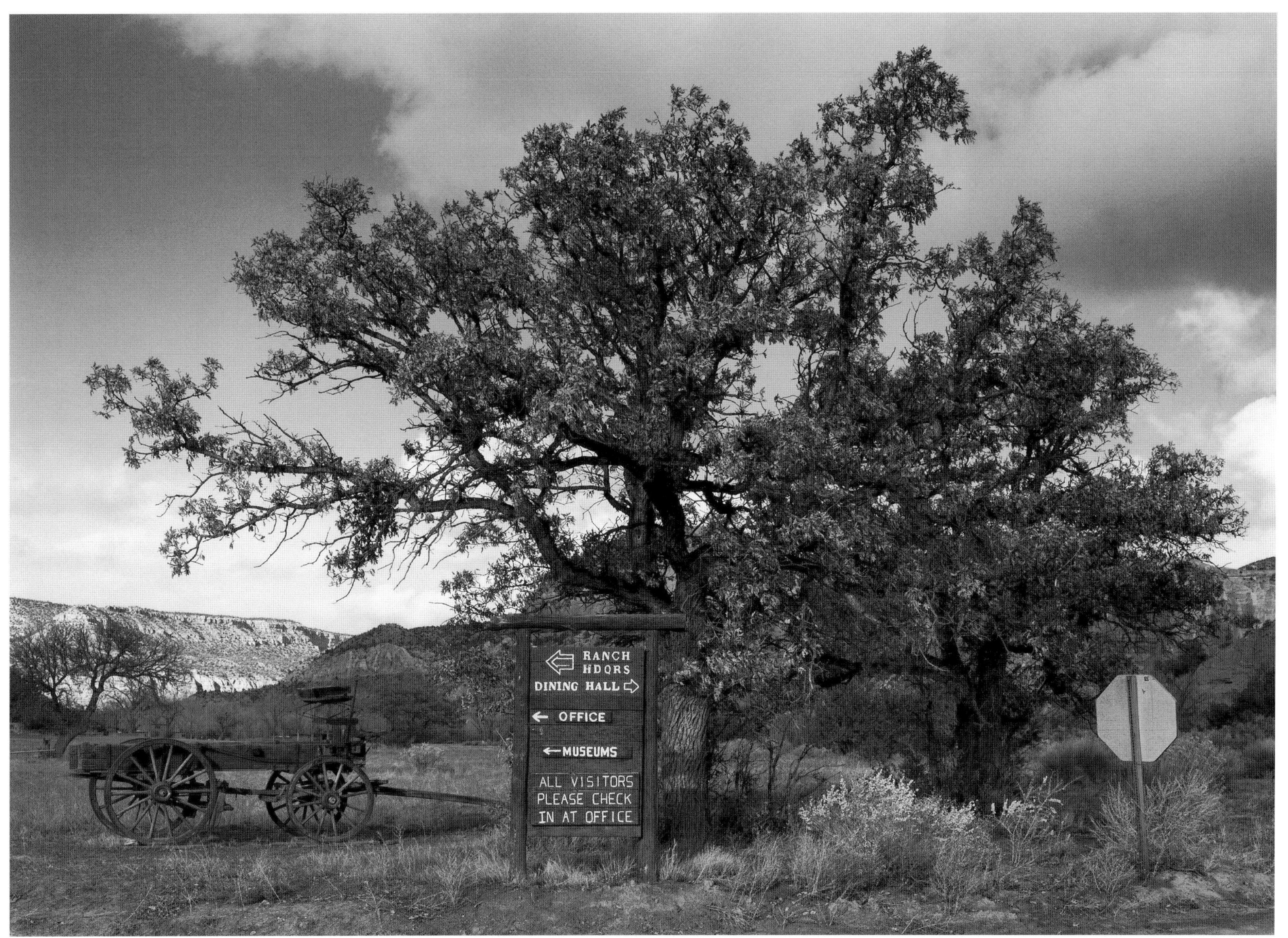

Plate 12: Directions, Ghost Ranch, New Mexico, 2005

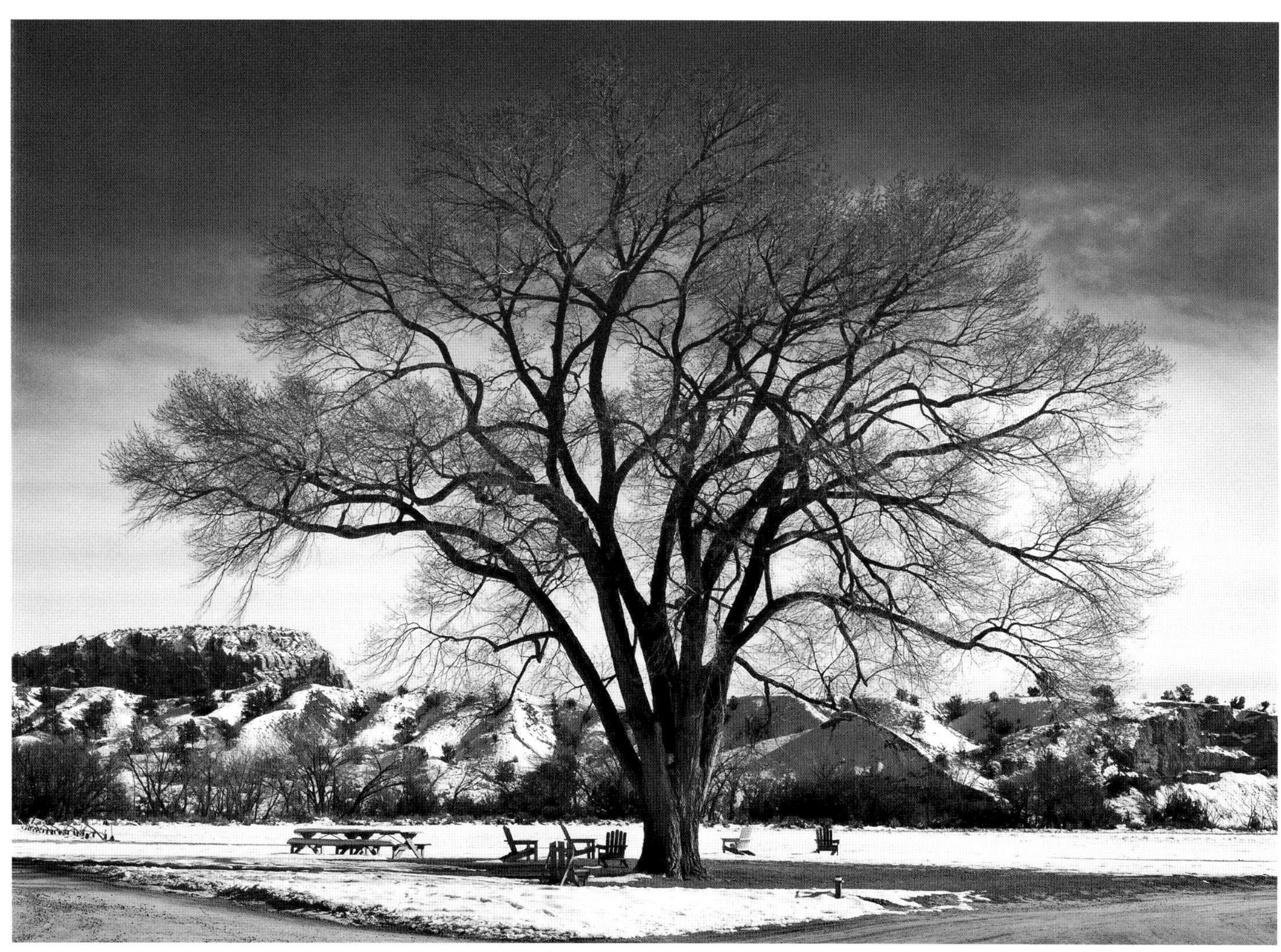

Plate 13: The Wisdom Tree, Winter, Ghost Ranch, New Mexico, 2005

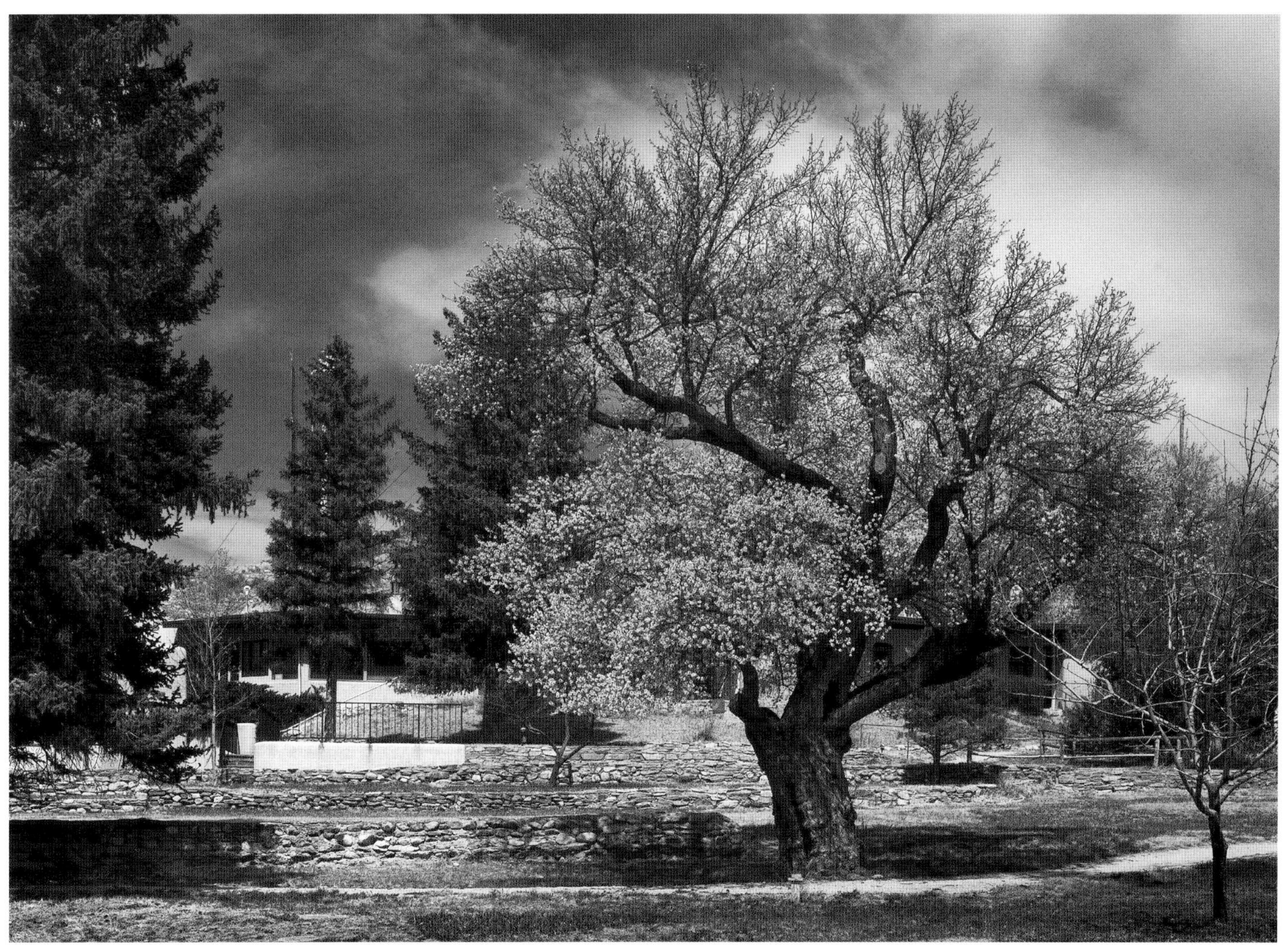

Plate 14: Fruit Tree in Bloom, Ranch Headquarters, Ghost Ranch, New Mexico, 2005

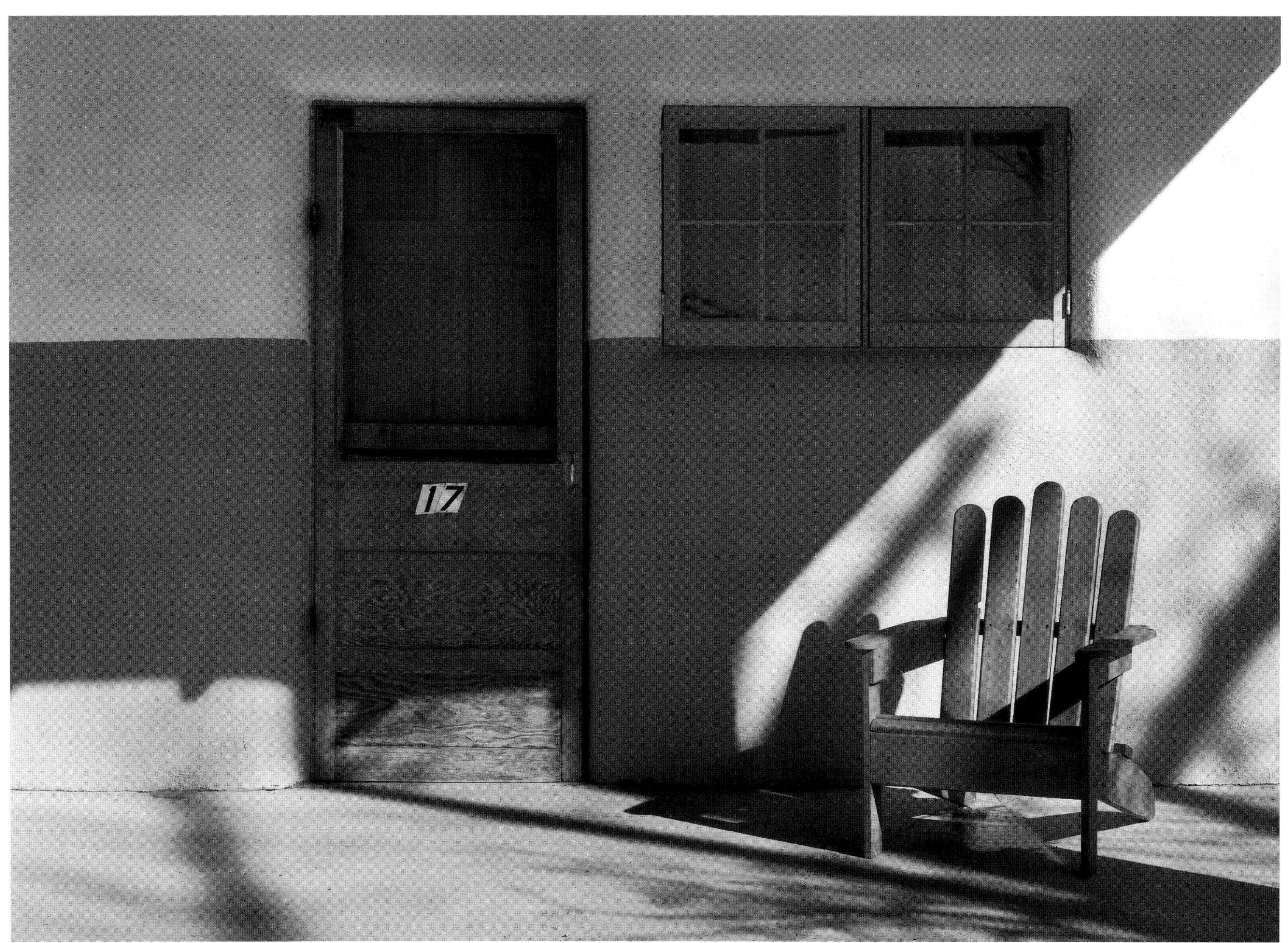

Plate 15: Room 17, Corral Block, Ghost Ranch, New Mexico, 2005

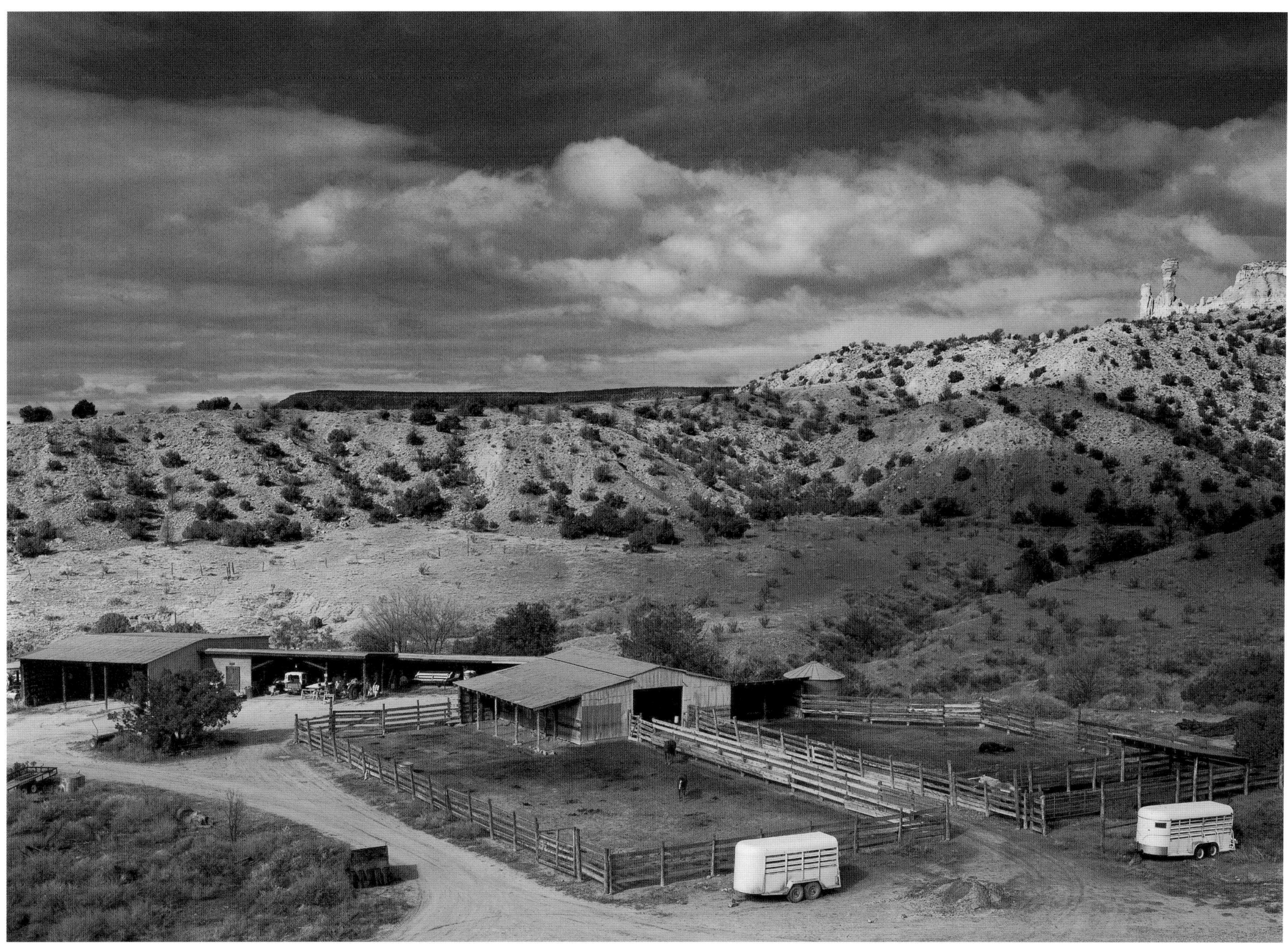

Plate 16: Overlooking the Horse Barn and Corrals, Ghost Ranch, New Mexico, 2005

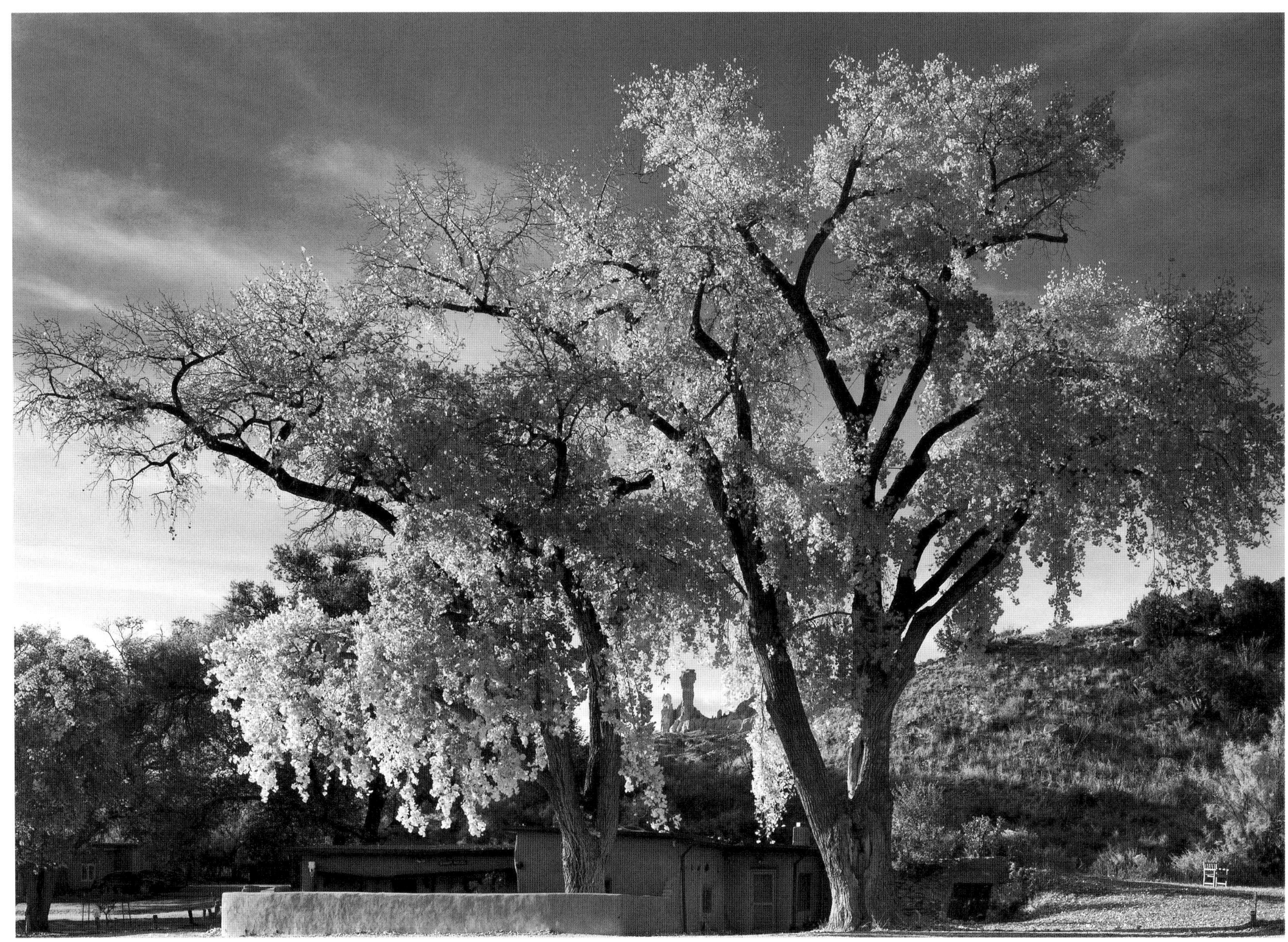

Plate 17: Cottonwoods at Ghost House, Ghost Ranch, New Mexico, 2006

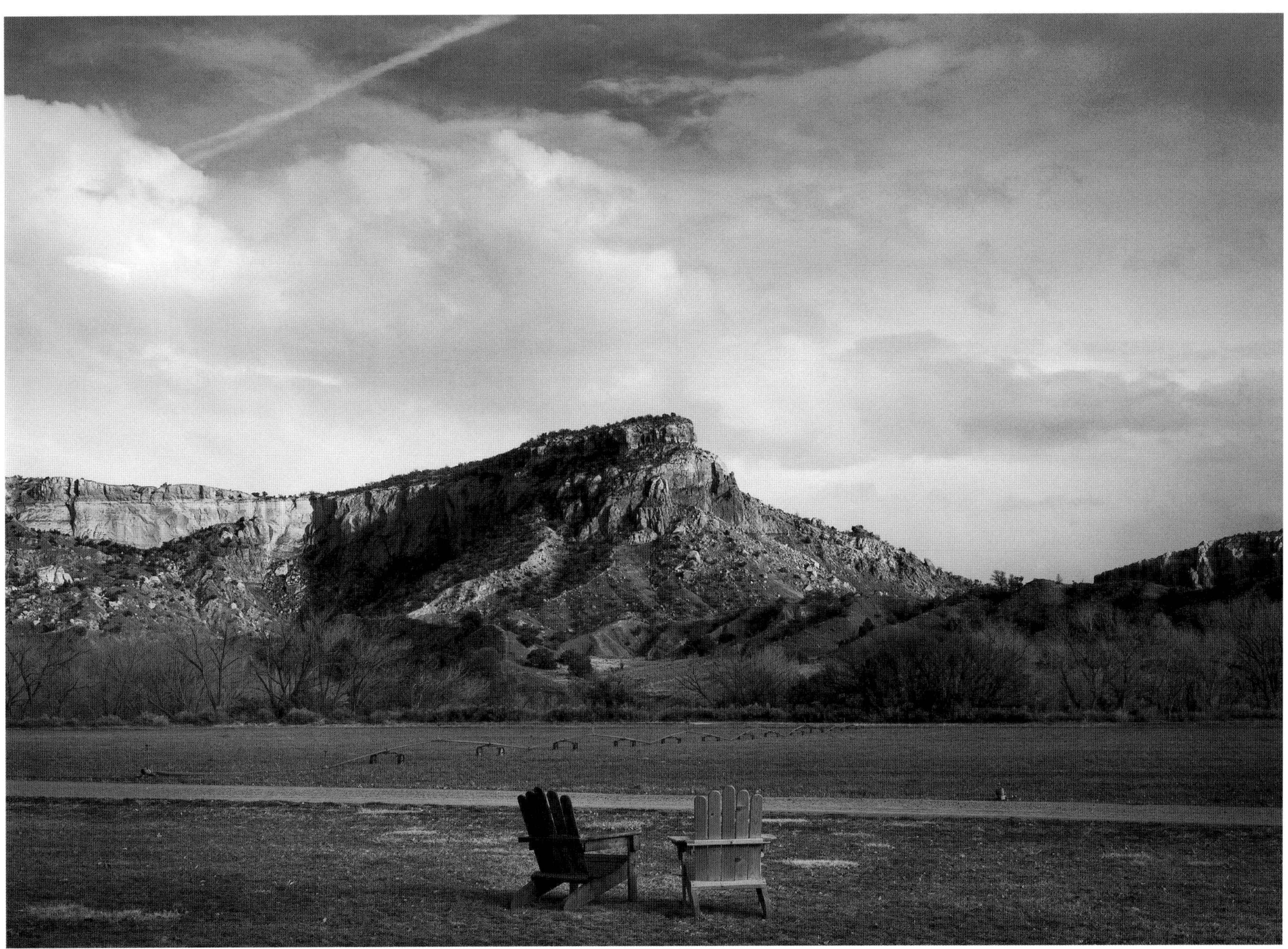

Plate 18: Pack's Point, Ghost Ranch, New Mexico, 2005

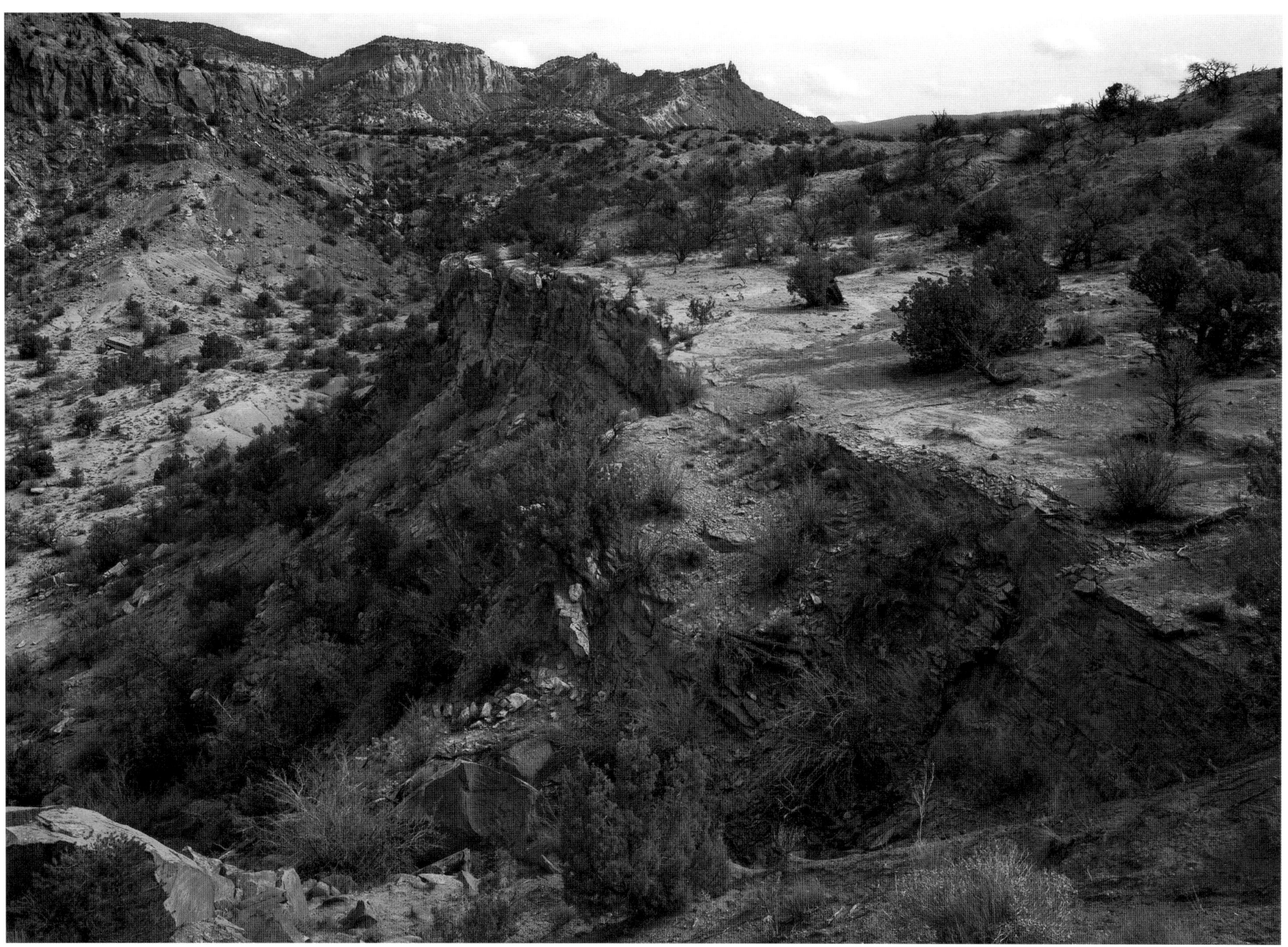

Plate 19: Comanche Canyon, Ghost Ranch, New Mexico, 2007

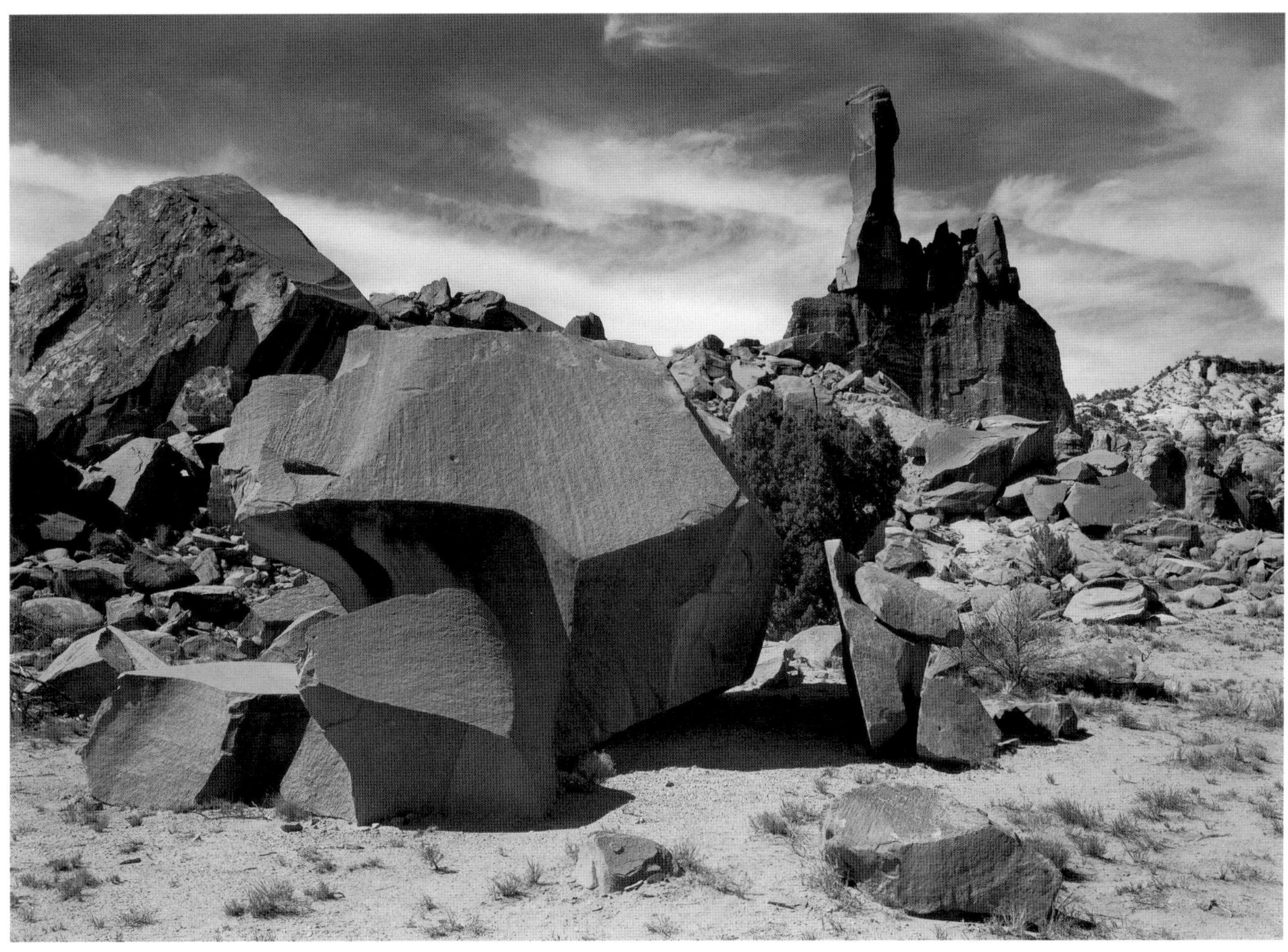

Plate 20: Boulders and Rock Forms, Comanche Canyon, Ghost Ranch, New Mexico, 2007

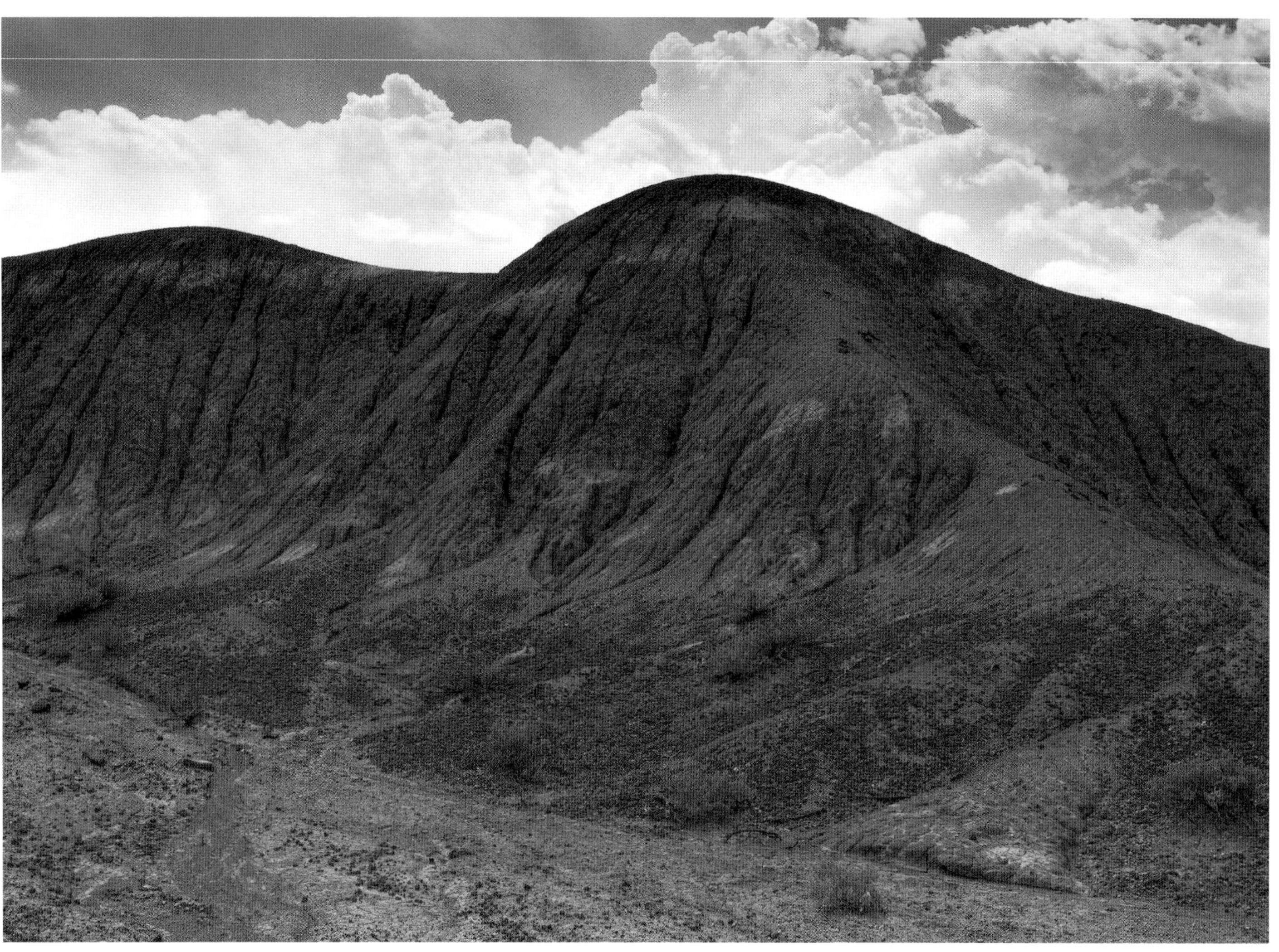

Plate 21: Red Hills and Clouds, Afternoon, Ghost Ranch, New Mexico, 2005

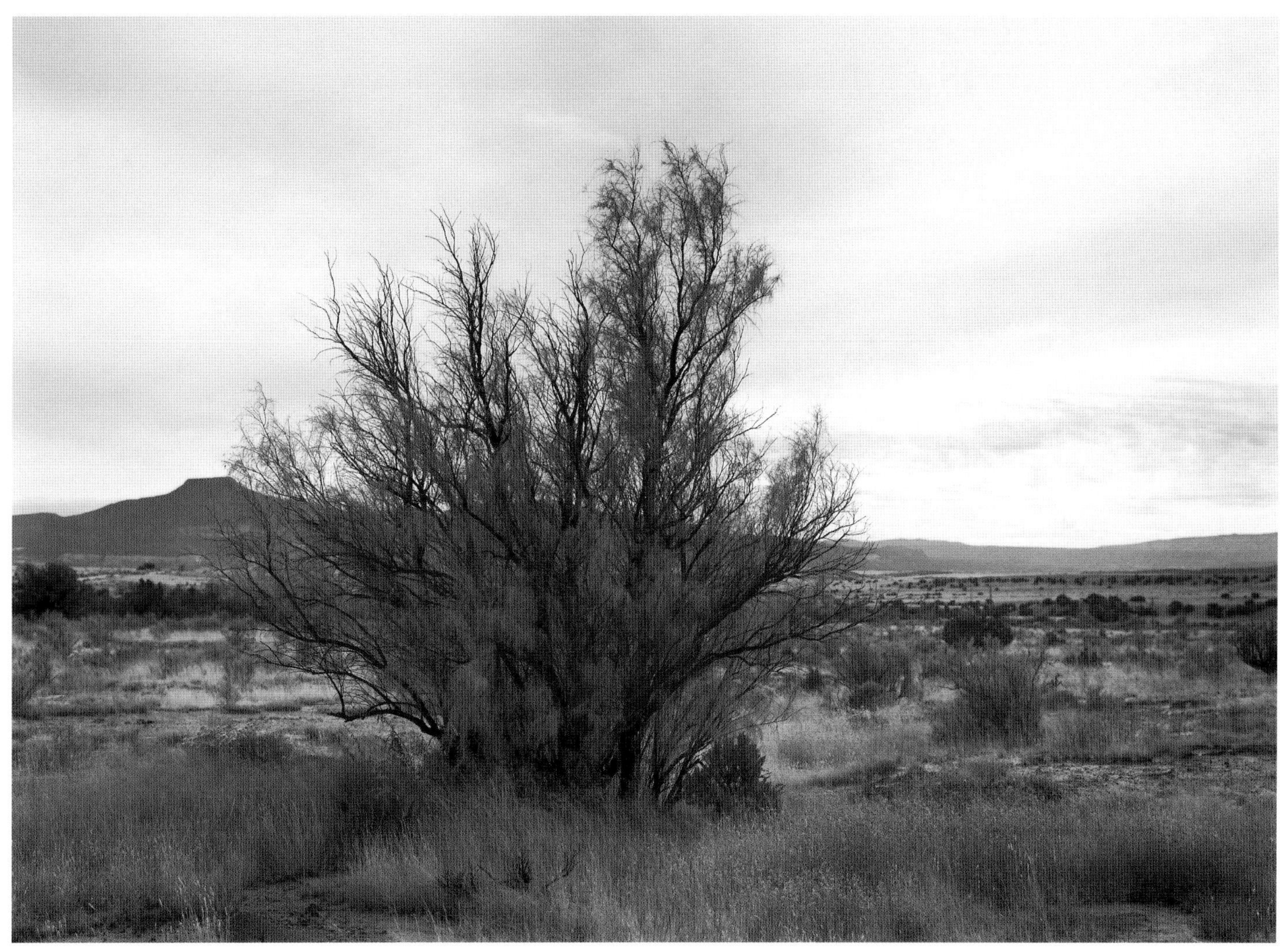

Plate 22: Salt Cedar, Ghost Ranch, New Mexico, 2006

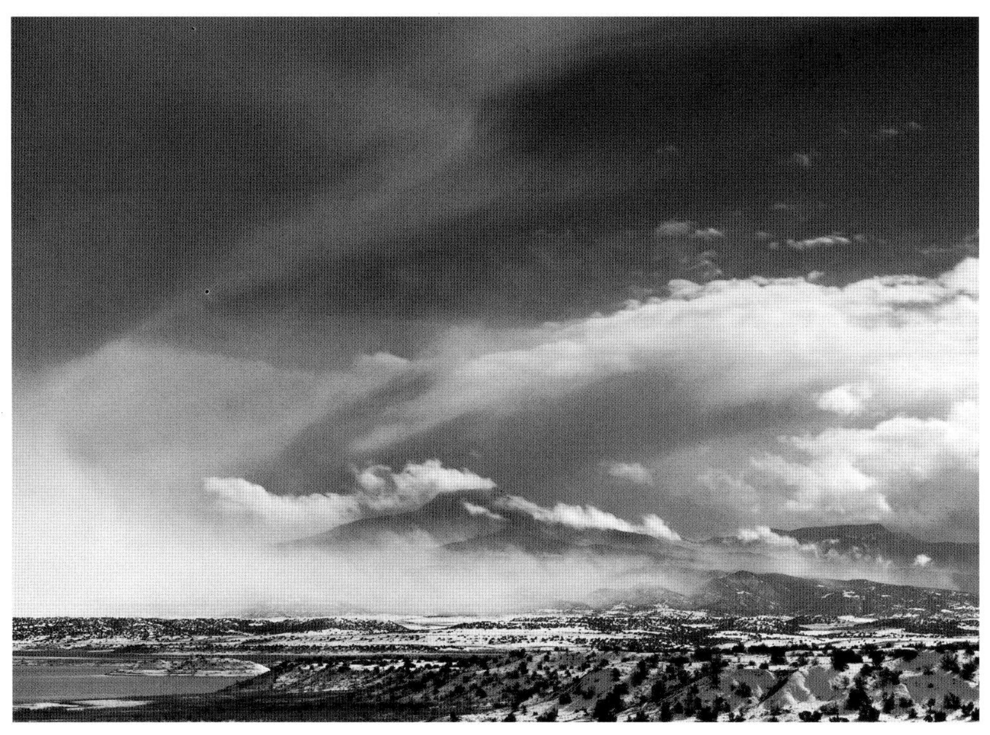

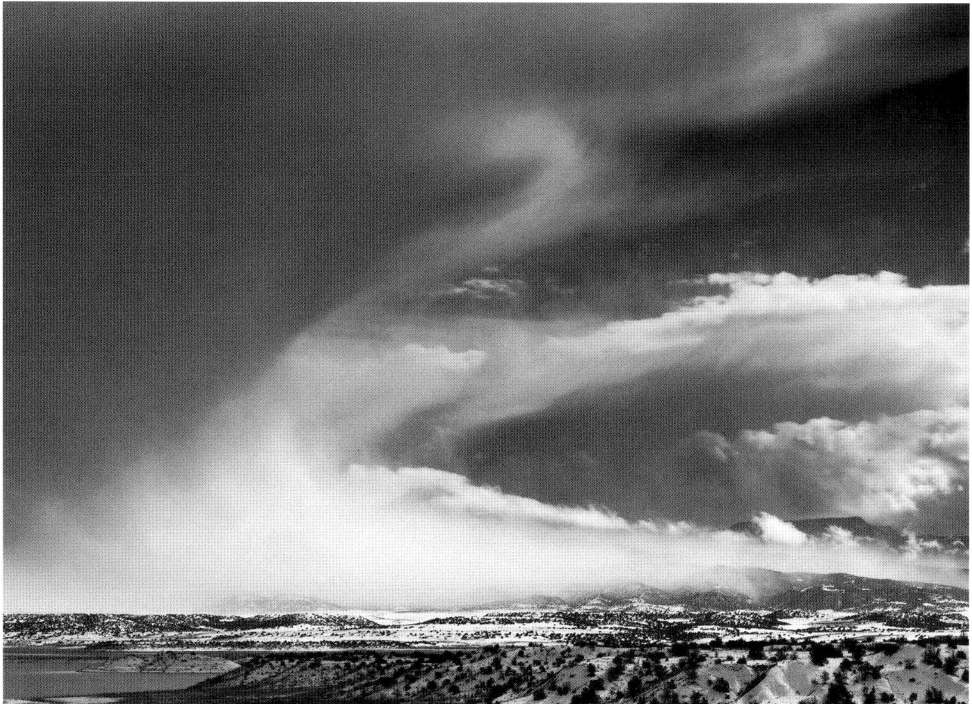

Plate 23–25: Winter Storm Series, Ghost Ranch, New Mexico, 2005

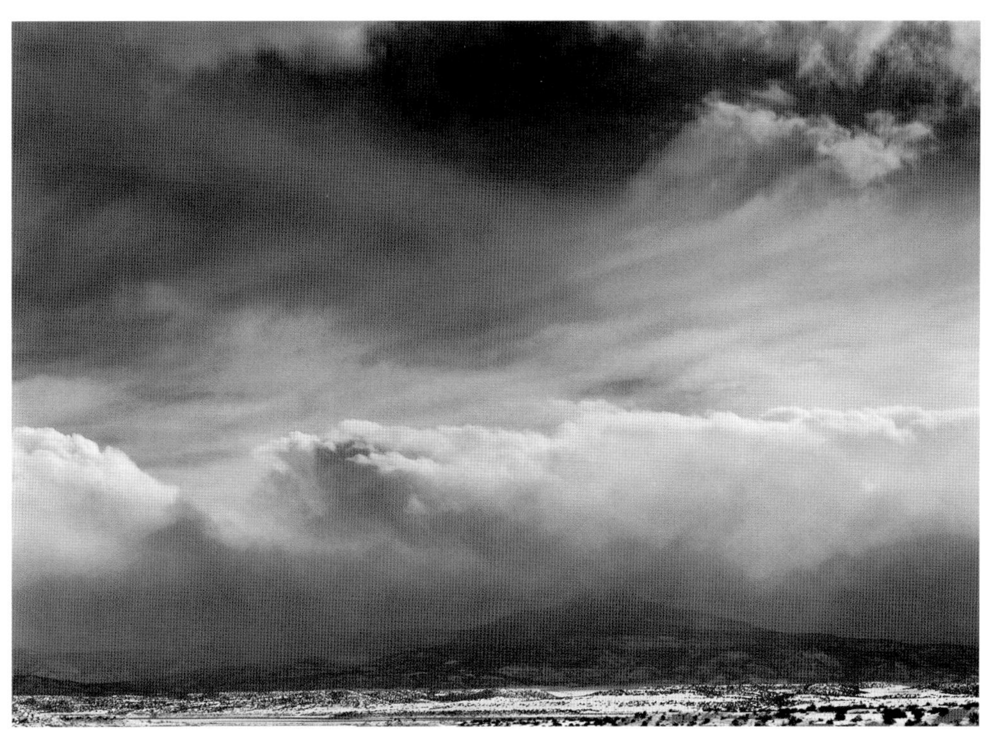

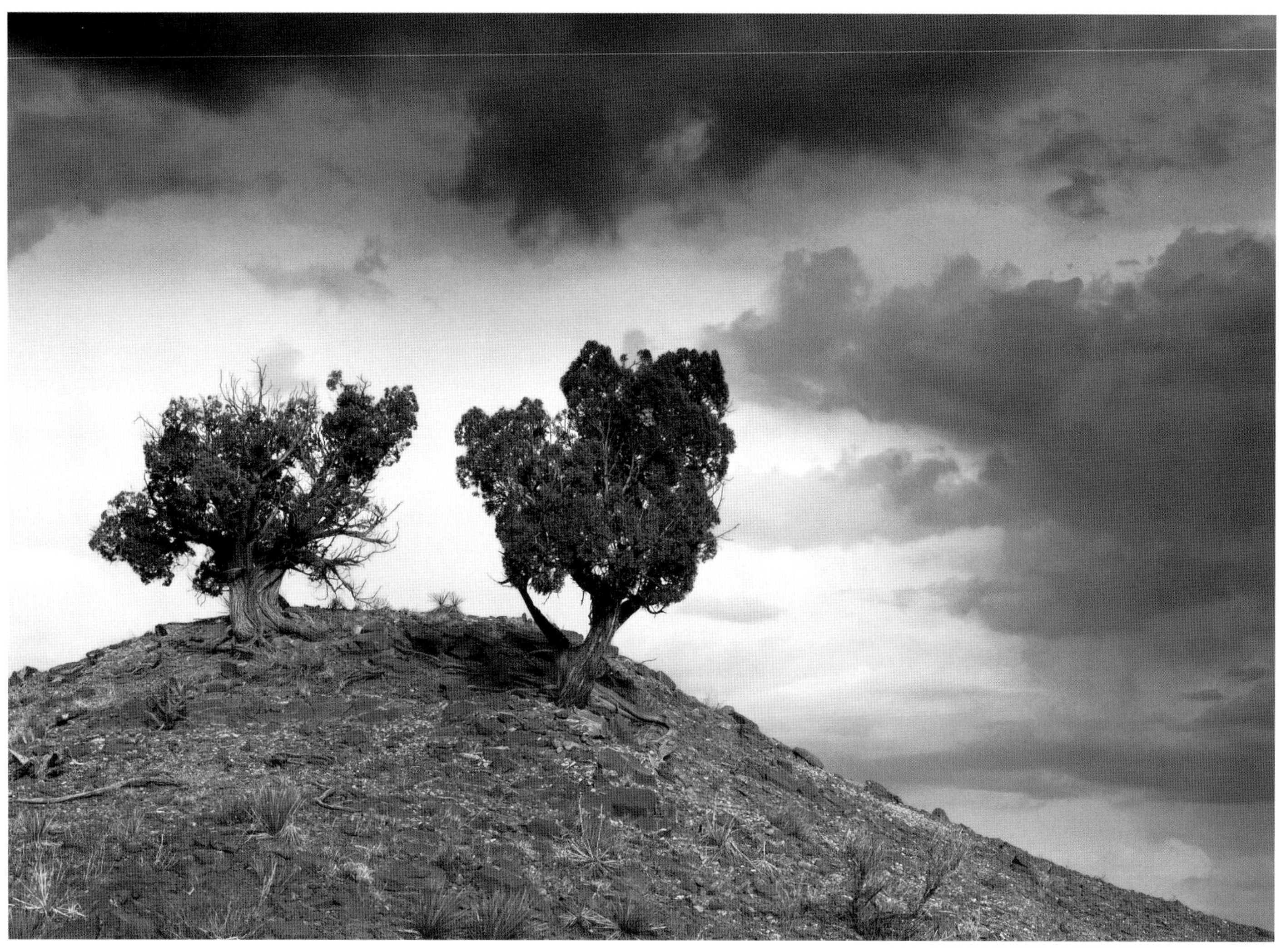

Plate 26: Two Trees, Afternoon Storm, Ghost Ranch, New Mexico, 2004

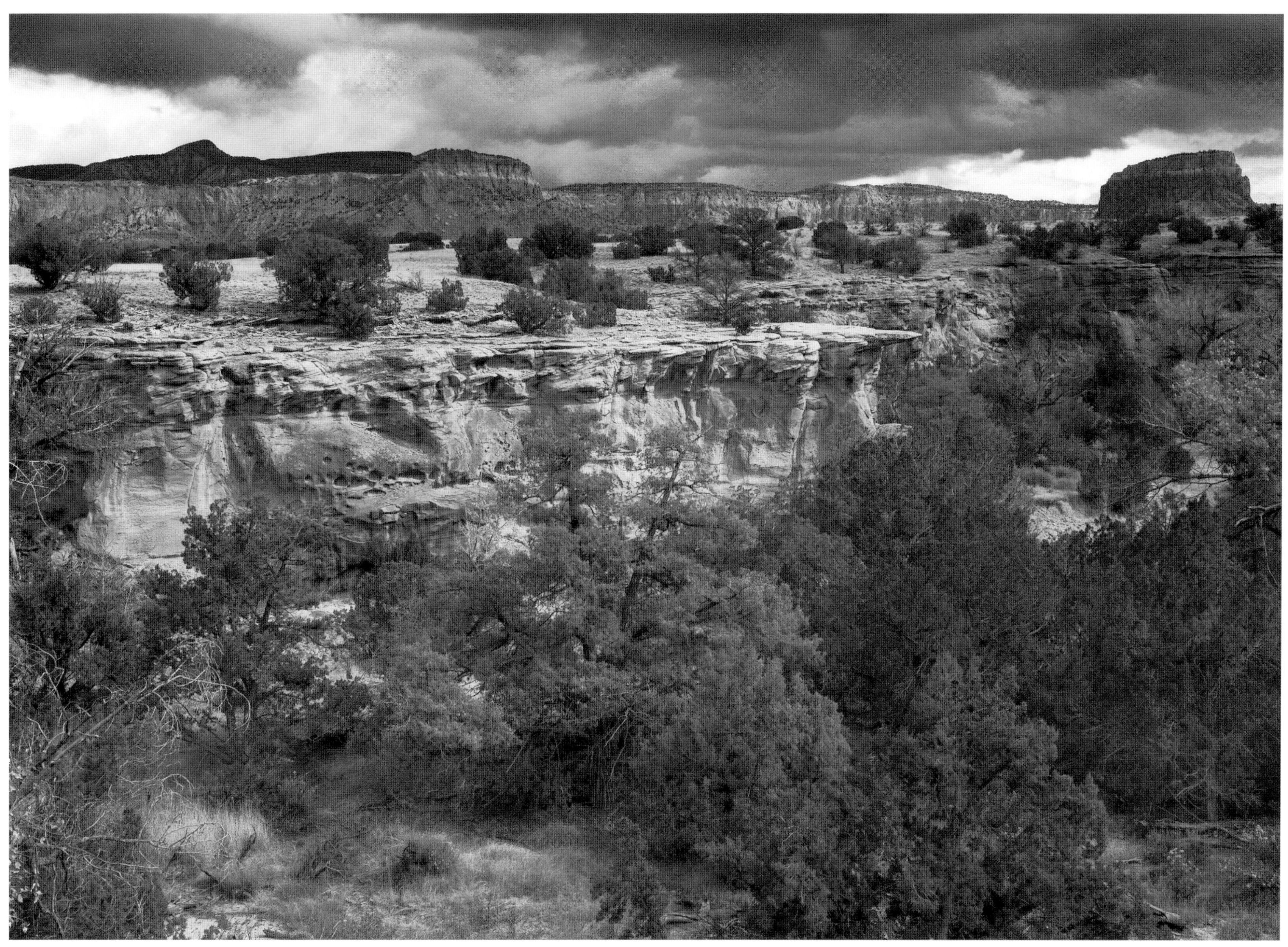

Plate 27: Pack's Point and Orphan Mesa, Arroyo Seco Pasture, Ghost Ranch, New Mexico, 2007

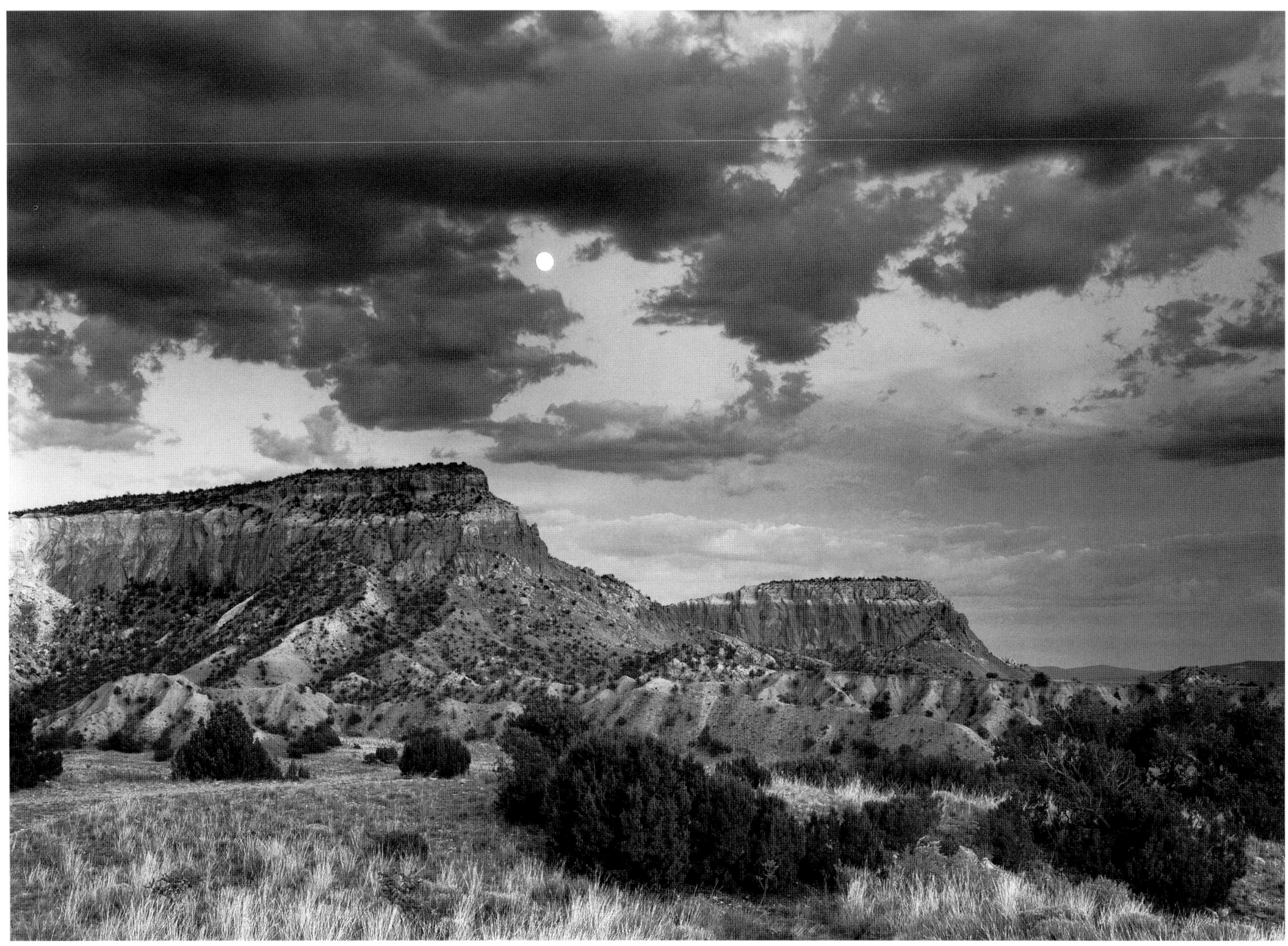

Plate 28: Moonrise over Pack's Point, Ghost Ranch, New Mexico, 2006

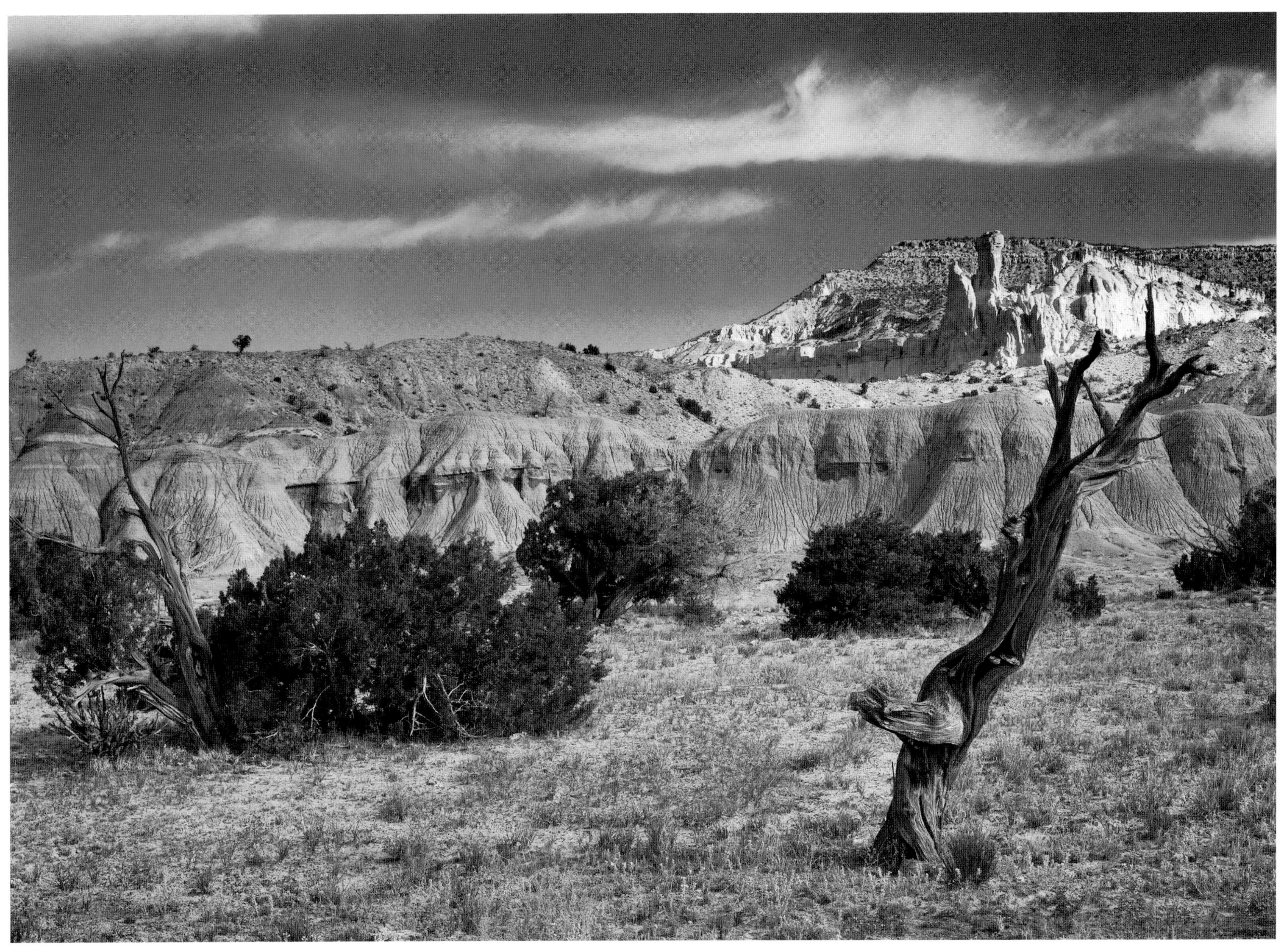

Plate 29: Juniper Tree and Chimney Rock, Ghost Ranch, New Mexico, 2005

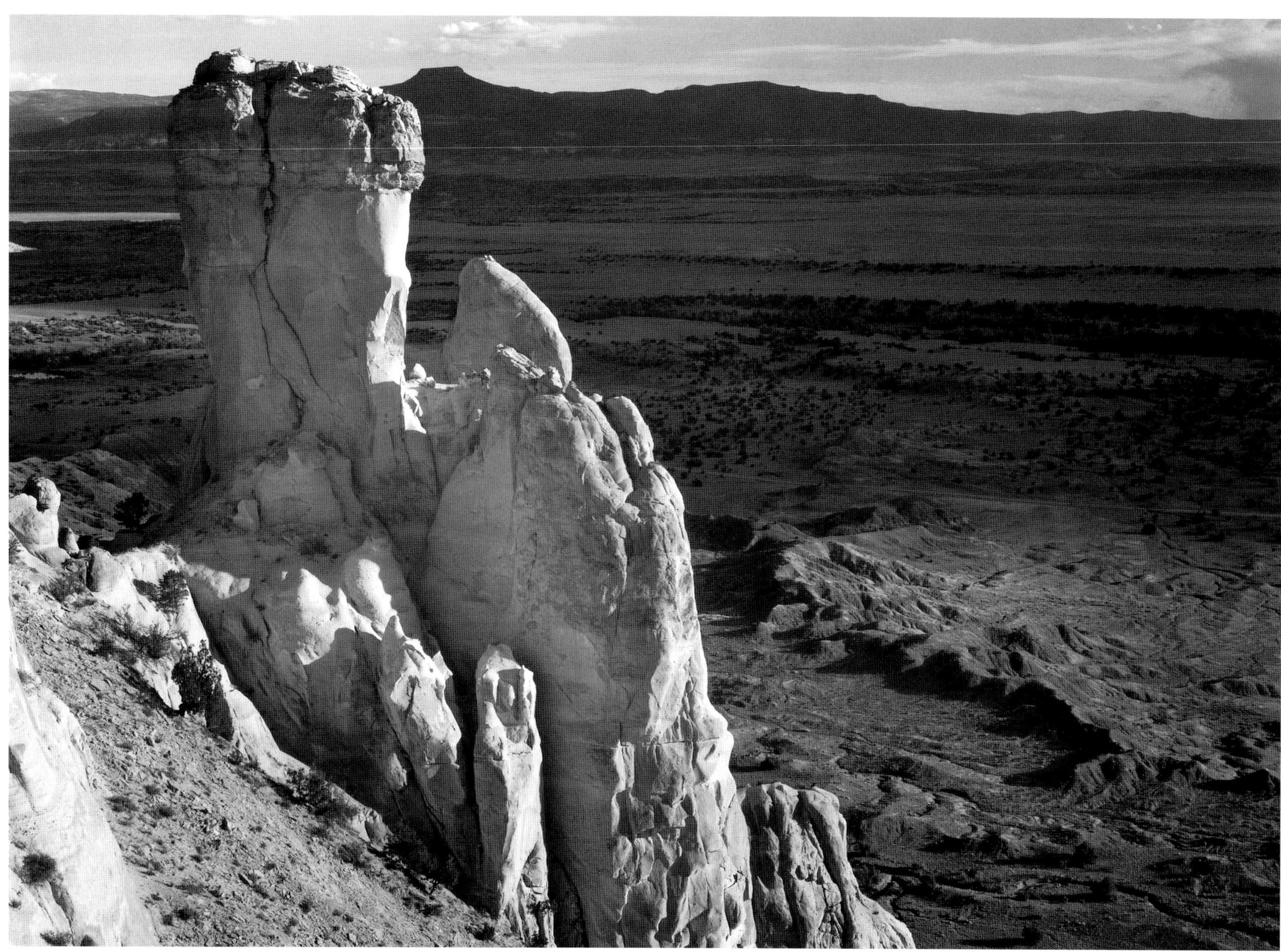

Plate 30: Chimney Rock after Storm, Late Afternoon, Ghost Ranch, New Mexico, 2005

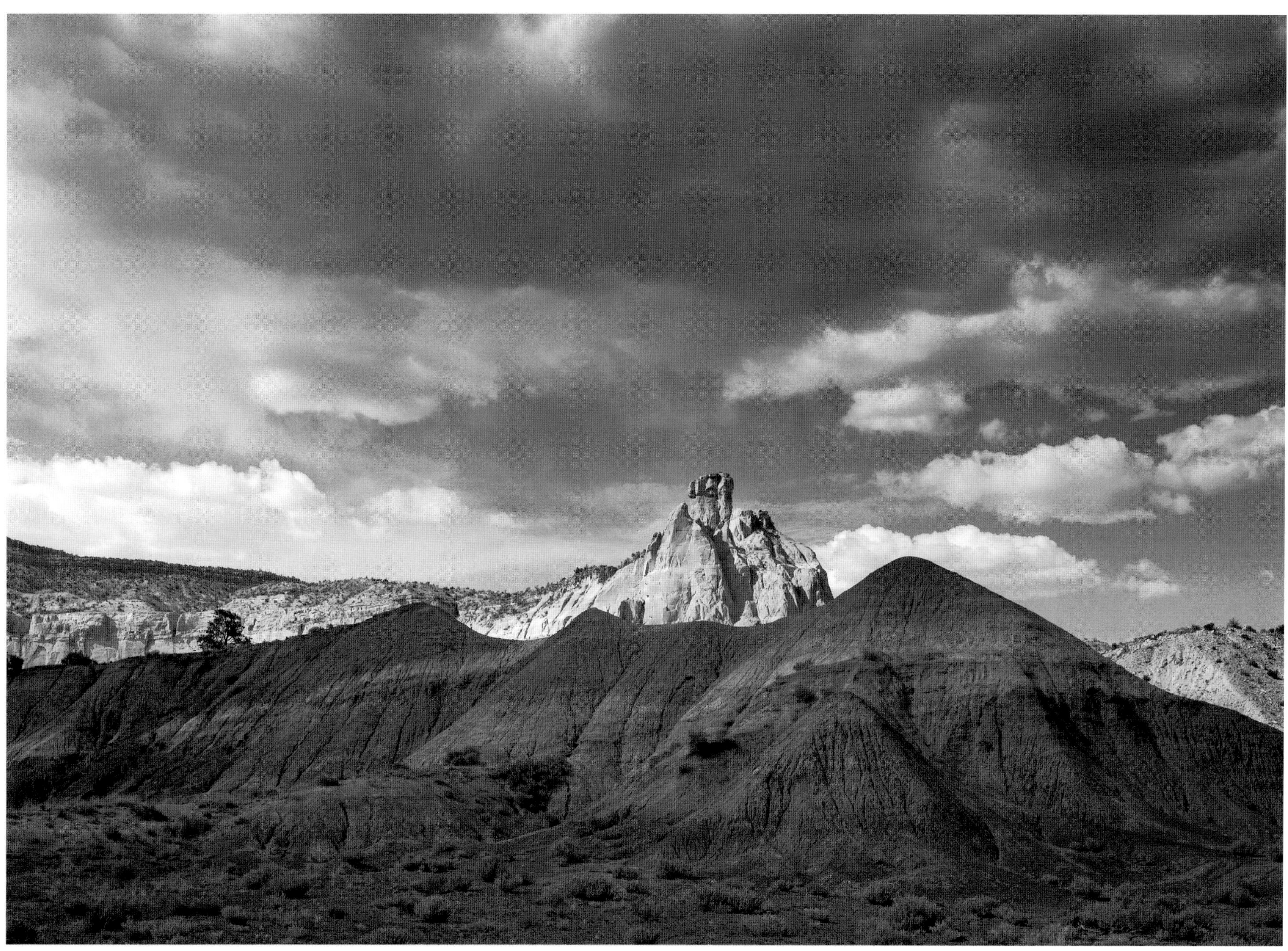

Plate 31: Red Hills and Chimney Rock, Ghost Ranch, New Mexico, 2007

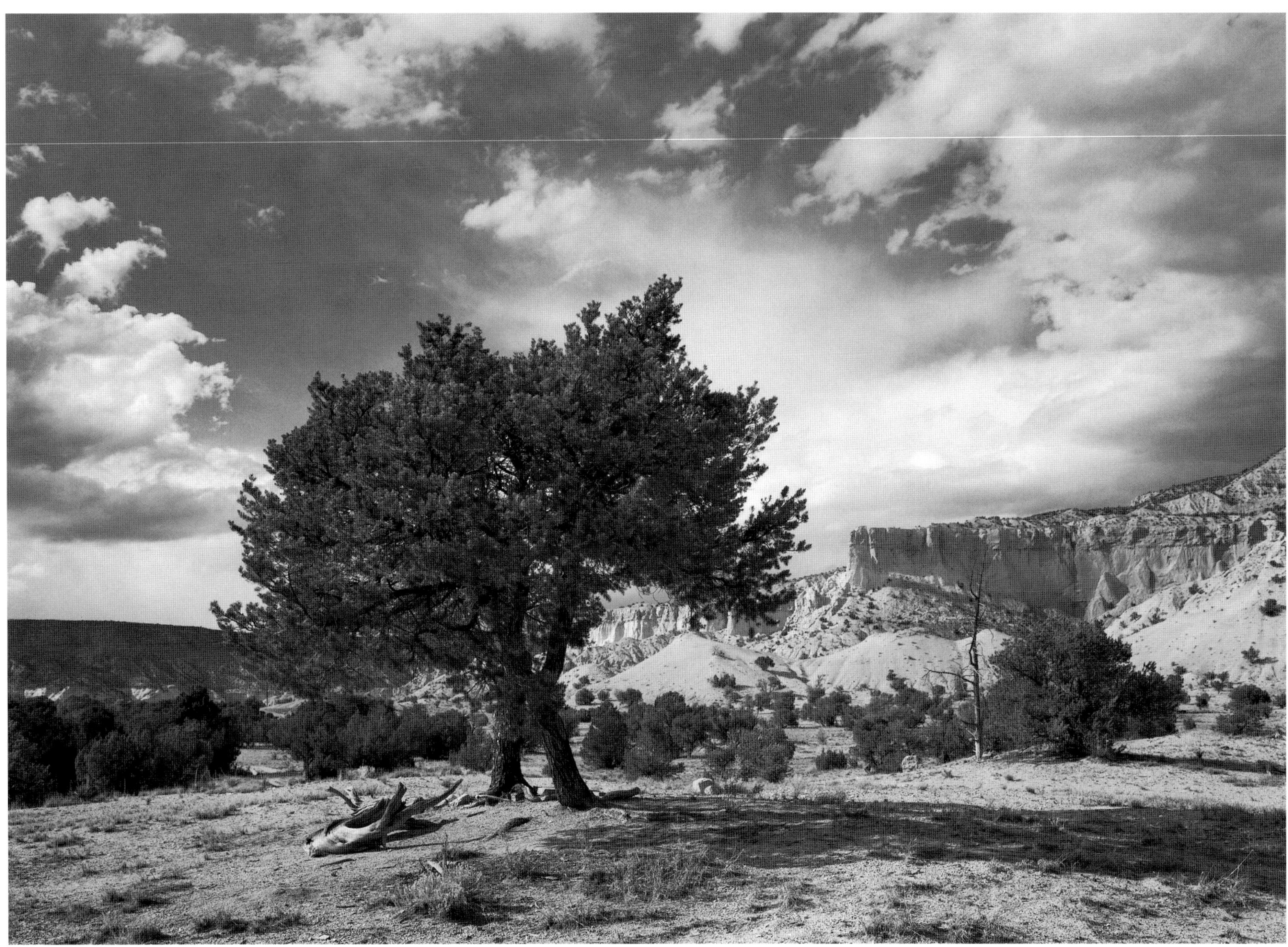

Plate 32: Twin Trees, Late Summer, Ghost Ranch, New Mexico, 2003

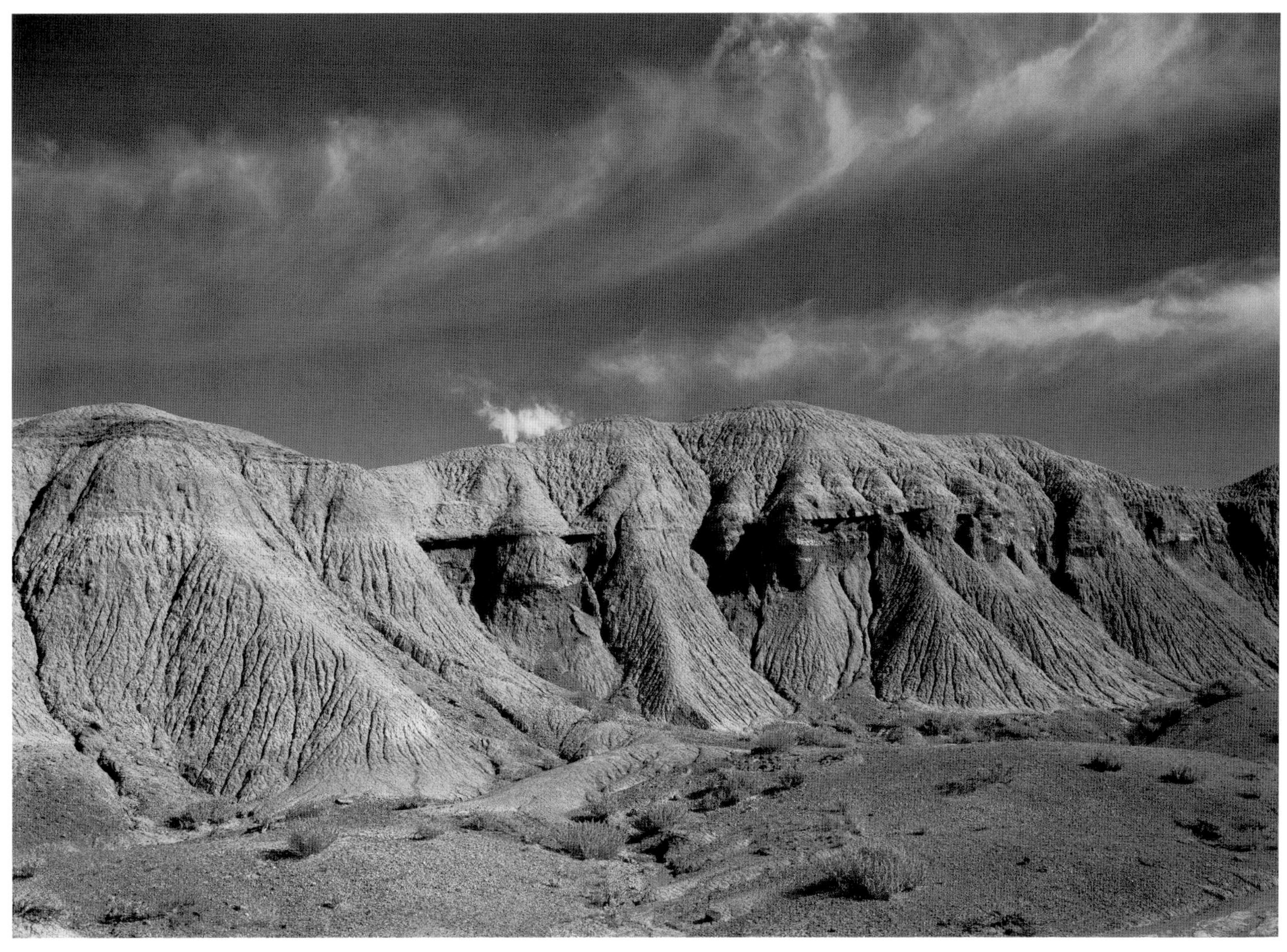

Plate 33: Lavendar Hills and Clouds, Ghost Ranch, New Mexico, 2004

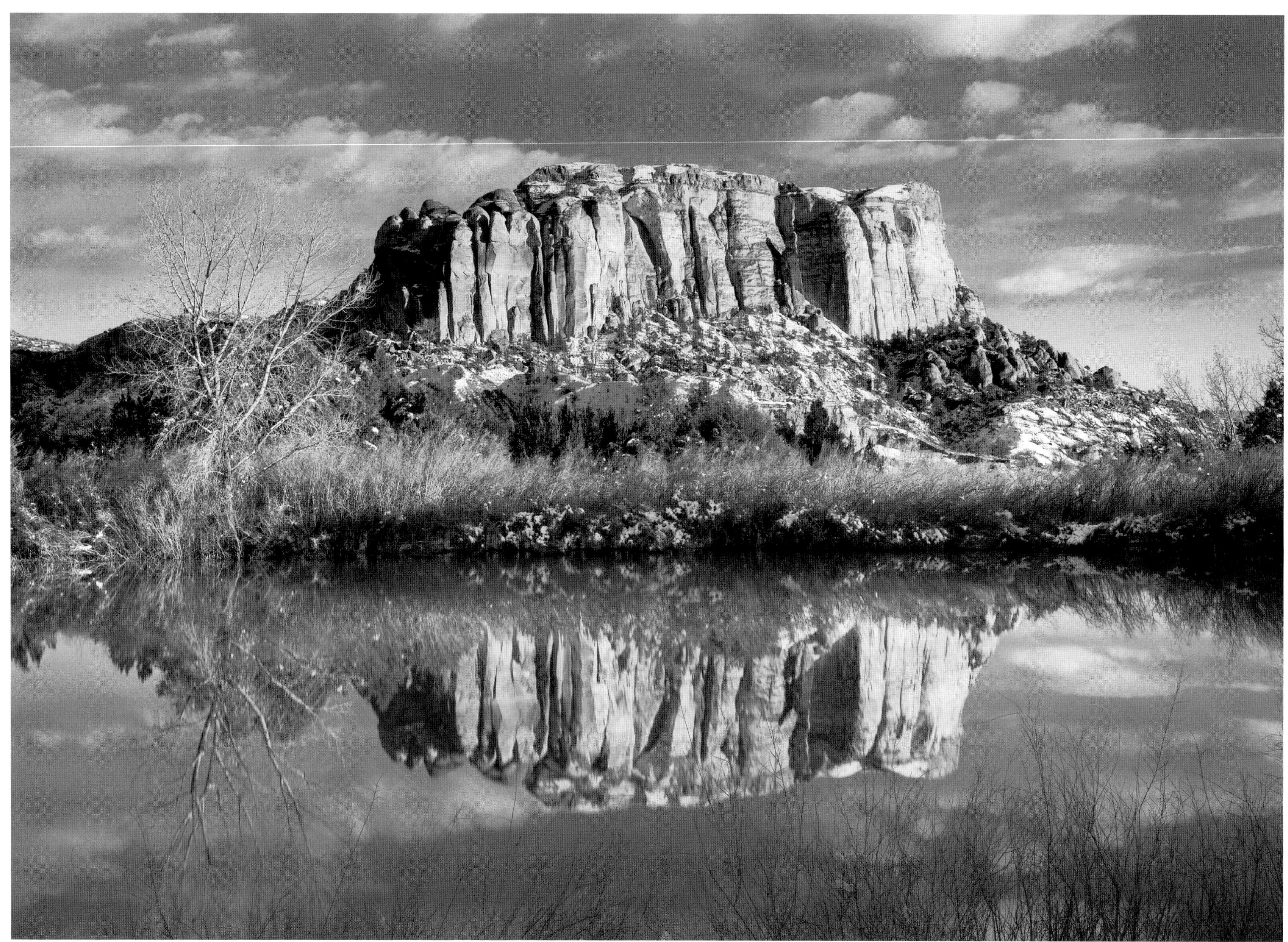

Plate 34: Kitchen Mesa (Ice Cream Rock) Reflection, Winter, Ghost Ranch, New Mexico, 2004

Peggy Pack McKinley, who lived at Ghost Ranch as a child during the 1930s, remembers that Kitchen Mesa was also called Ice Cream Rock.

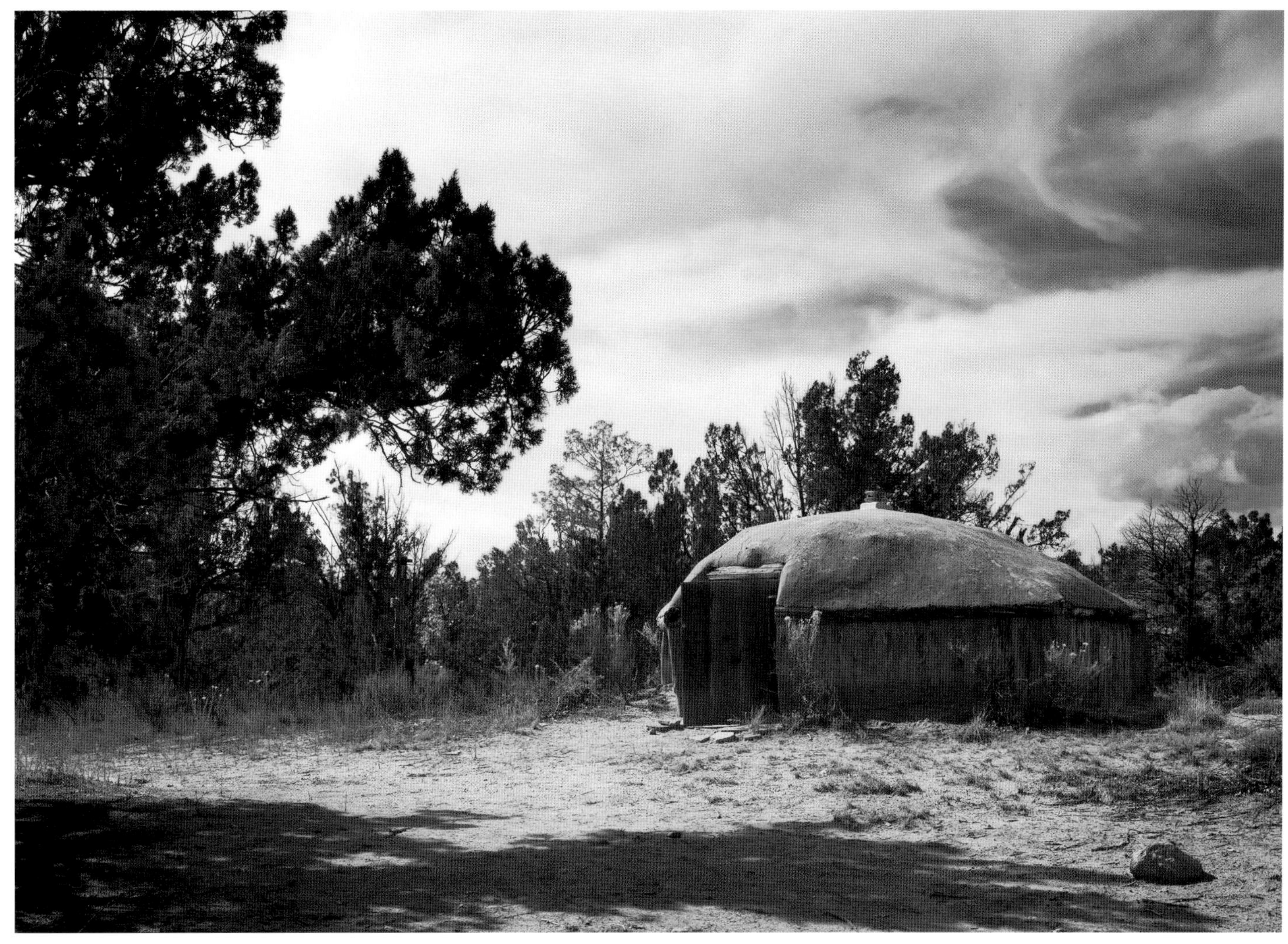

Plate 35: Hogan, Box Canyon Trail, Ghost Ranch, New Mexico, 2005

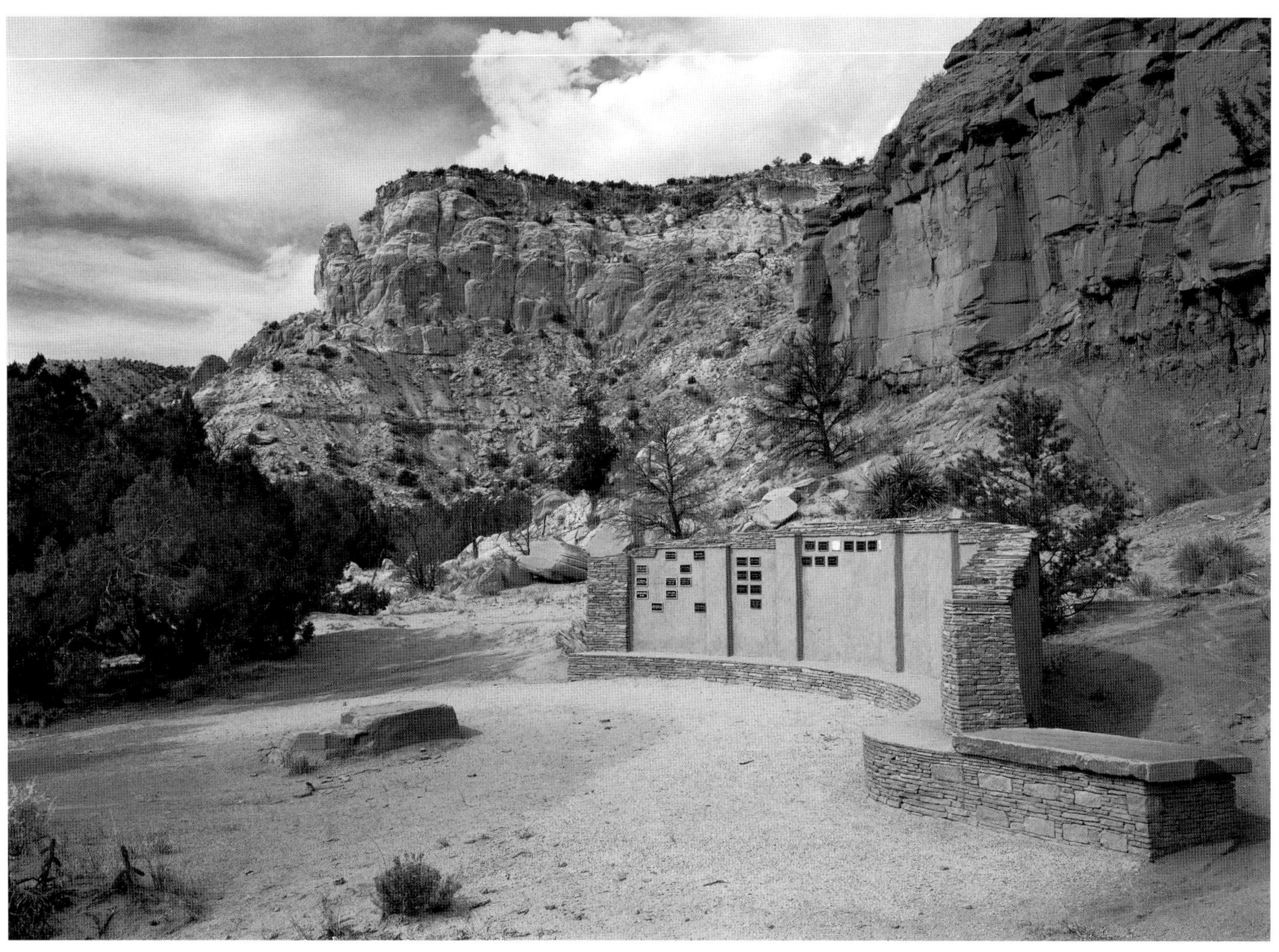

Plate 36: Campo Santo, Yeso Canyon, Ghost Ranch, New Mexico, 2005

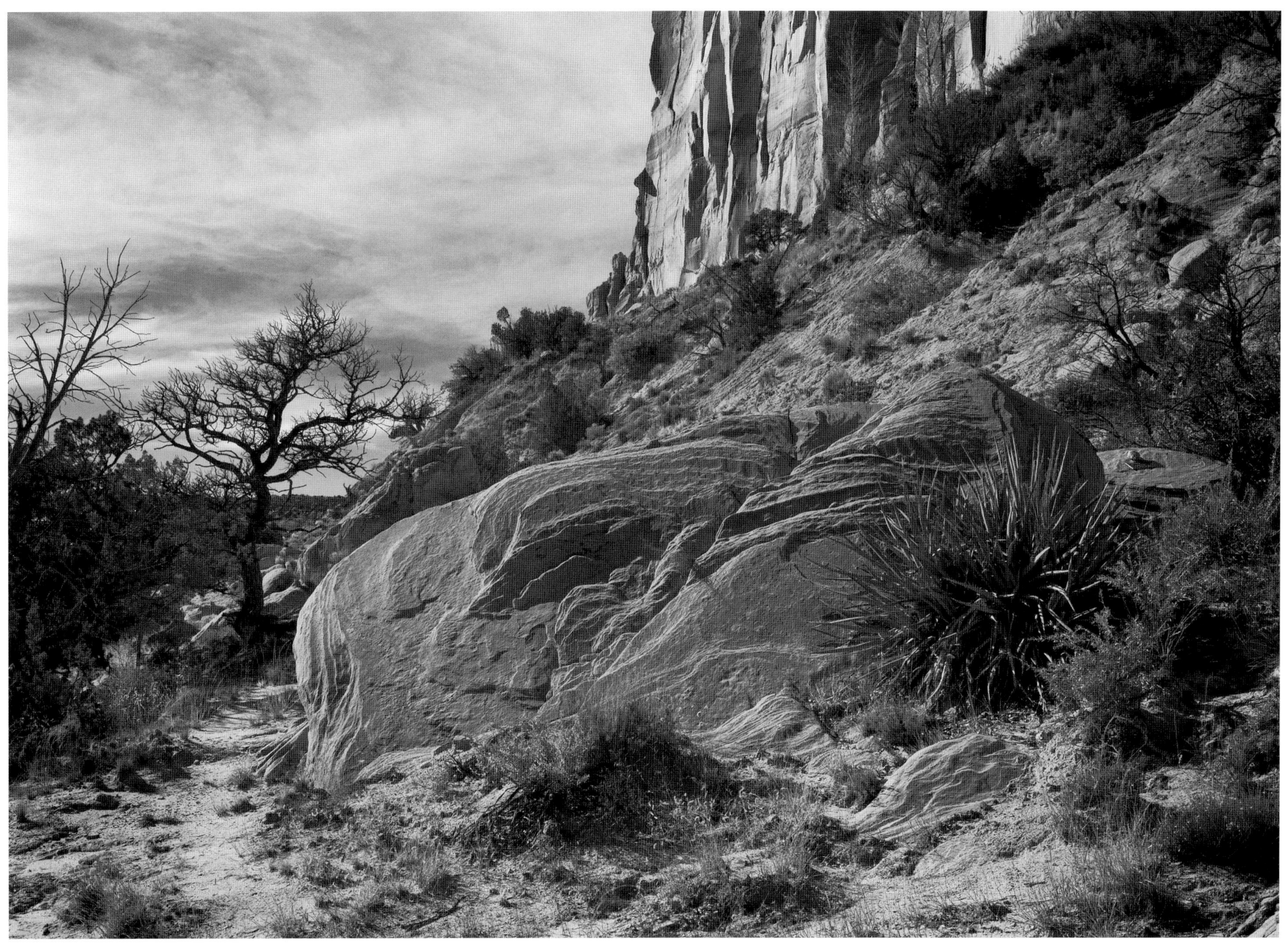

Plate 37: Boulder, Yeso Canyon, Ghost Ranch, New Mexico, 2007

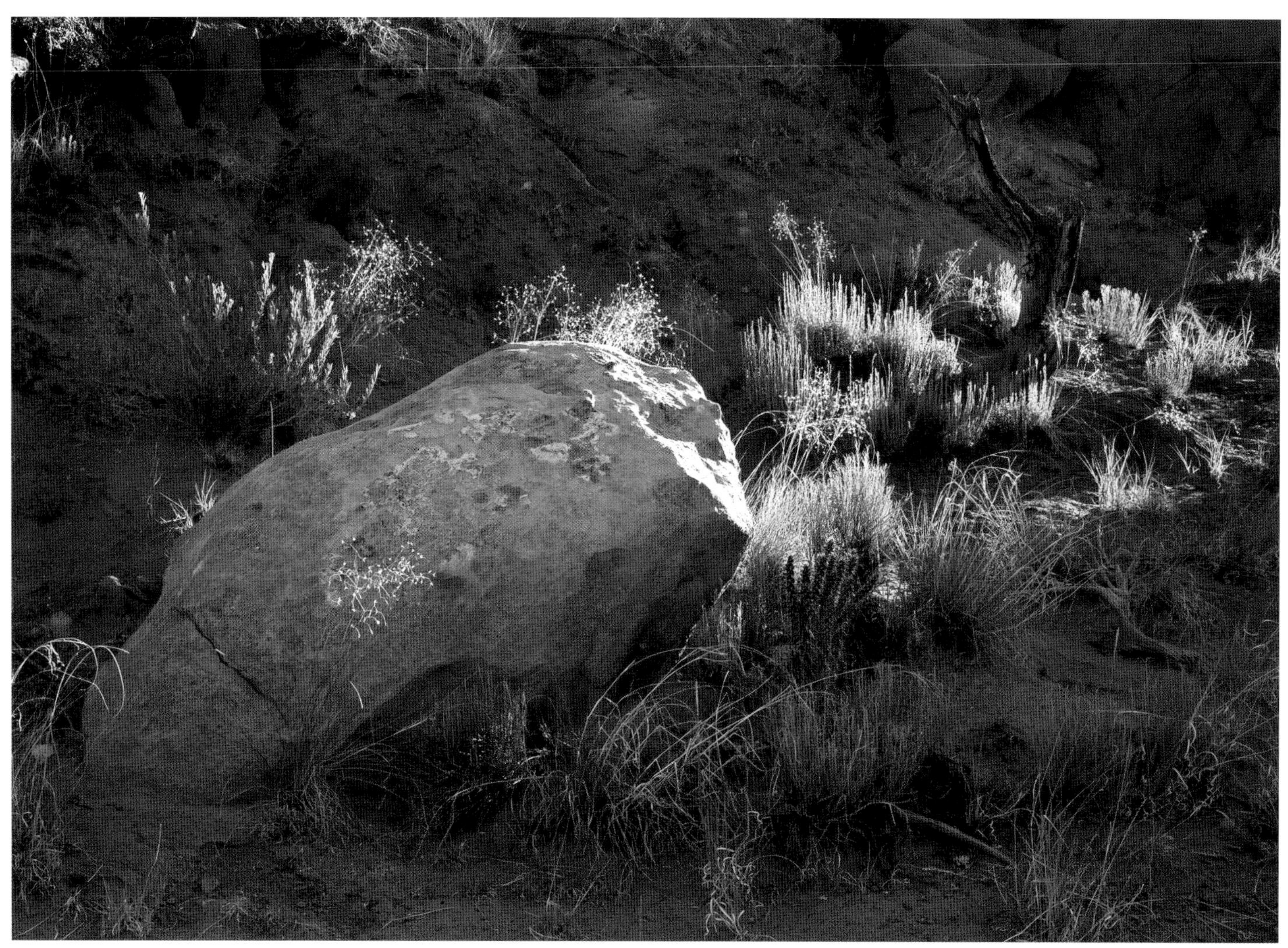

Plate 38: Rock and Grass Study, Yeso Canyon, Summer, Ghost Ranch, New Mexico, 2005

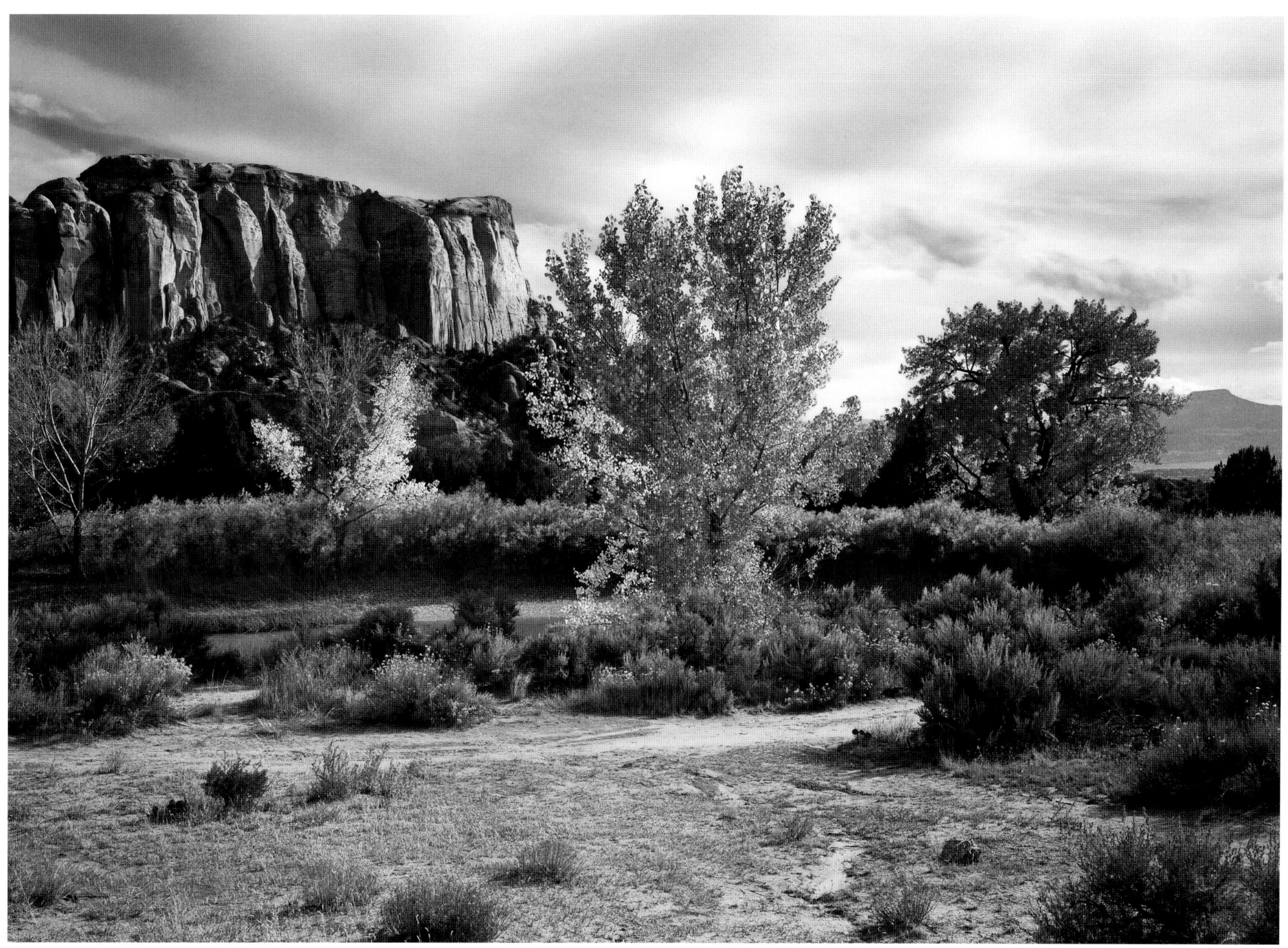

Plate 39: Box Canyon Trail past Kitchen Mesa, Ghost Ranch, New Mexico, 2007

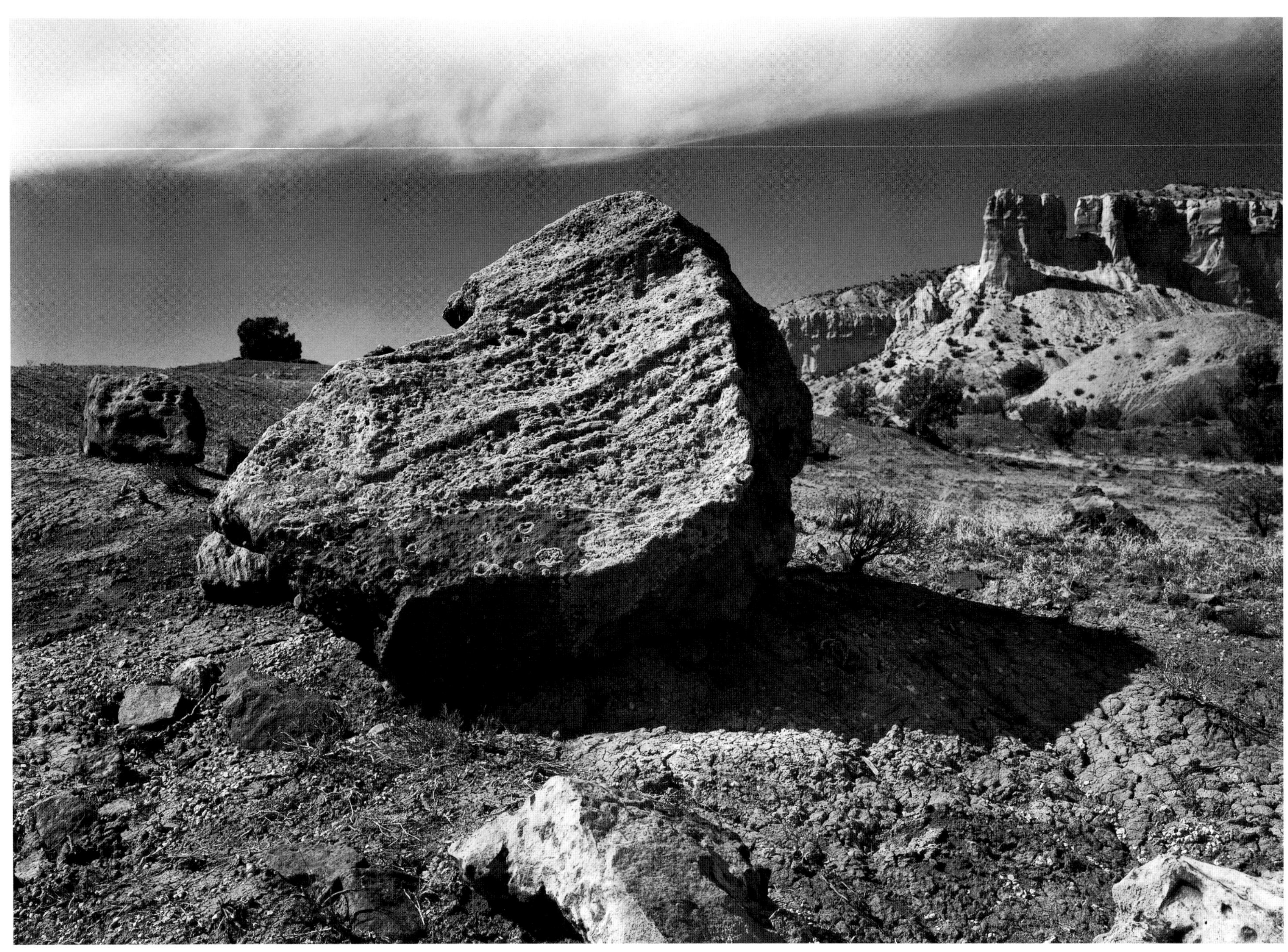

Plate 40: Boulder and Puerta del Cielo (Bennett Chimneys), Ghost Ranch, New Mexico, 2007

The stone spires forming Puerta del Cielo have also been referred to as the Bennett Chimneys, after Edward Bennett, who in 1934 built the house that sits directly beneath them.

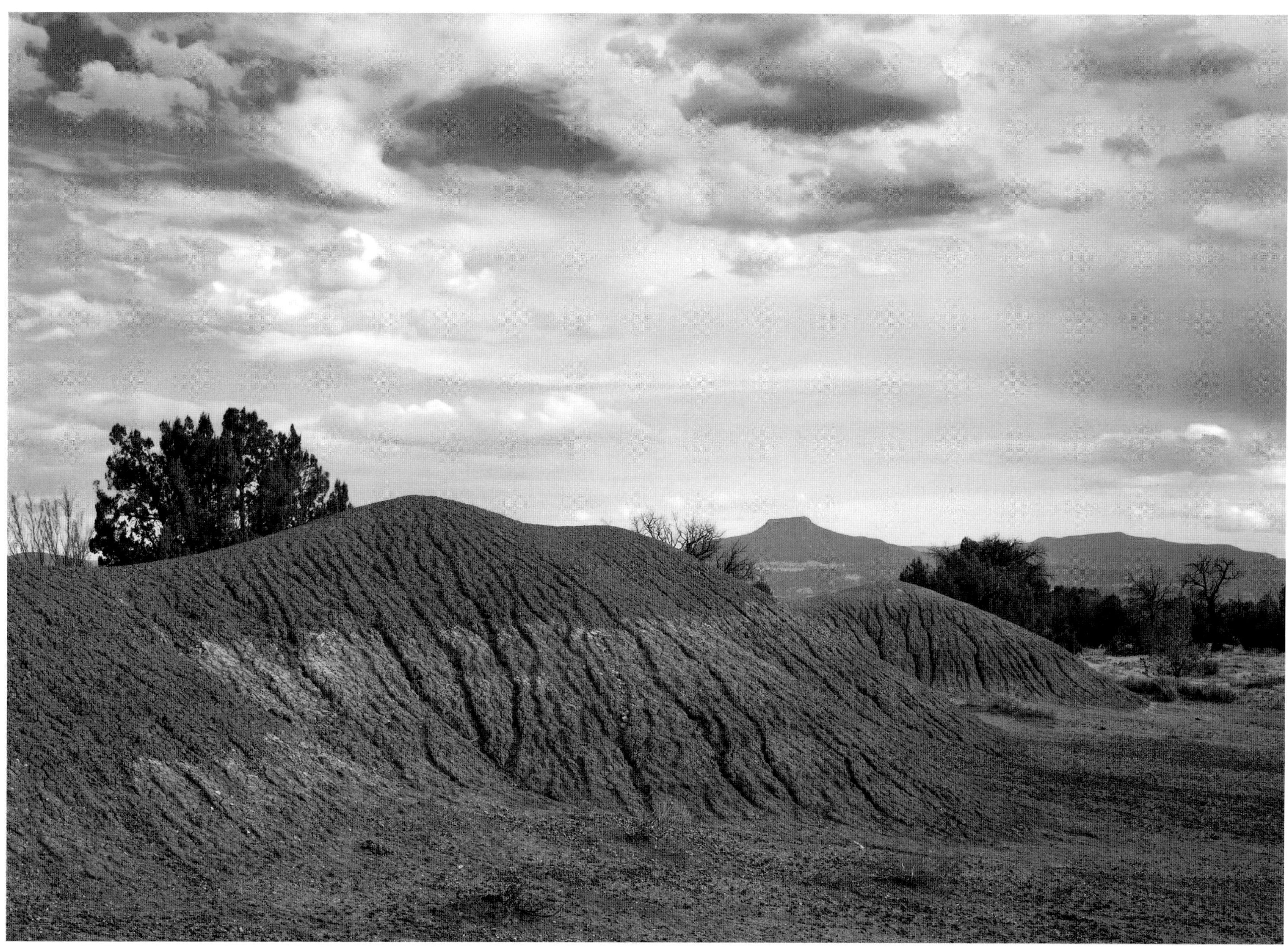

Plate 41: Red Hills and Cerro Pedernal, Ghost Ranch, New Mexico, 2006

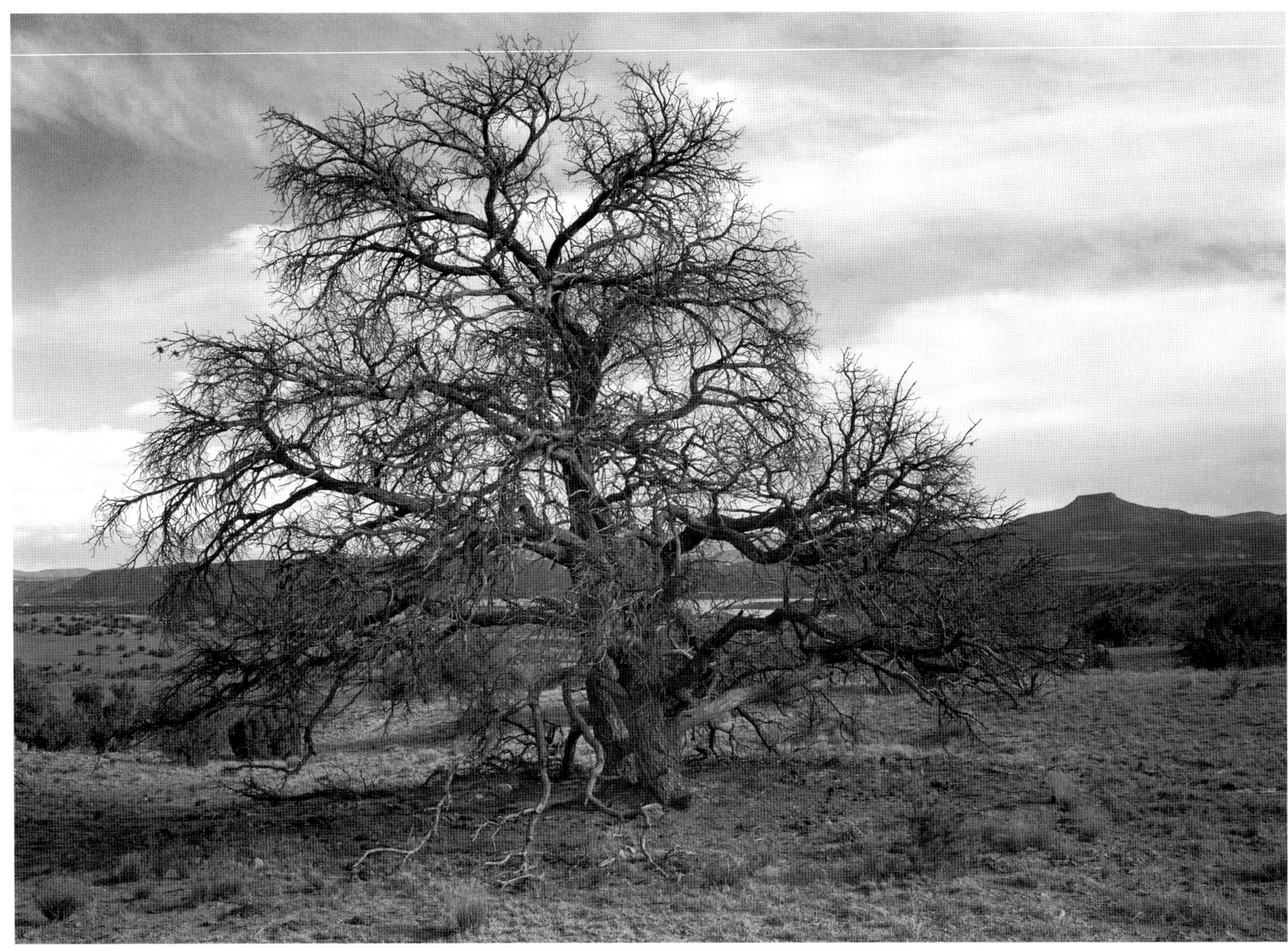

Plate 42: Skeleton Tree, Ghost Ranch, New Mexico, 2004

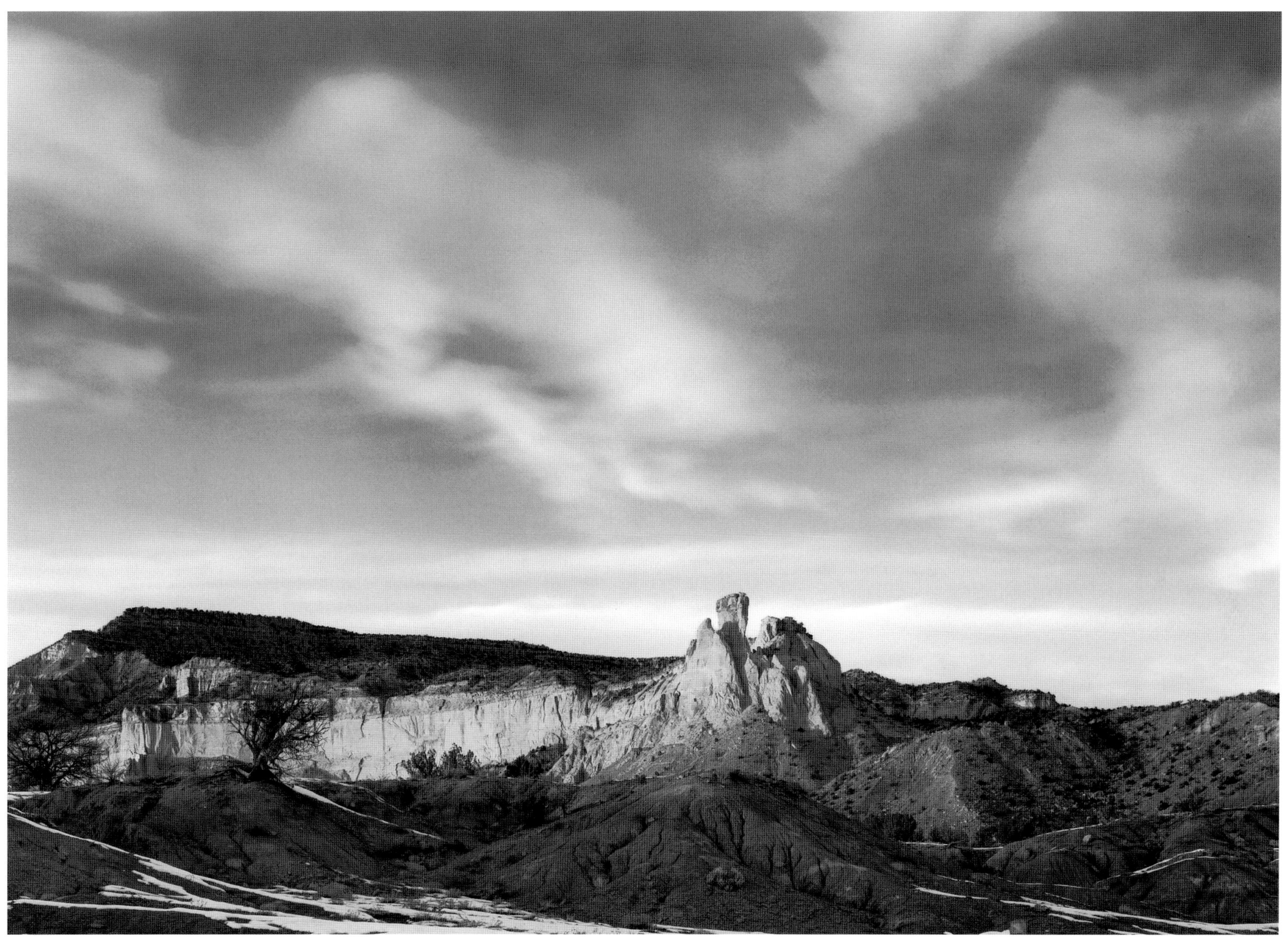

Plate 43: Chimney Rock after Winter Storm, Ghost Ranch, New Mexico, 2006

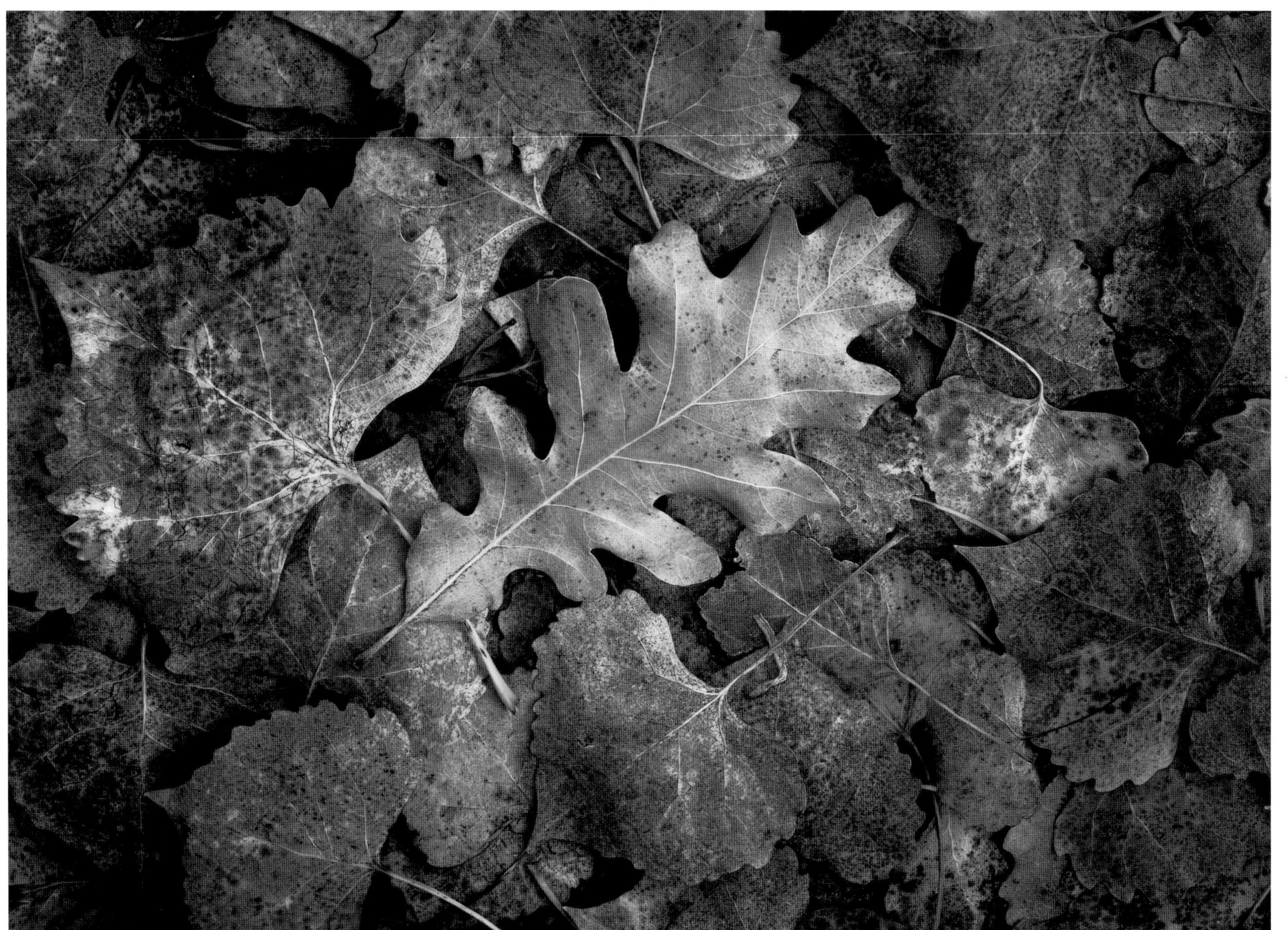

Plate 44: Oak Leaf and Cottonwoods, Ghost Ranch, New Mexico, 2001

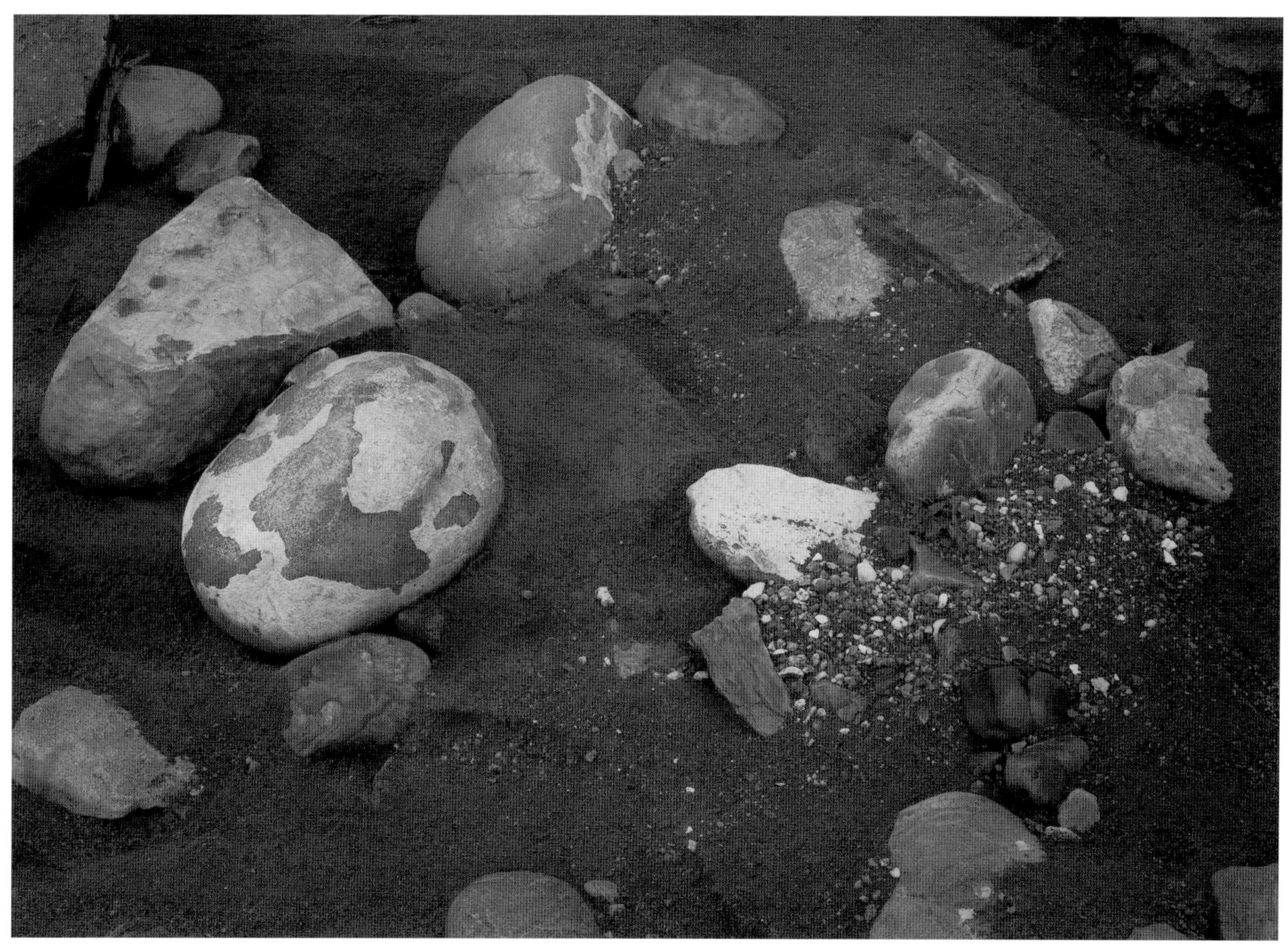

Plate 45: Arroyo Rock Study, Ghost Ranch, New Mexico, 2005

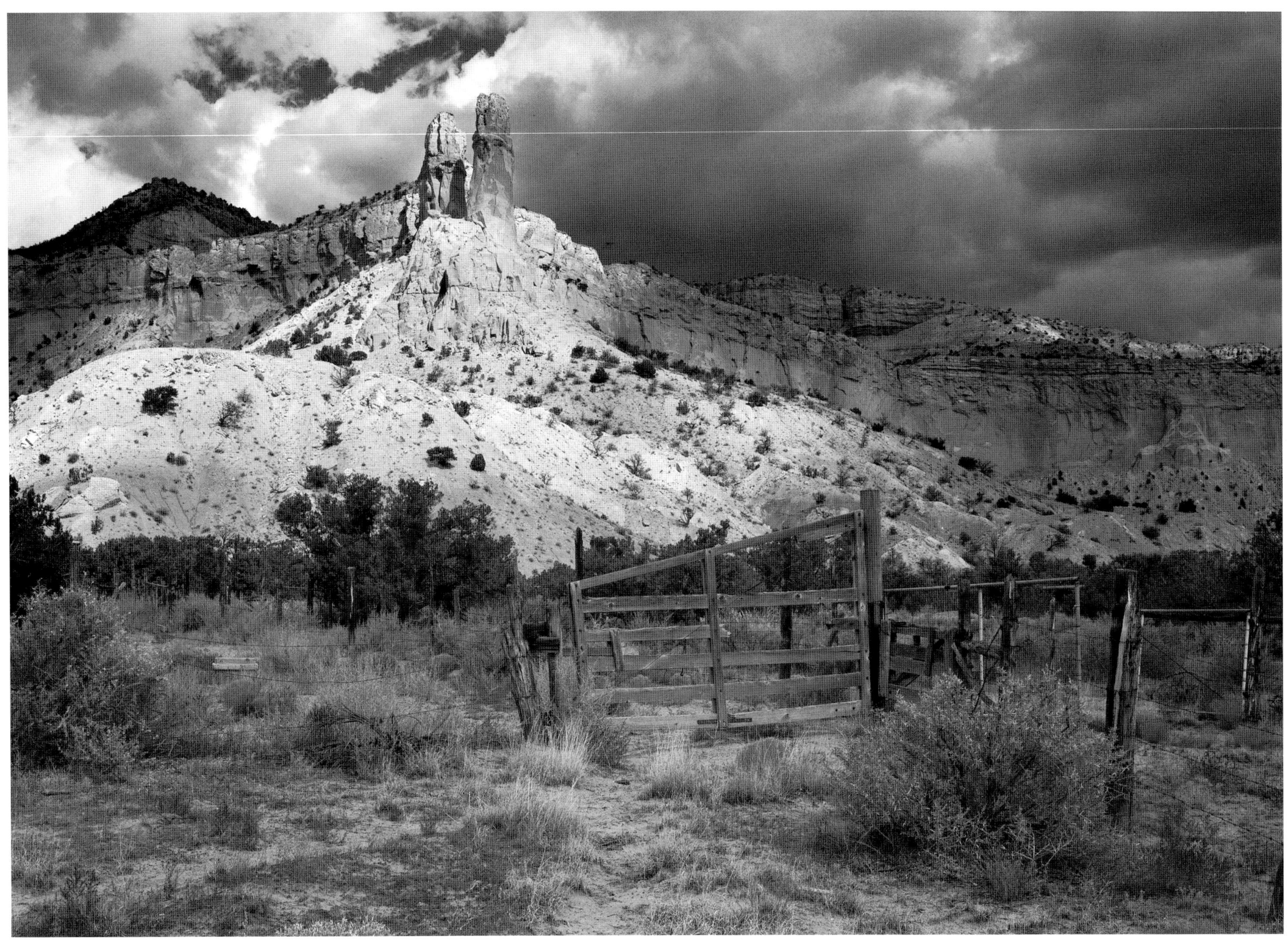

Plate 46: Puerta del Cielo (Bennett Chimneys) and Corral Gate, Ghost Ranch, New Mexico, 2005

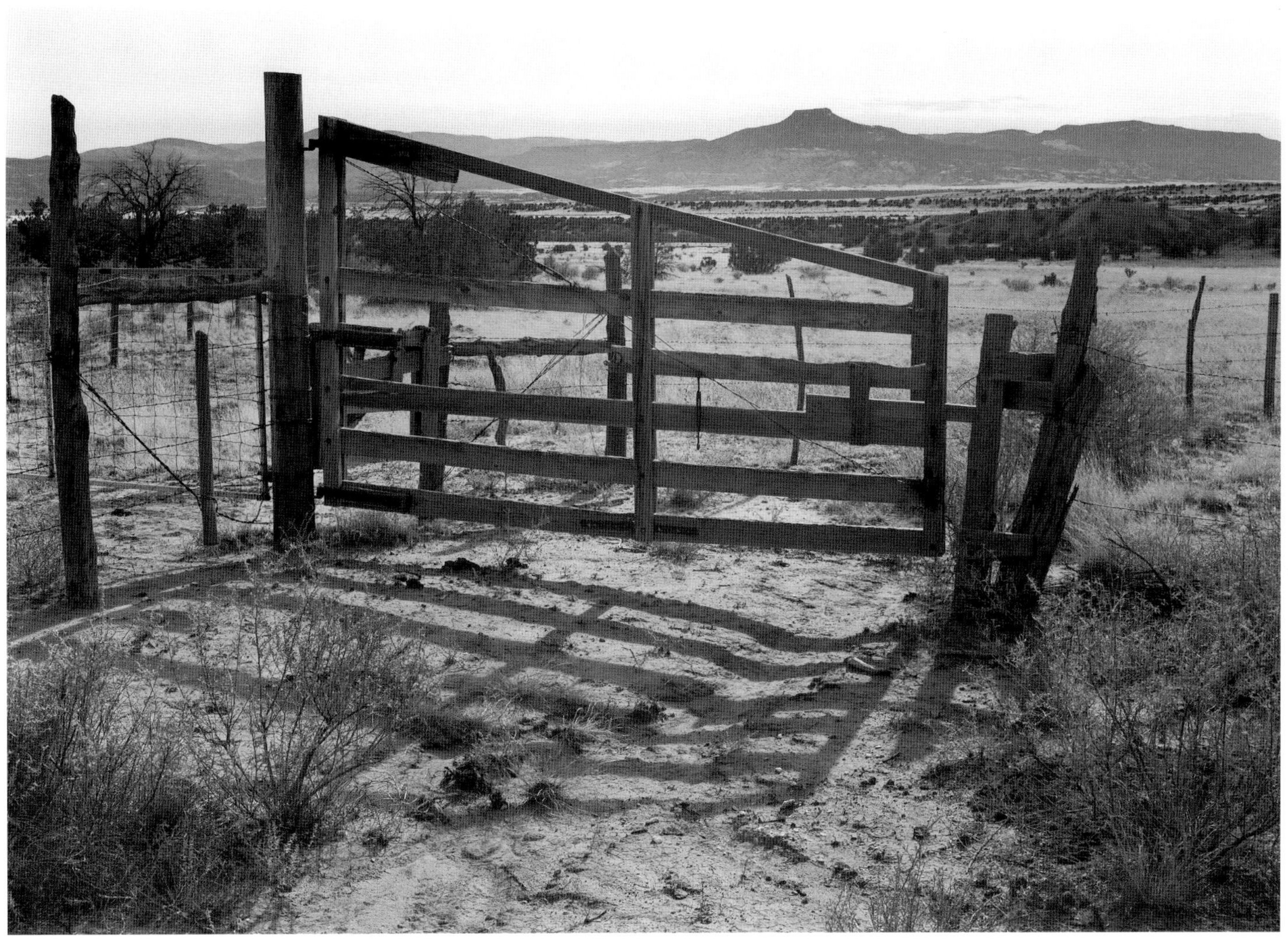

Plate 47: Corral Gate, Ghost Ranch, New Mexico, 2005

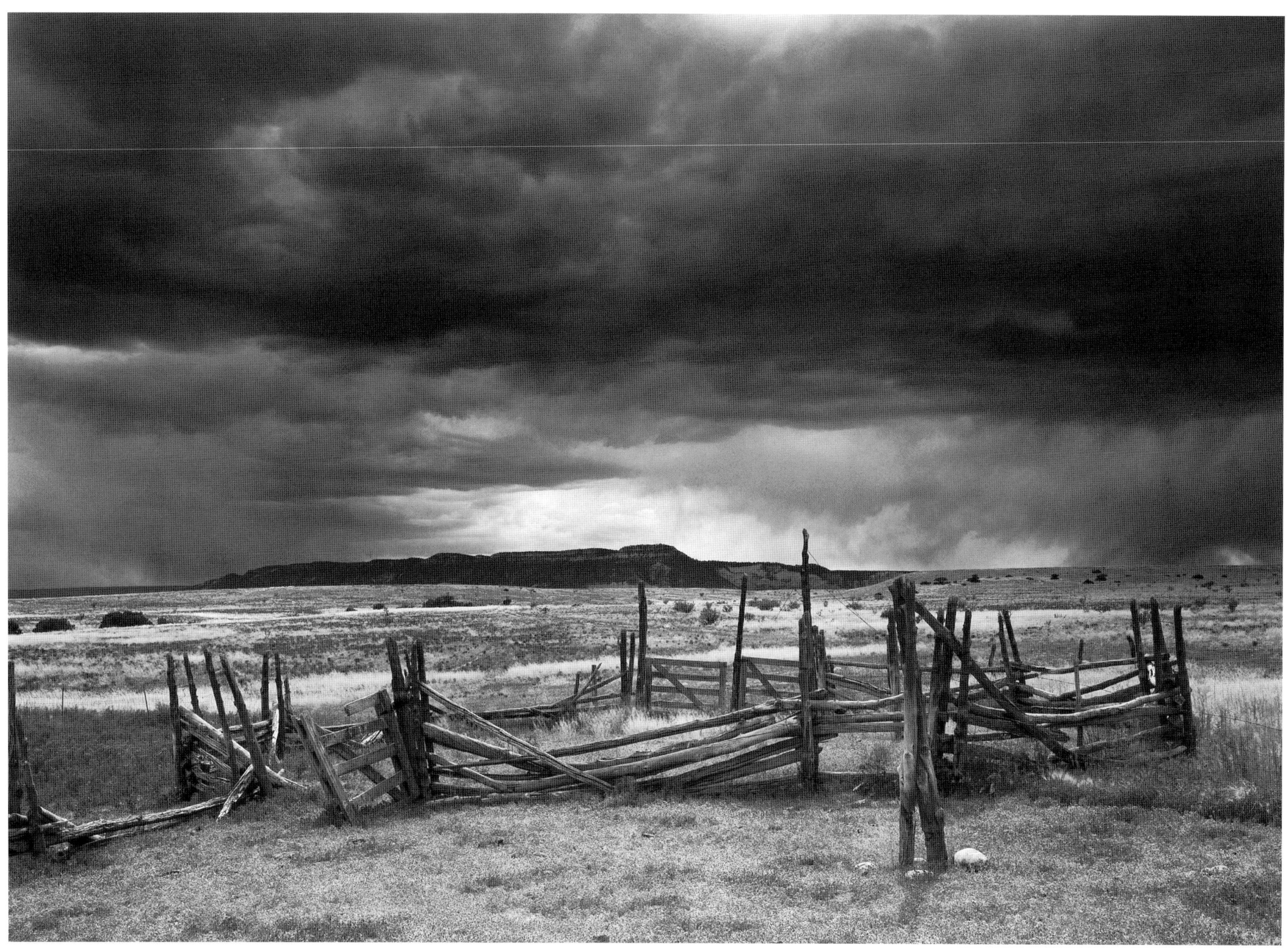

Plate 48: Old Corral and Approaching Storm, Antelope Flats (Llano Pasture), Ghost Ranch, New Mexico, 2005

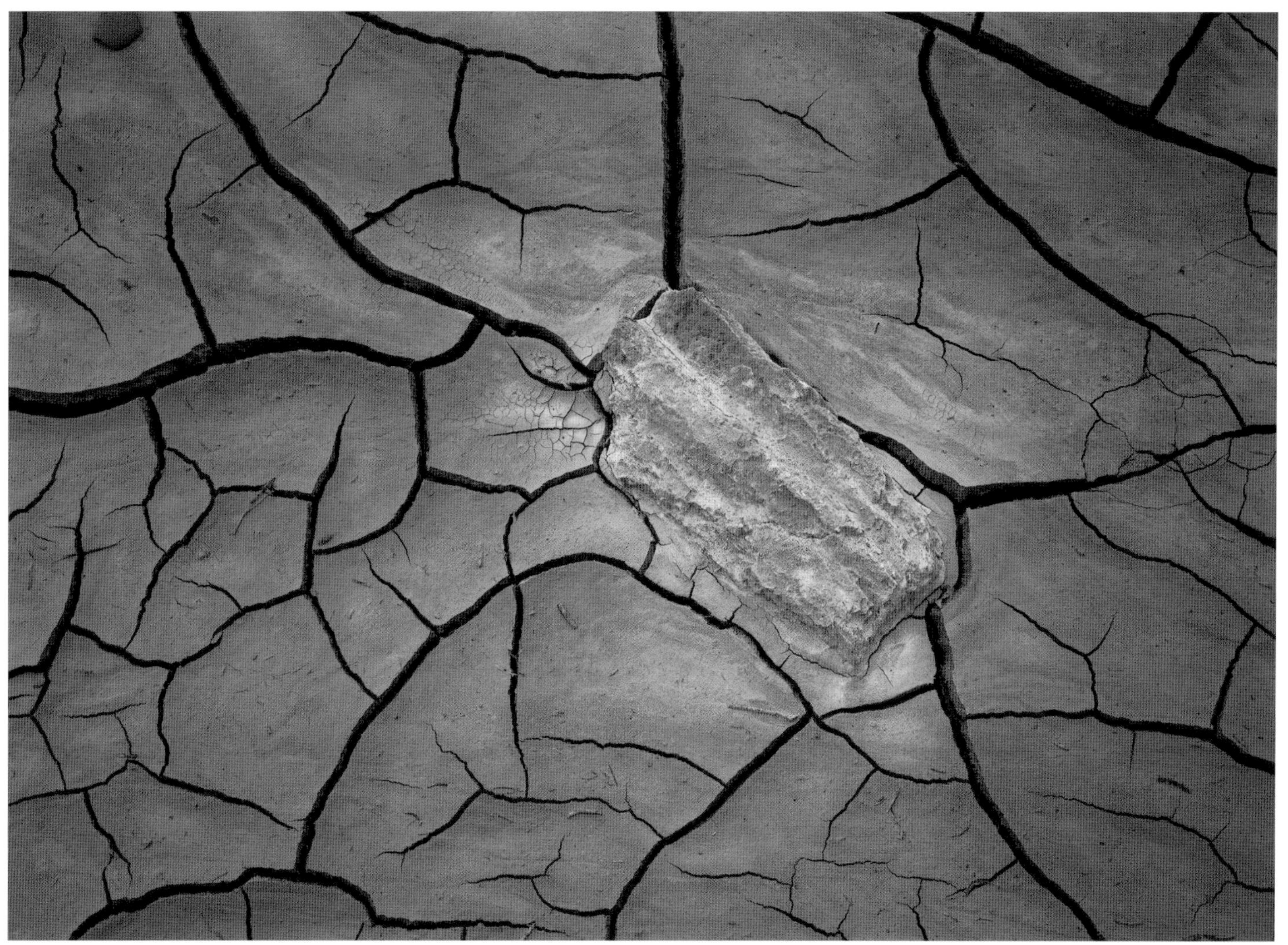

Plate 49: Rock and Mud Cracks, Summer, Ghost Ranch, New Mexico, 2006

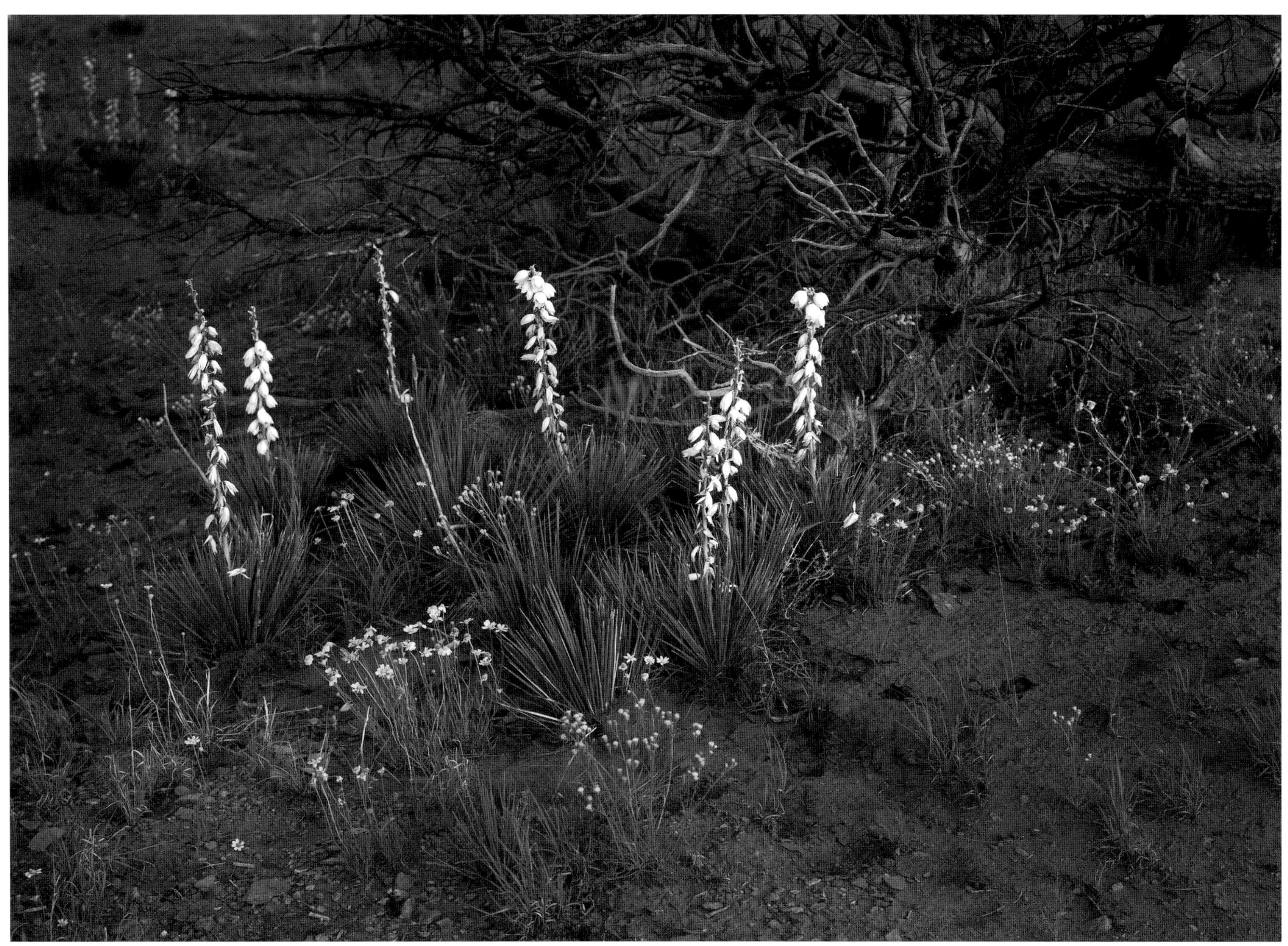

Plate 50: Yuccas, Summer, Ghost Ranch, New Mexico, 2007

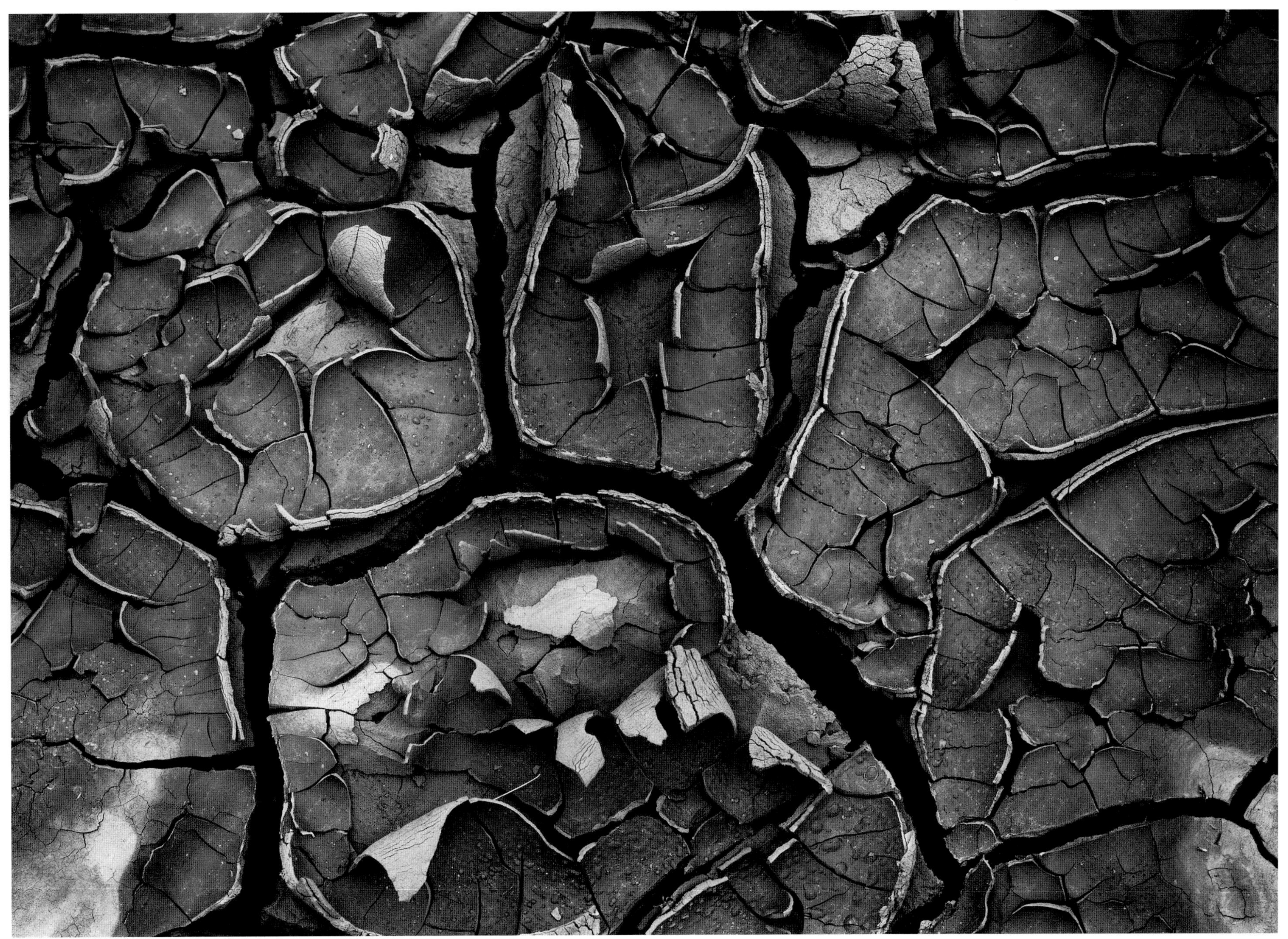

Plate 51: Sun-Baked Earth, Painted Desert, Ghost Ranch, New Mexico, 2006

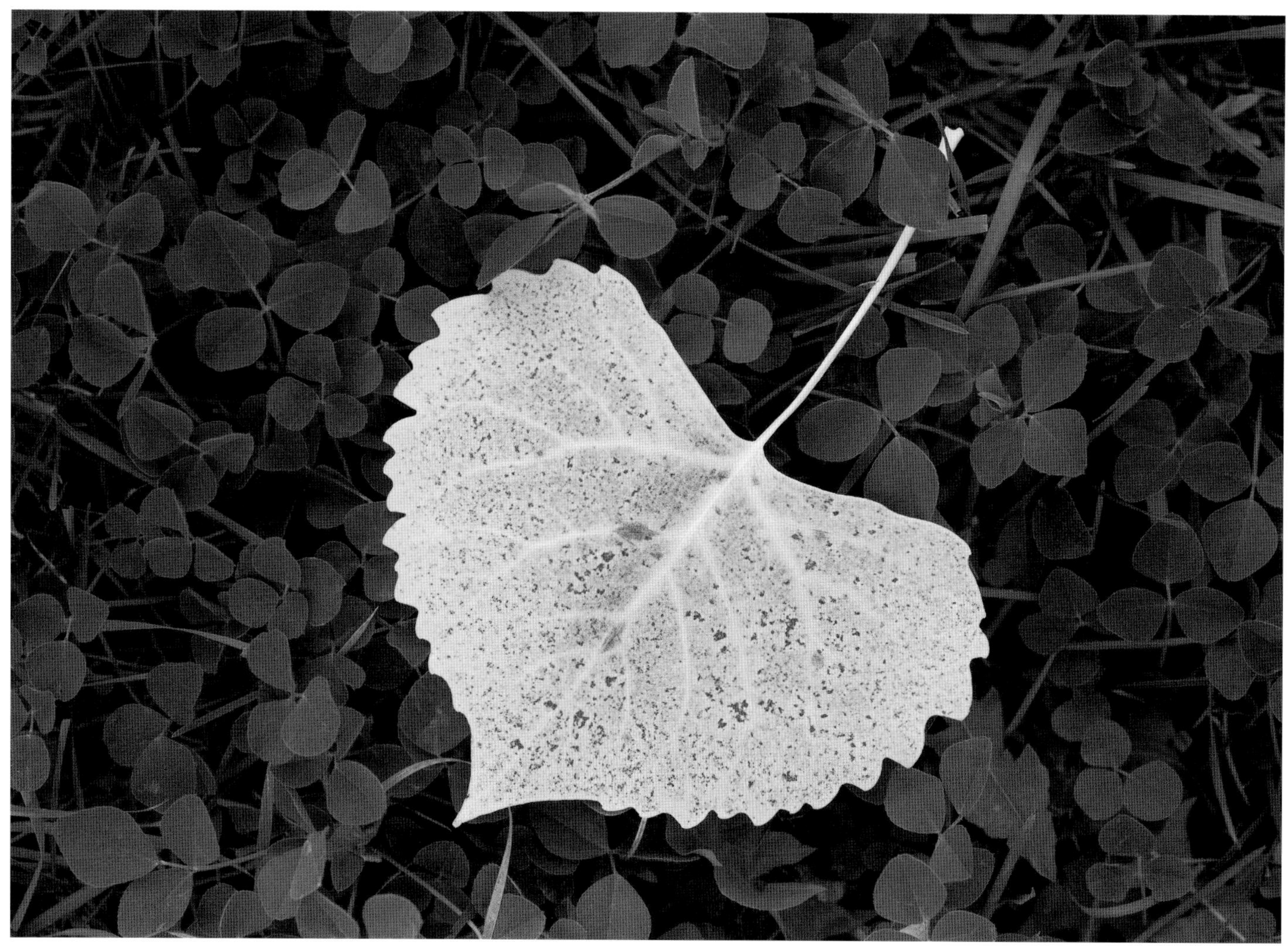

Plate 52: Autumn Cottonwood Leaf, Ghost Ranch, New Mexico, 2006

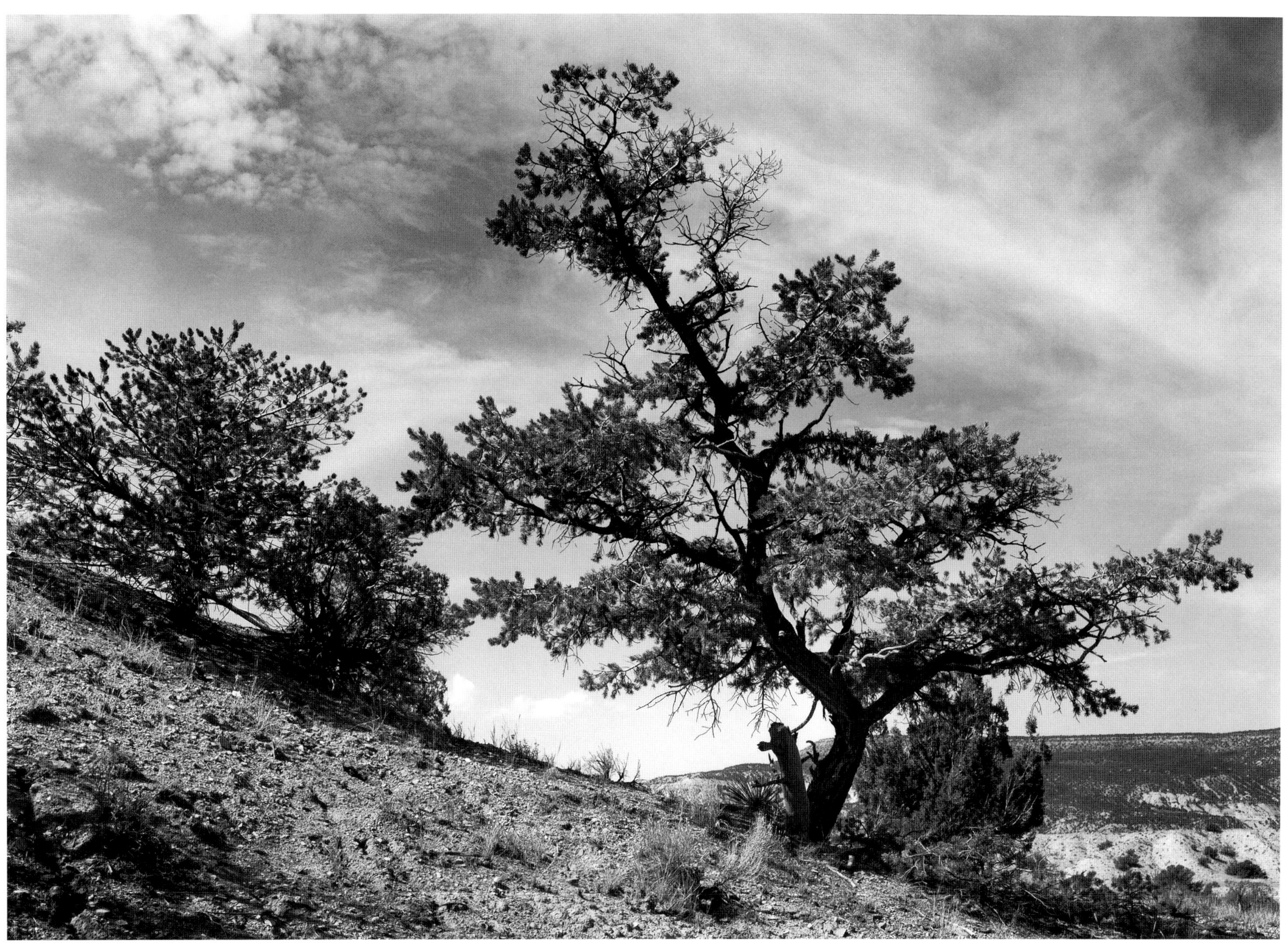

Plate 53: Pine Tree, Ghost Ranch, New Mexico, 2007

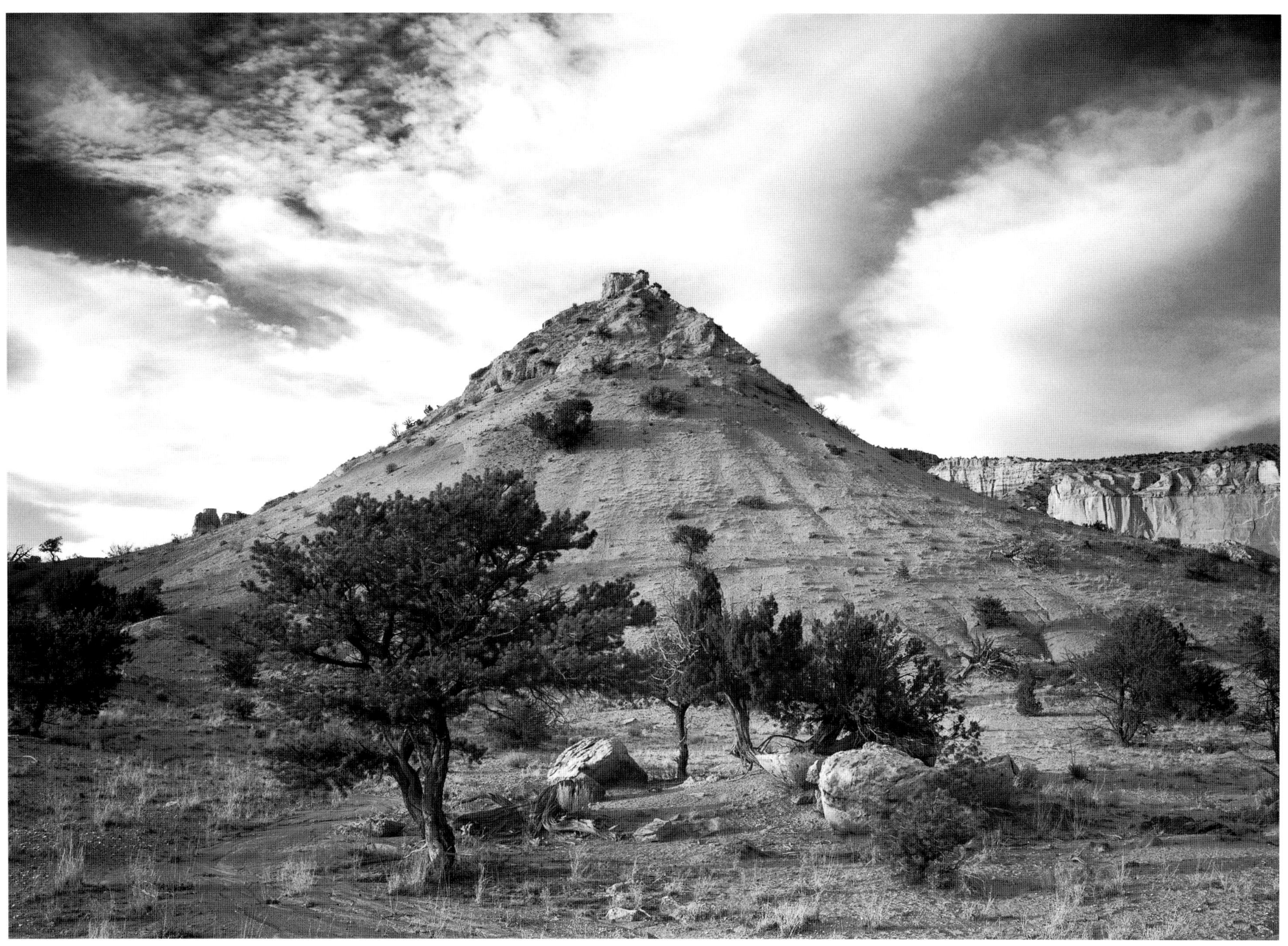

Plate 54: Red Hill and Juniper (Arroyo Seco Pasture), Ghost Ranch, New Mexico, 2005

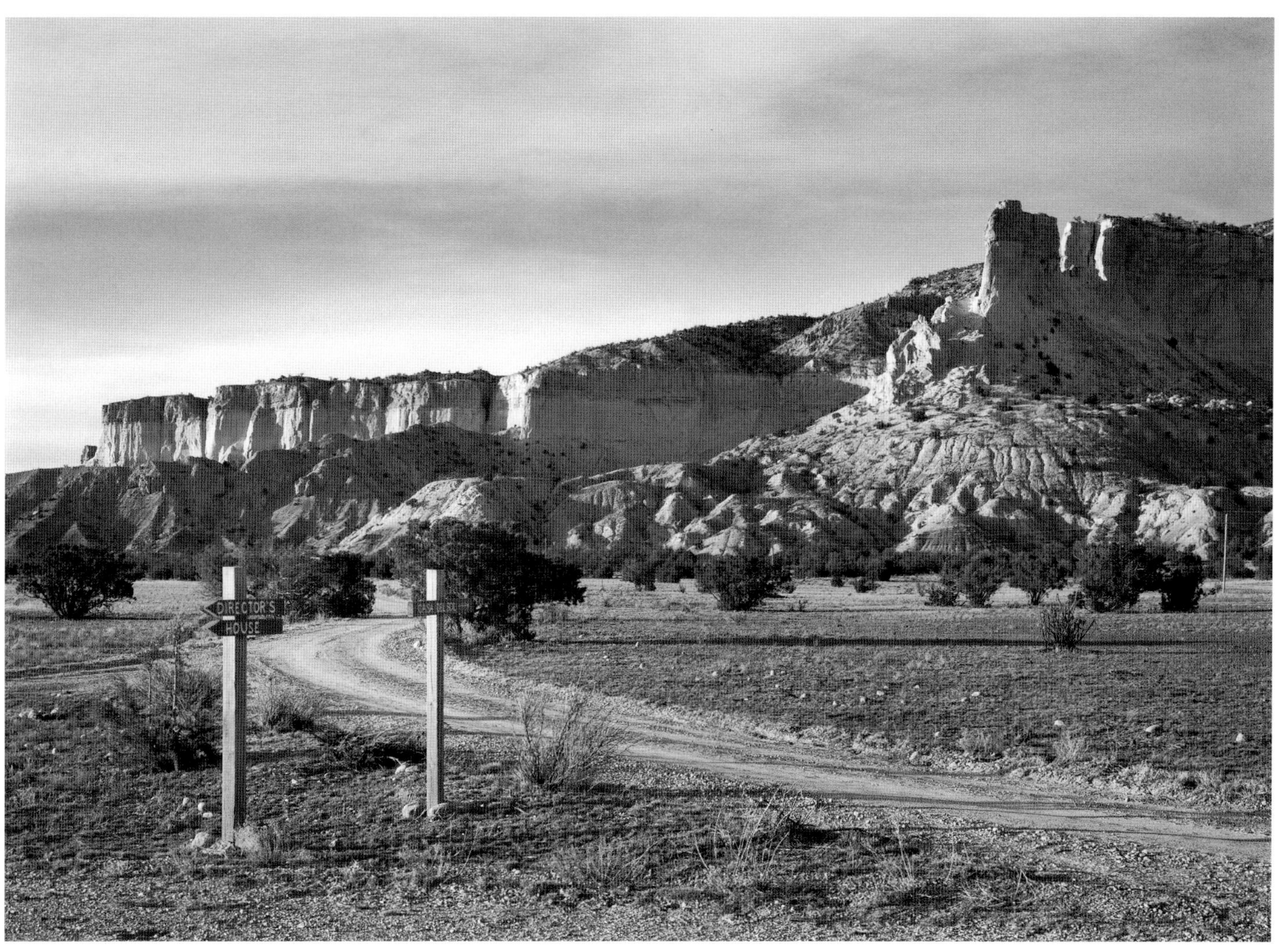

Plate 55: Road to Director's House and Casa del Sol, Ghost Ranch, New Mexico, 2006

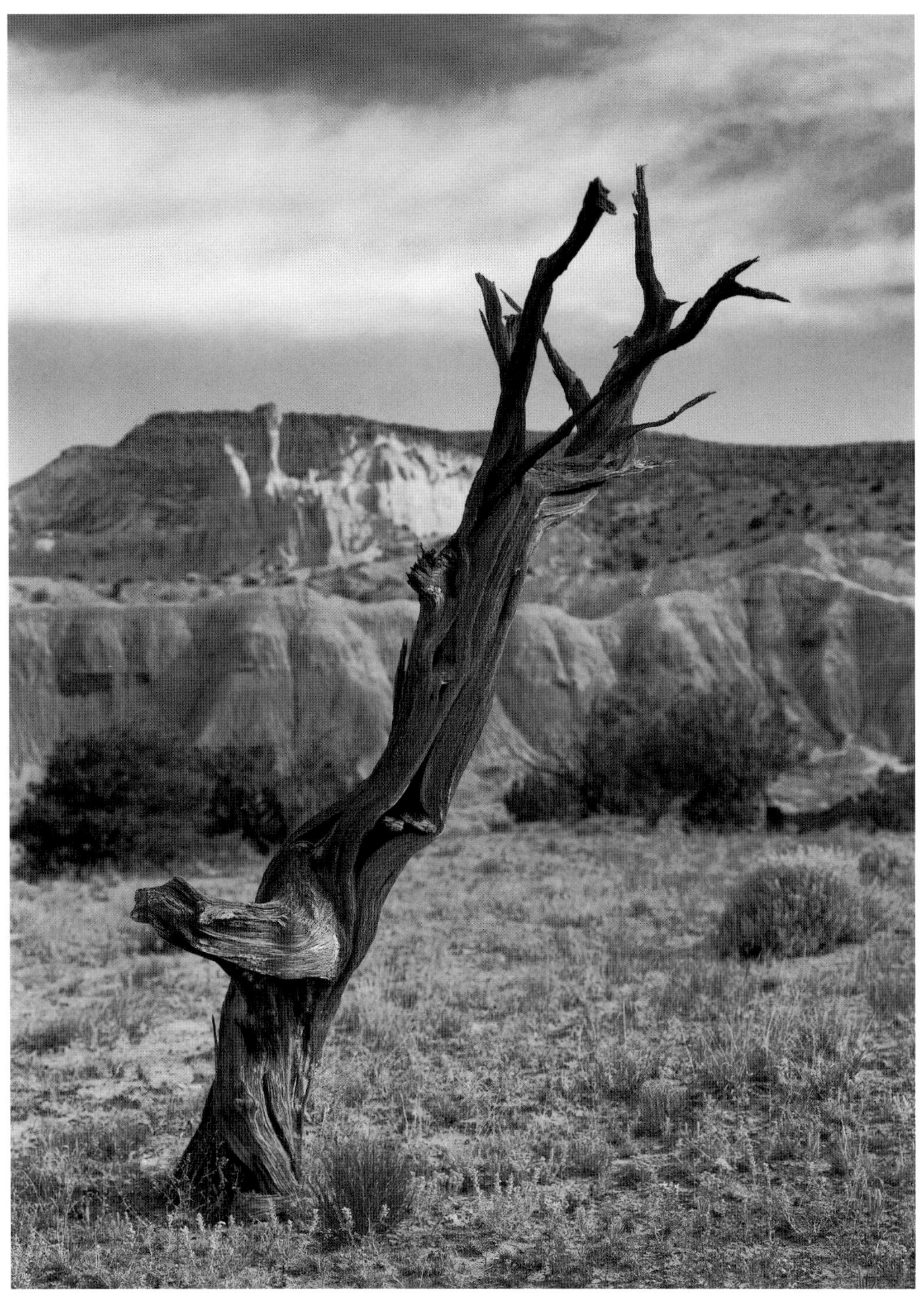

Plate 56: Juniper Tree with Lavender Hills, Ghost Ranch, New Mexico, 2005

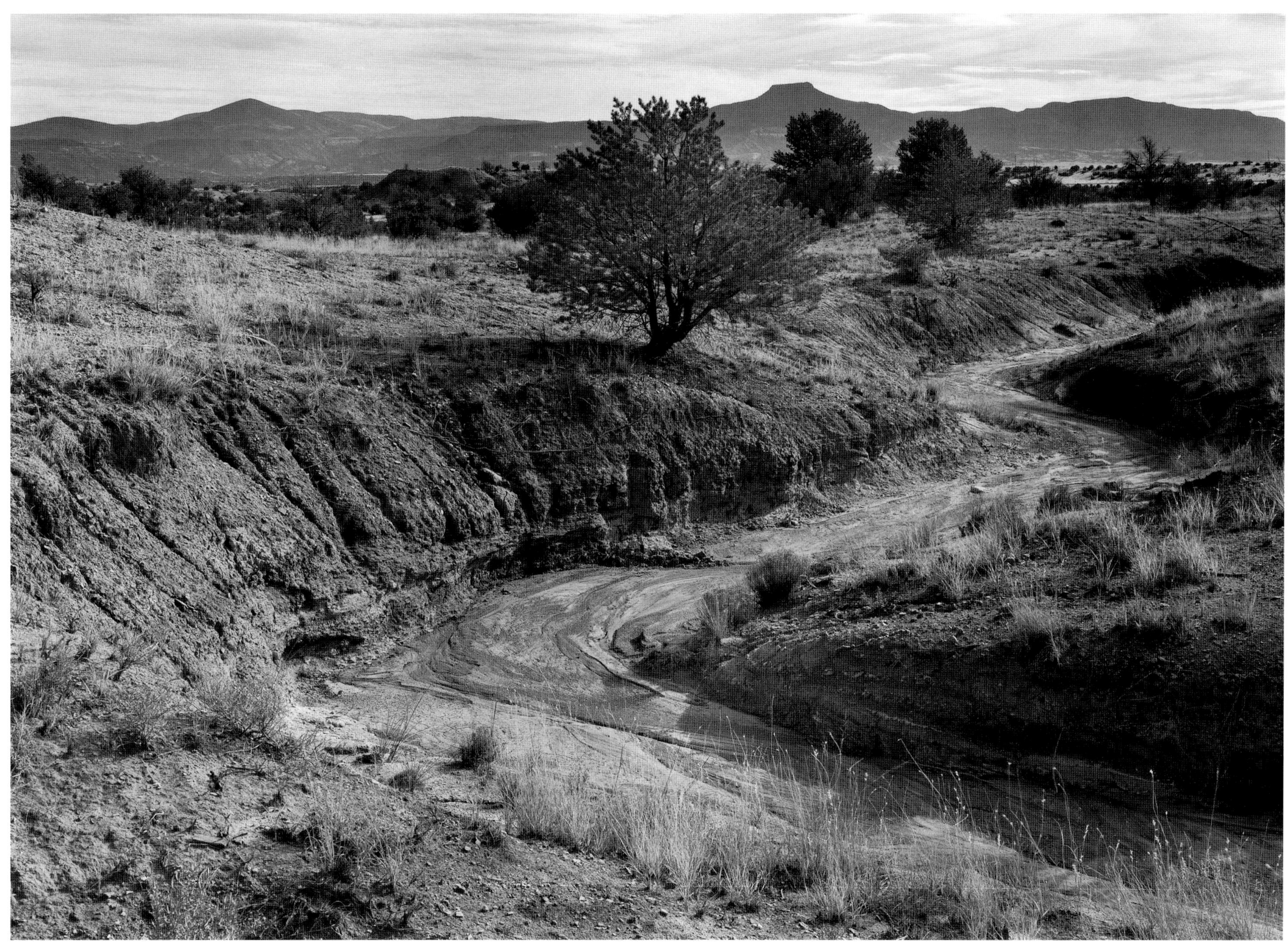

Plate 57: Dry Arroyo and Cerro Pedernal, Late Summer, Ghost Ranch, New Mexico, 2005

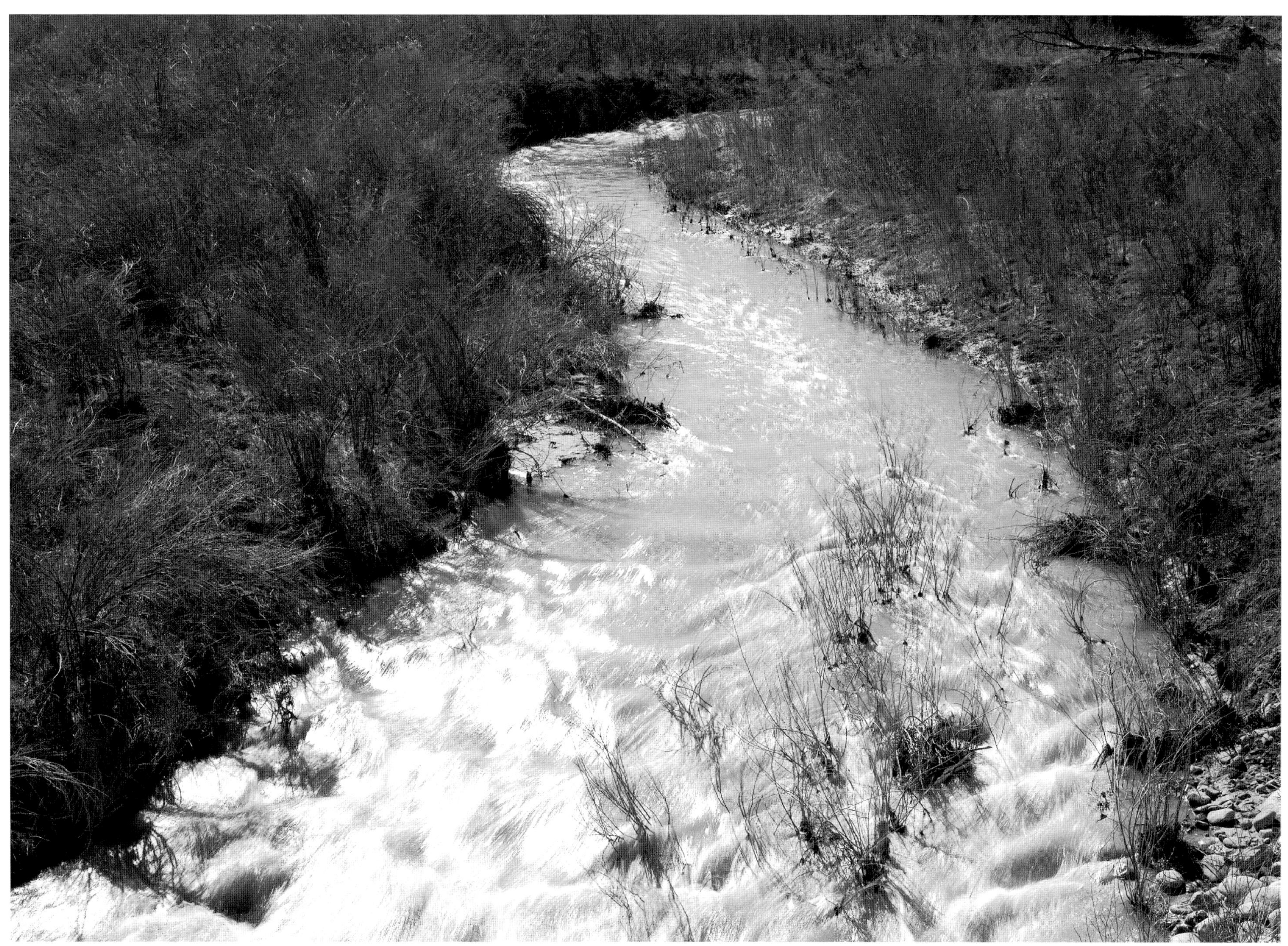

Plate 58: Arroyo Seco Creek after Summer Rainstorm, Ghost Ranch, New Mexico, 2005

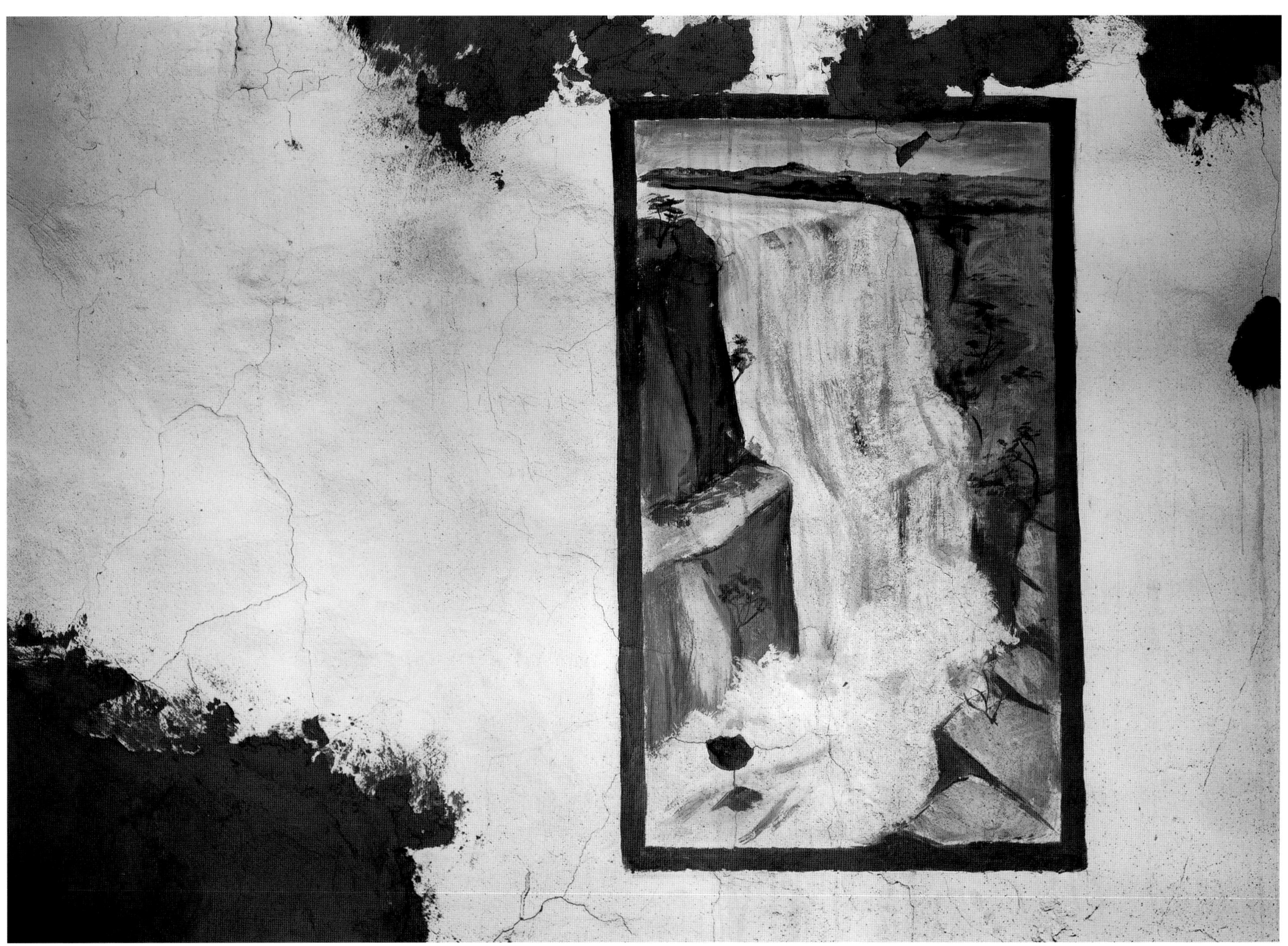

Plate 59: Waterfall Mural inside Burnham Homestead, Ghost Ranch, New Mexico, 2006

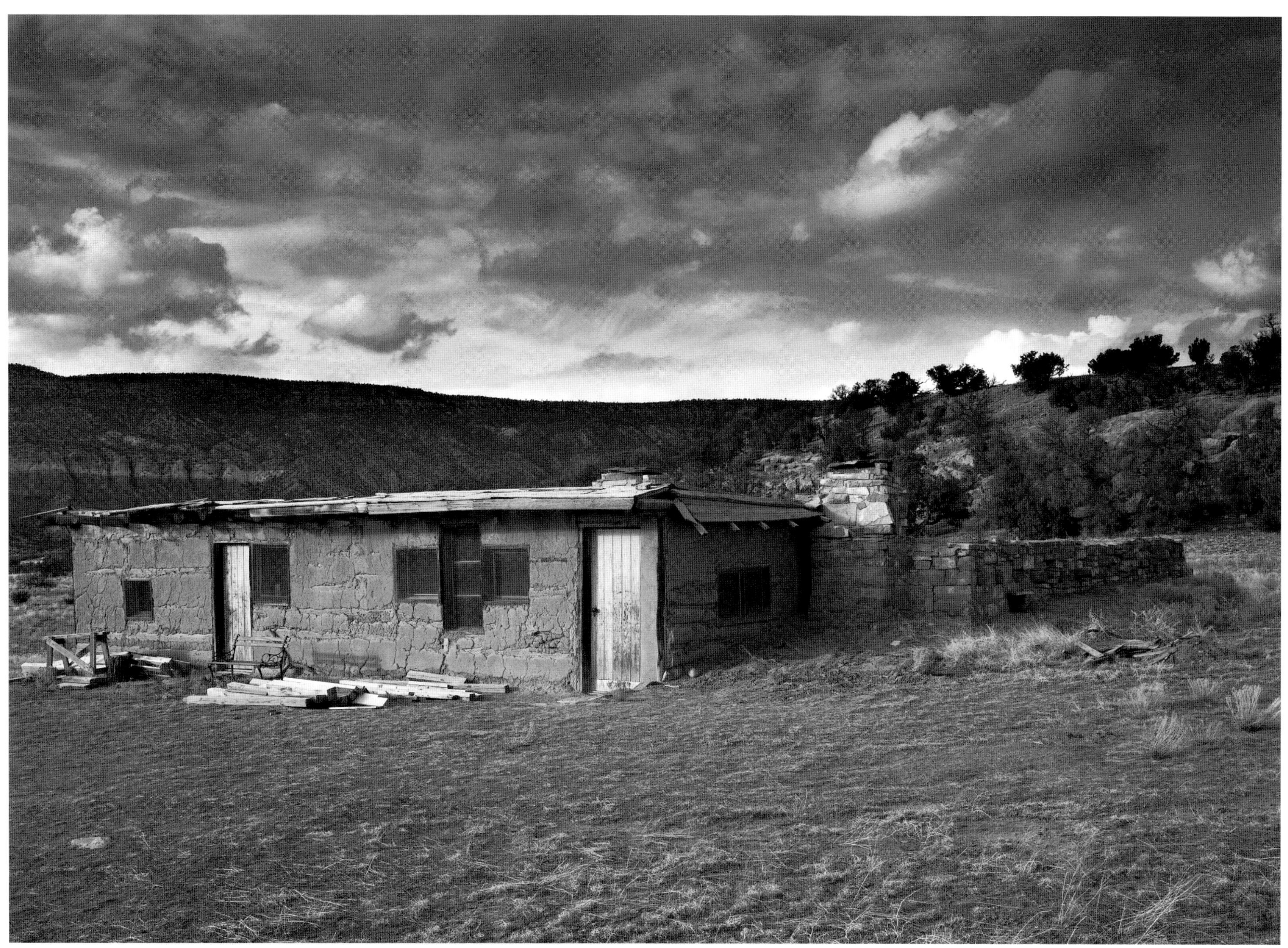

Plate 60: Blackie Burnham's Homestead, Ghost Ranch, New Mexico, 2006

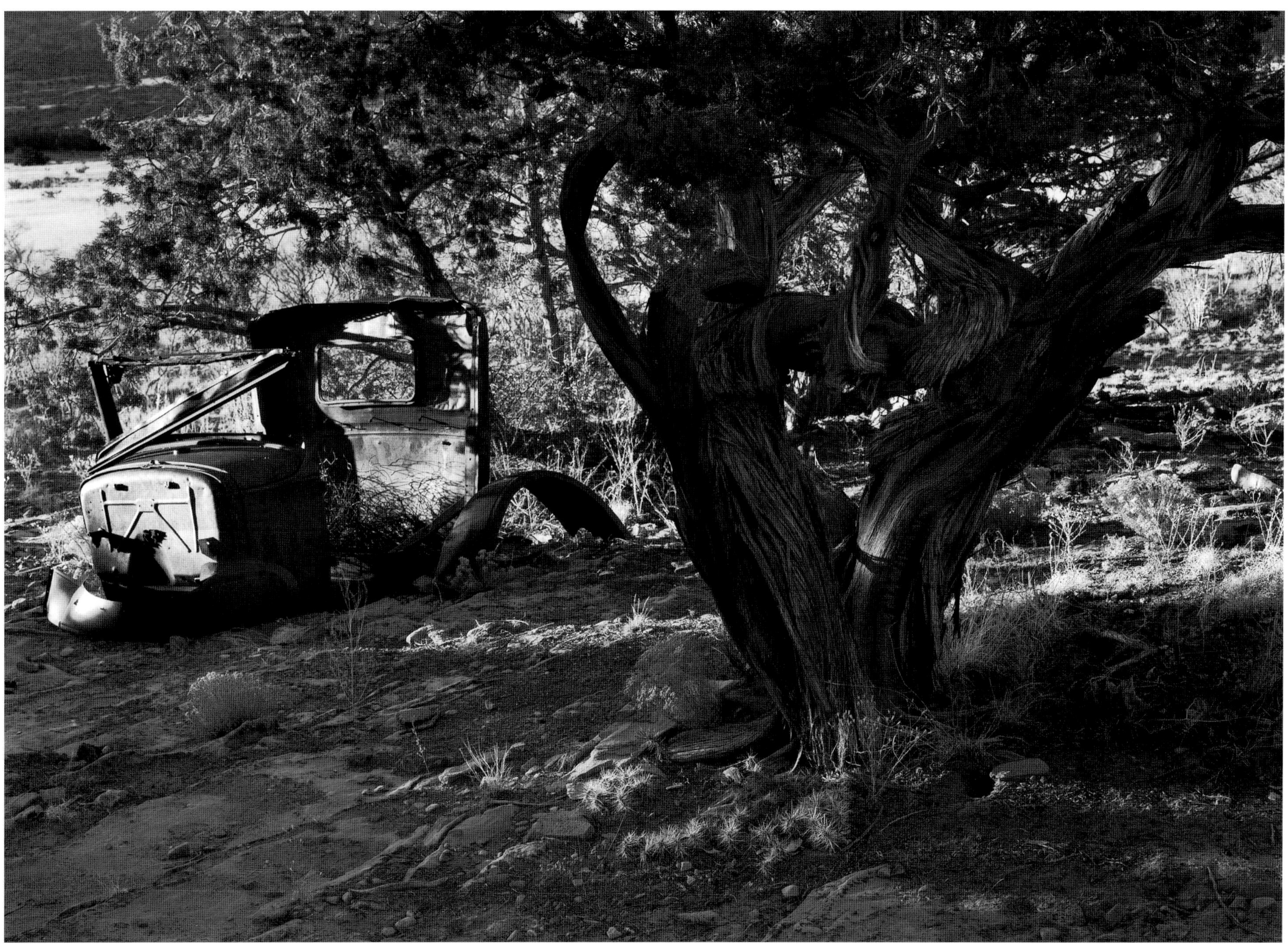

Plate 61: Old Juniper, Burnham Homestead, Ghost Ranch, New Mexico, 2005

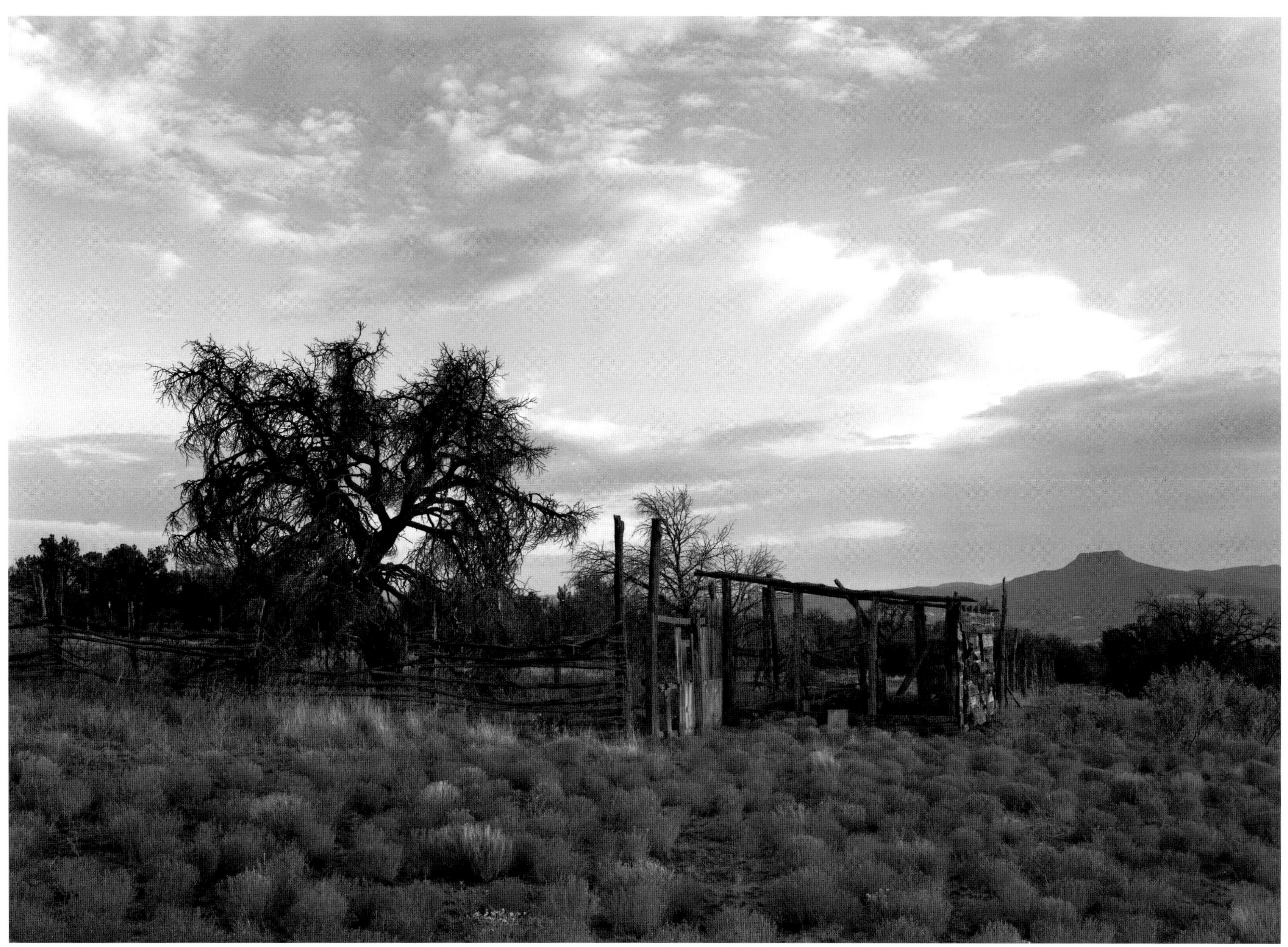

Plate 62: Corral, Burnham Homestead, Ghost Ranch, New Mexico, 2006

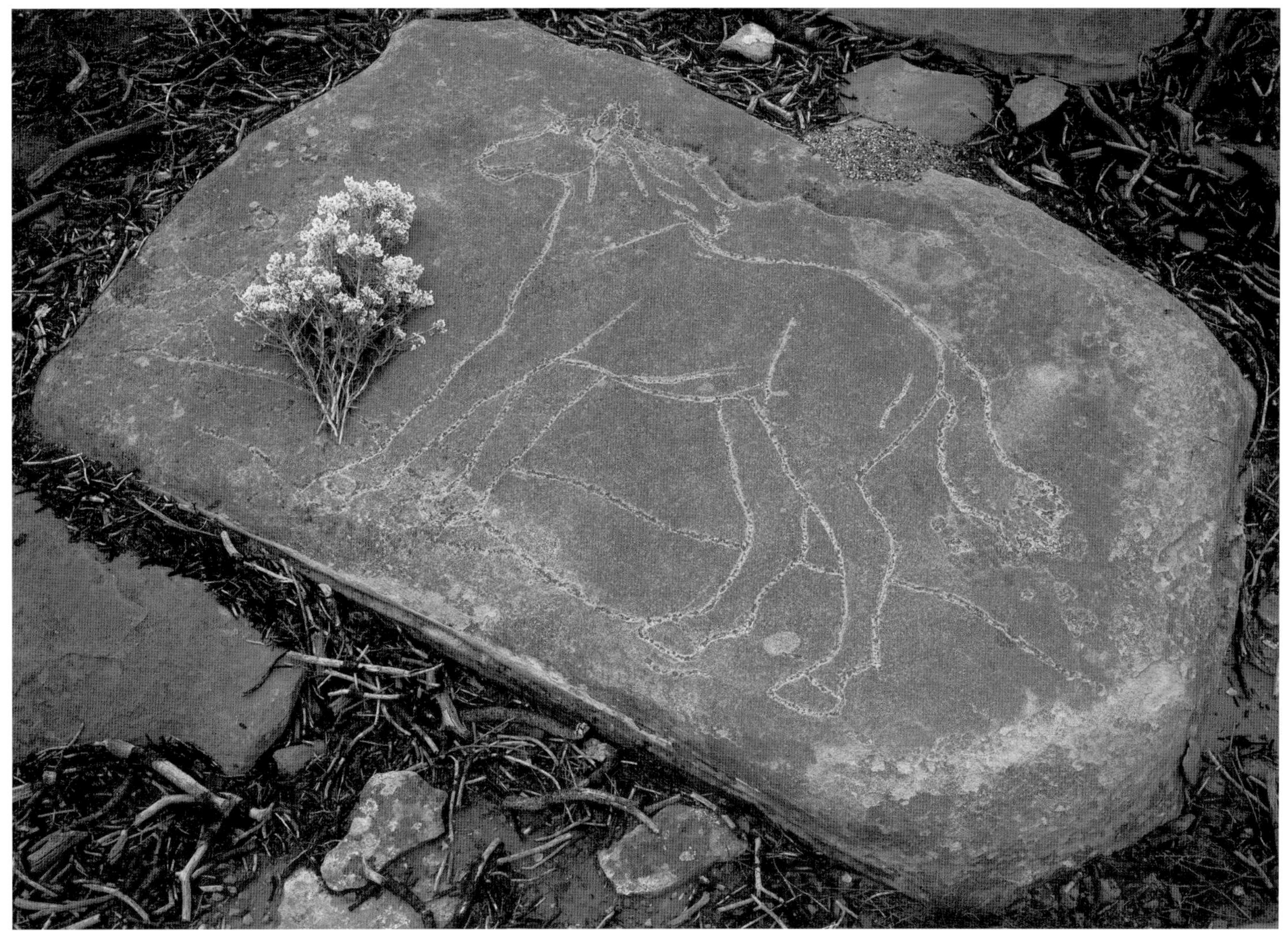

Plate 63: Dorthy Burnham's Horse, Burnham Homestead, Ghost Ranch, New Mexico, 2006

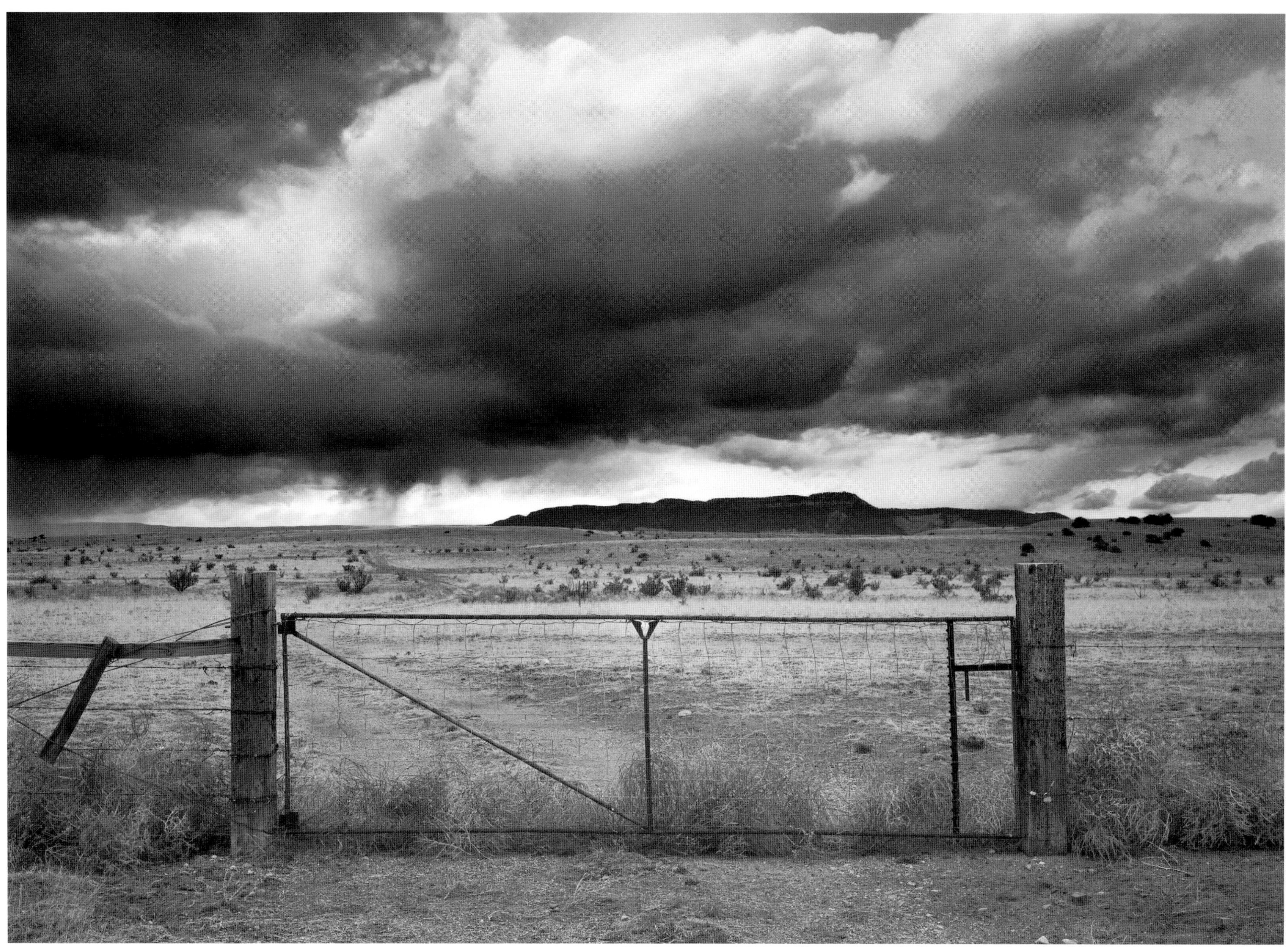

Plate 64: Llano Gate and Approaching Storm, Ghost Ranch, New Mexico, 2004

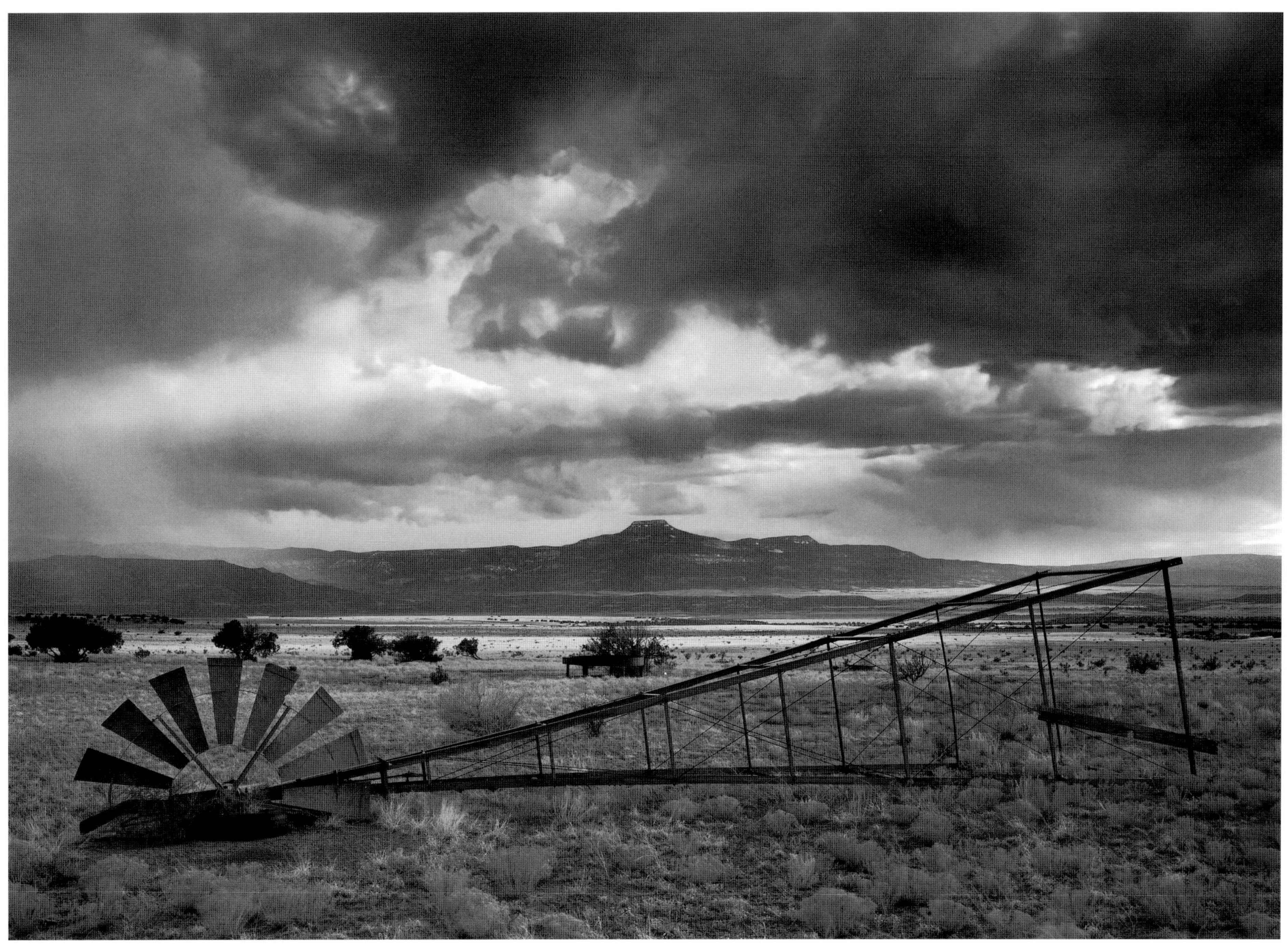

Plate 65: Fallen Windmill and Cerro Pedernal (East Pasture), Ghost Ranch, New Mexico, 2005

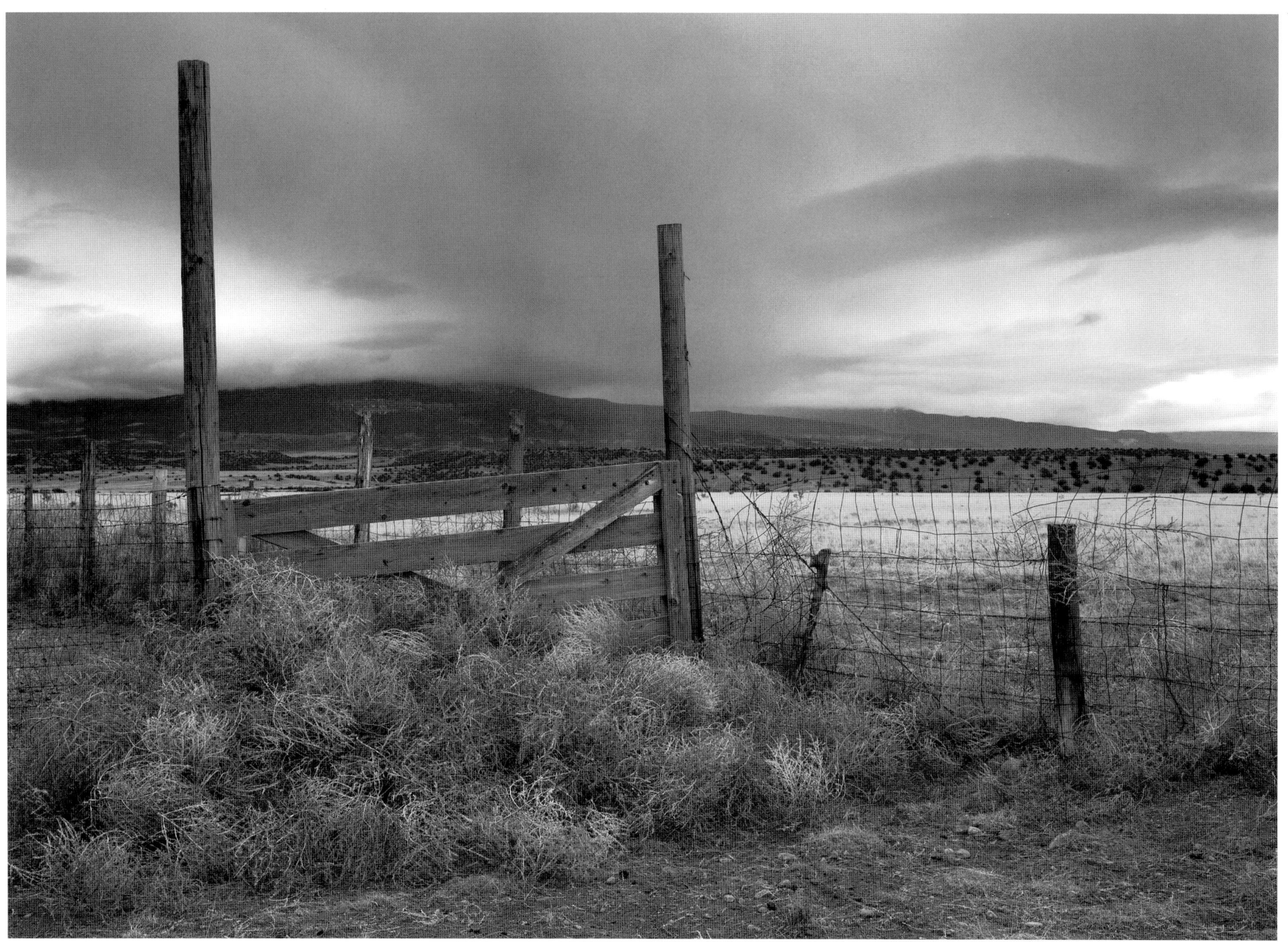

Plate 66: Tumbleweeds (Llano Pasture), Ghost Ranch, New Mexico, 2006

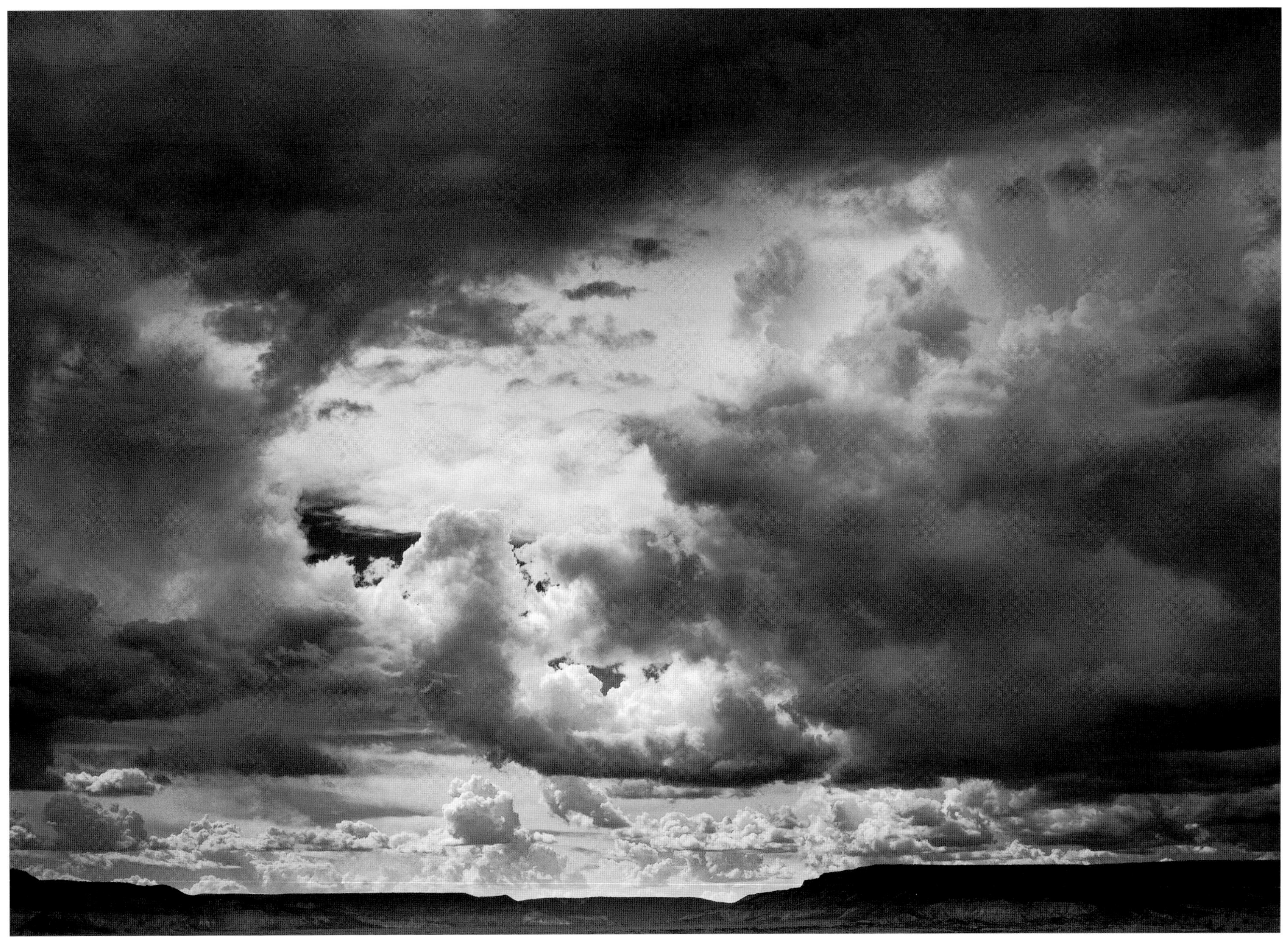

Plate 67: Storm over the Llano, Ghost Ranch, New Mexico, 2005

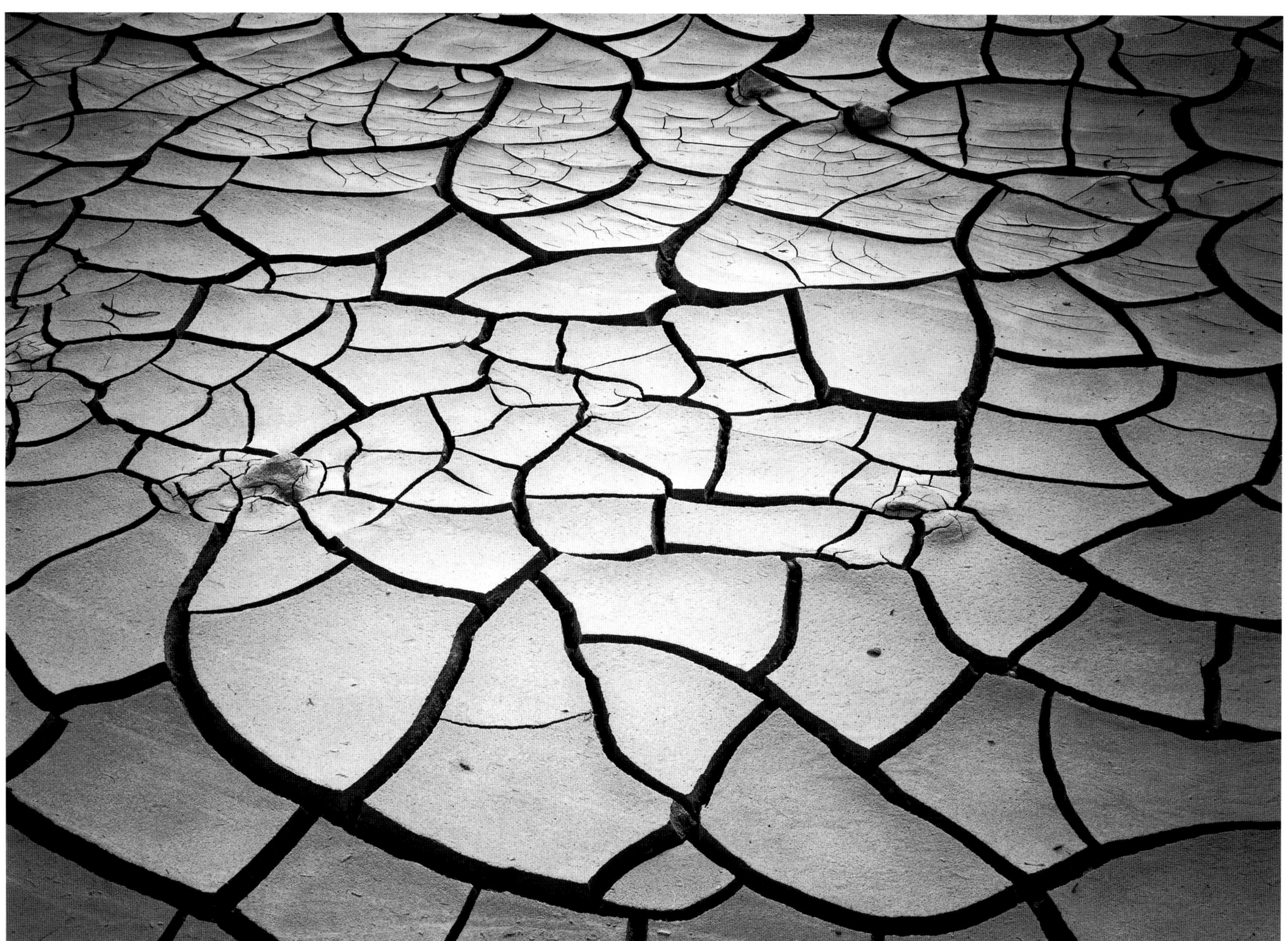

Plate 68: Dried Mud Patterns, Ghost Ranch, New Mexico, 2005

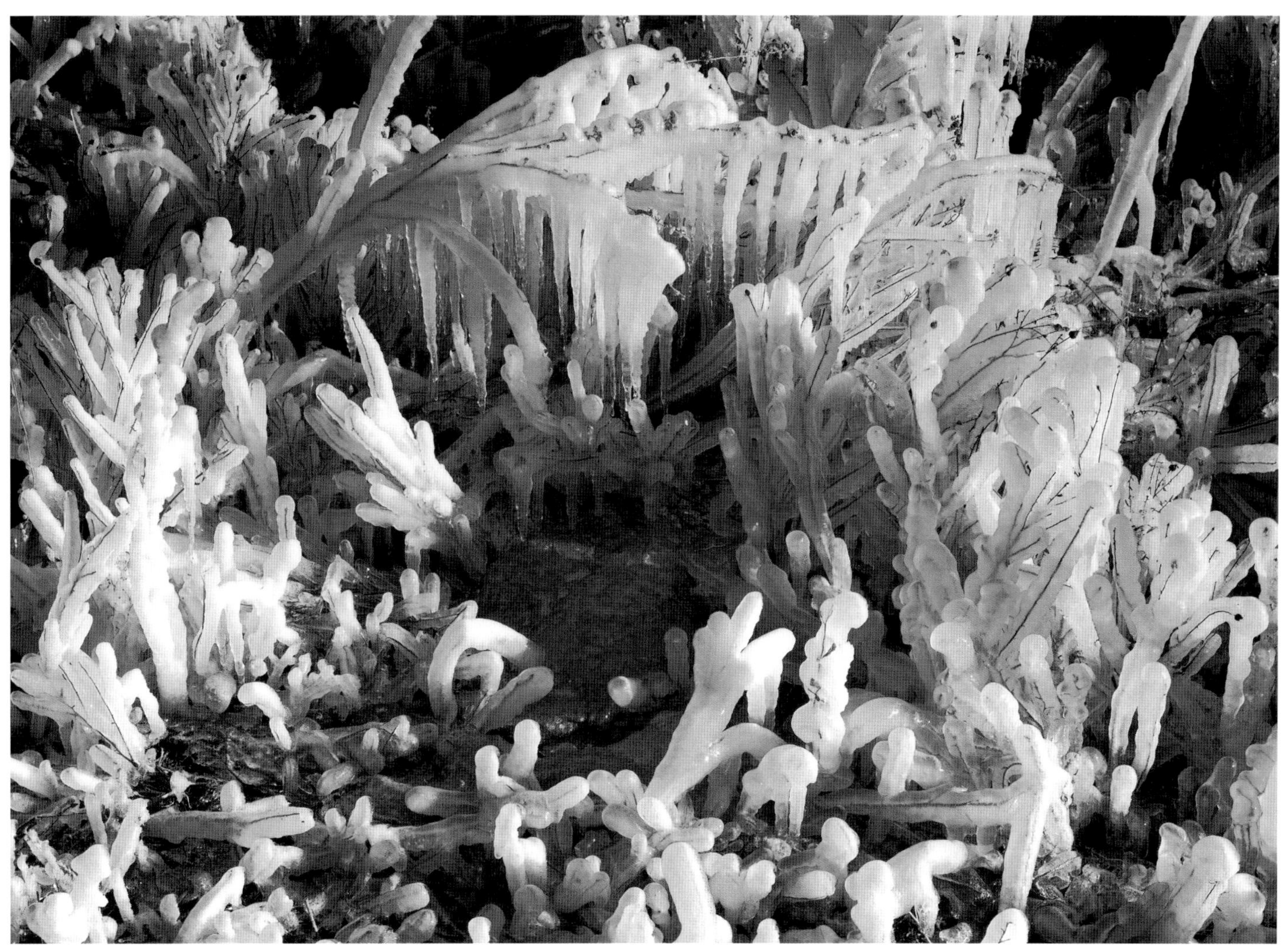

Plate 69: Icicles, Alfalfa Field, Ghost Ranch, New Mexico, 2006

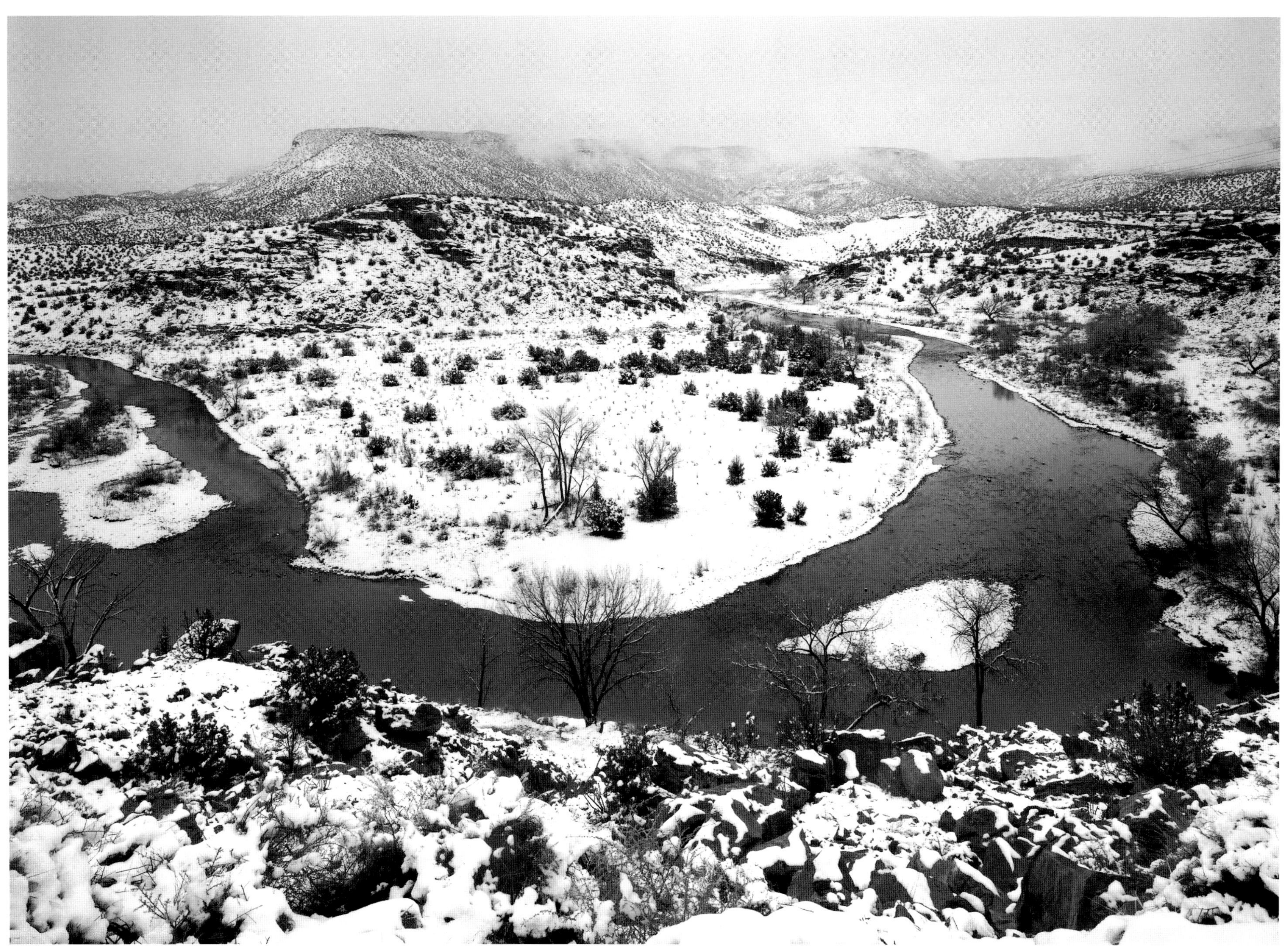

Plate 70: Rio Chama after Winter Snowstorm, Abiquiu, New Mexico, 2004

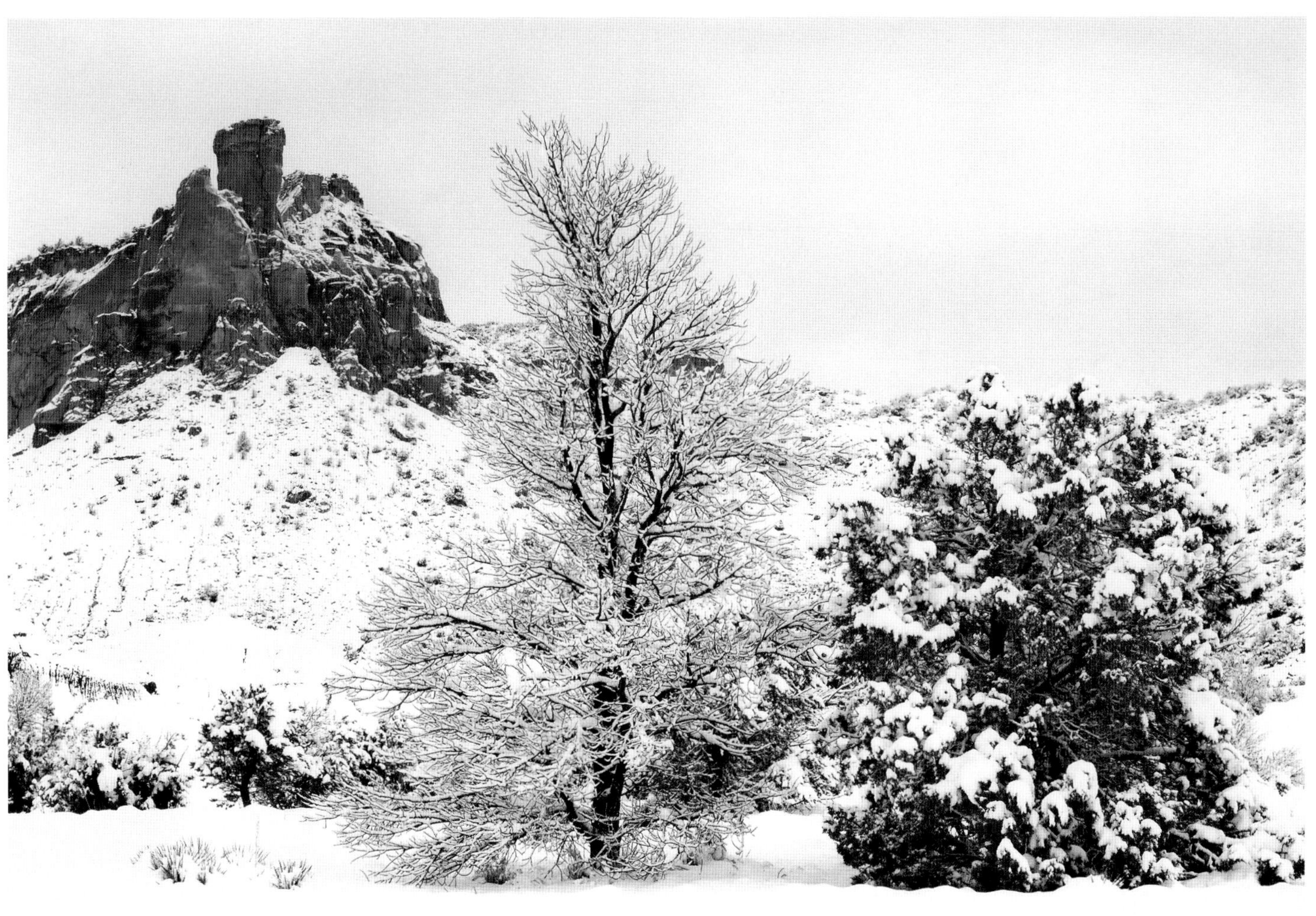

Plate 71: Trees below Chimney Rock, Winter, Ghost Ranch, New Mexico, 2005

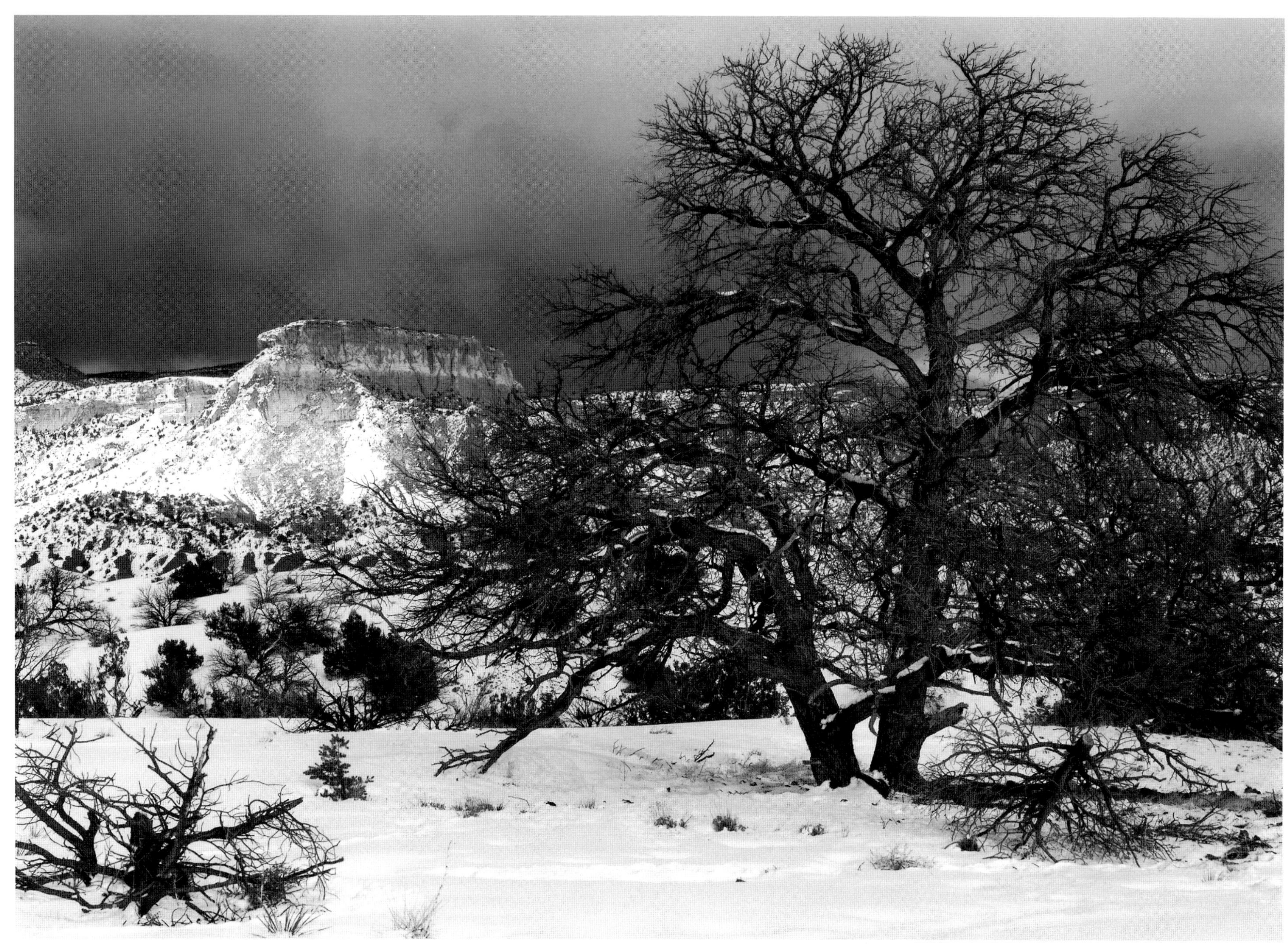

Plate 72: Pack's Point, Last Light, Winter, Ghost Ranch, New Mexico, 2007

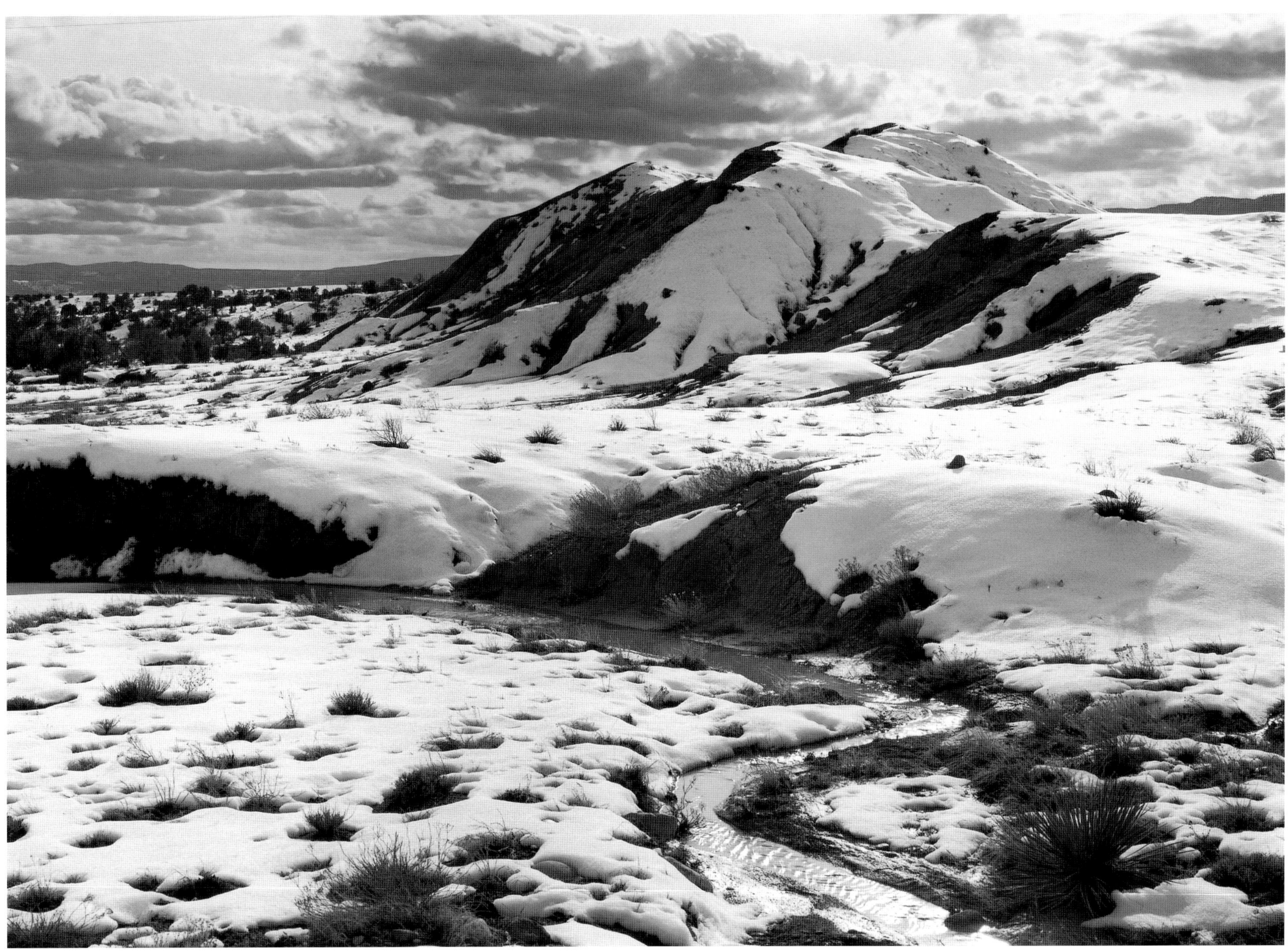

Plate 73: Painted Desert in Snow, Ghost Ranch, New Mexico, 2005

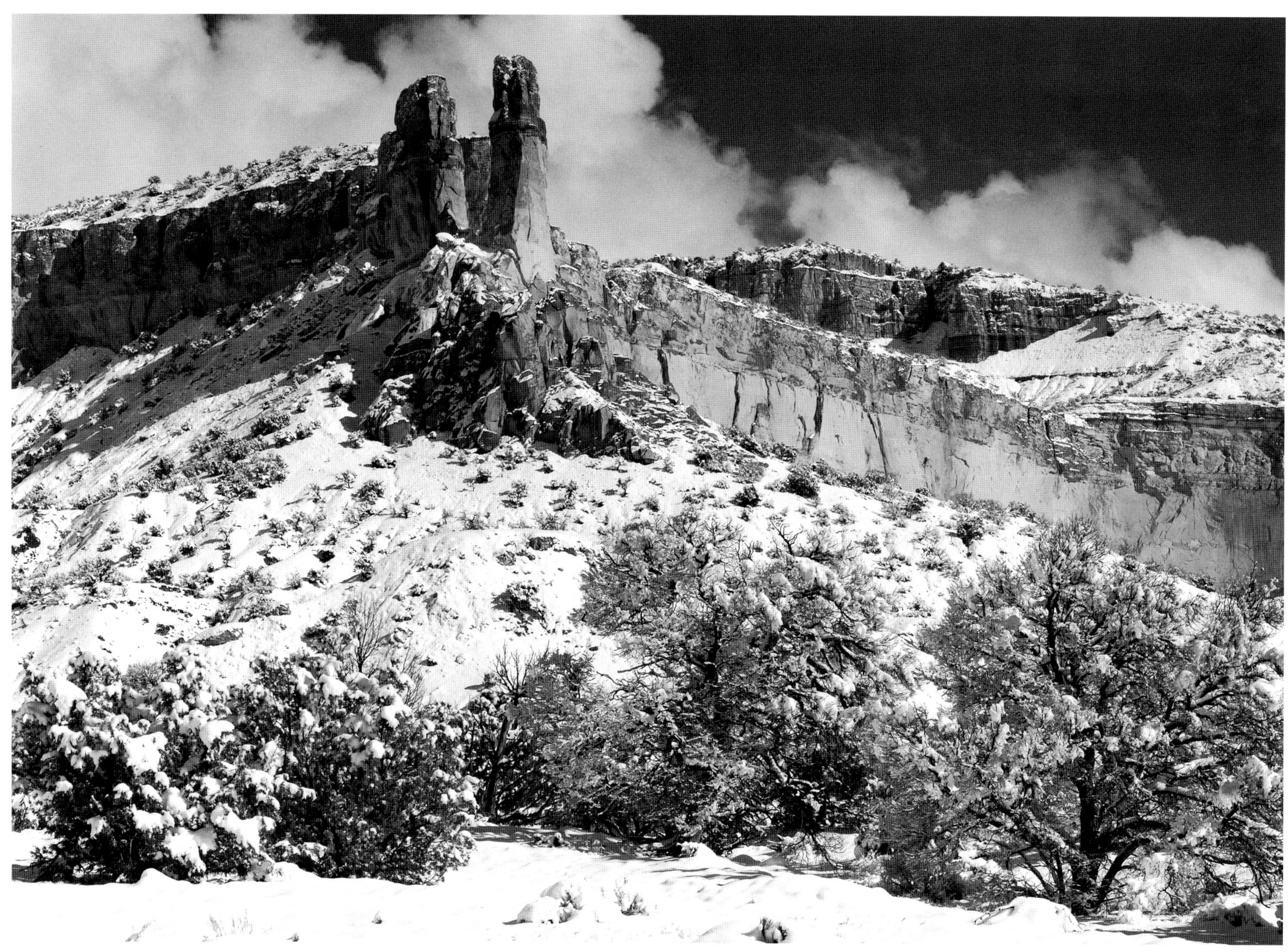

Plate 74: Puerta del Cielo (Bennett Chimneys), Winter, Ghost Ranch, New Mexico, 2006

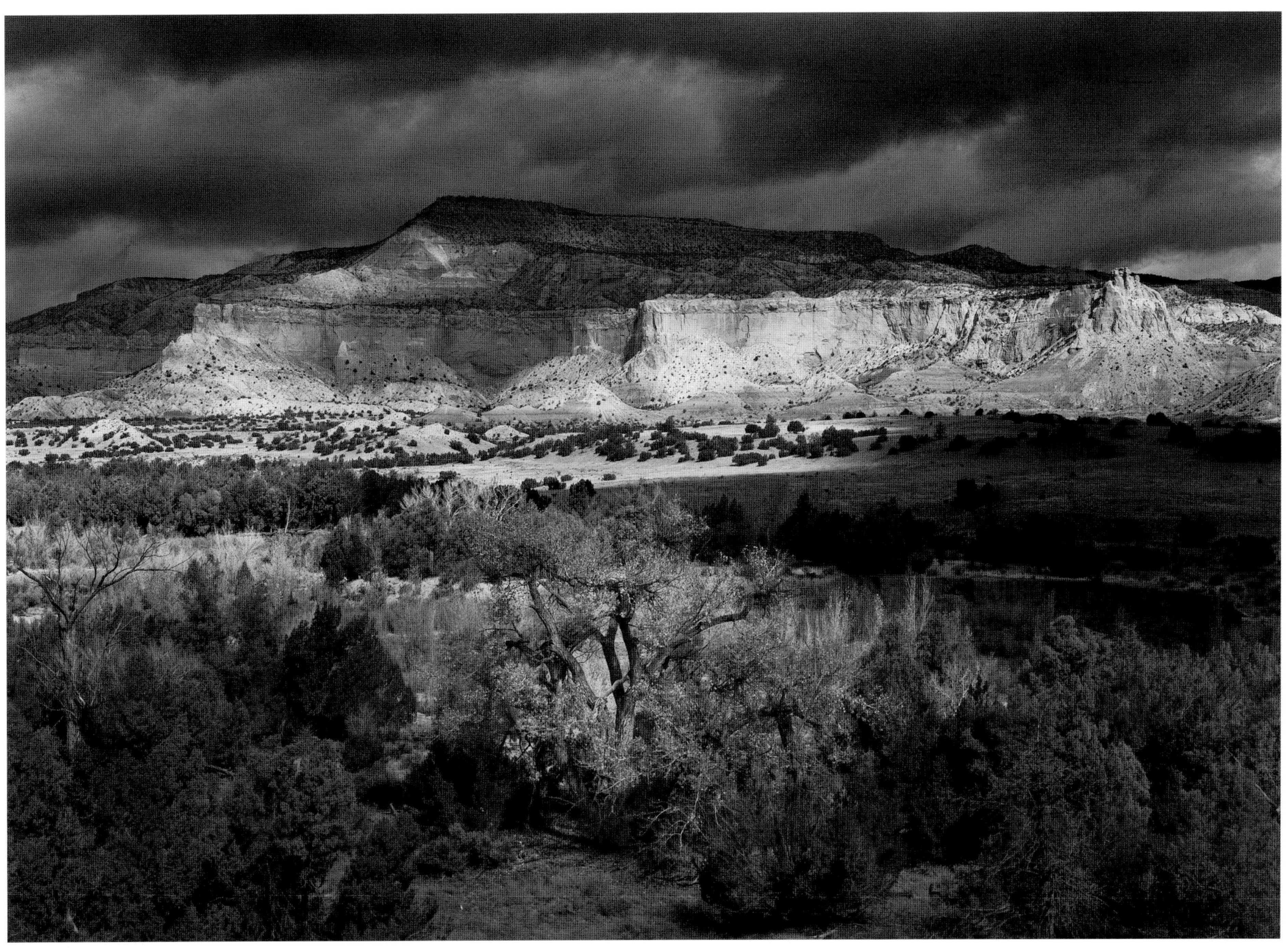

Plate 75: Tree Overlooking Painted Desert (Arroyo Seco Pasture), Ghost Ranch, New Mexico, 2007

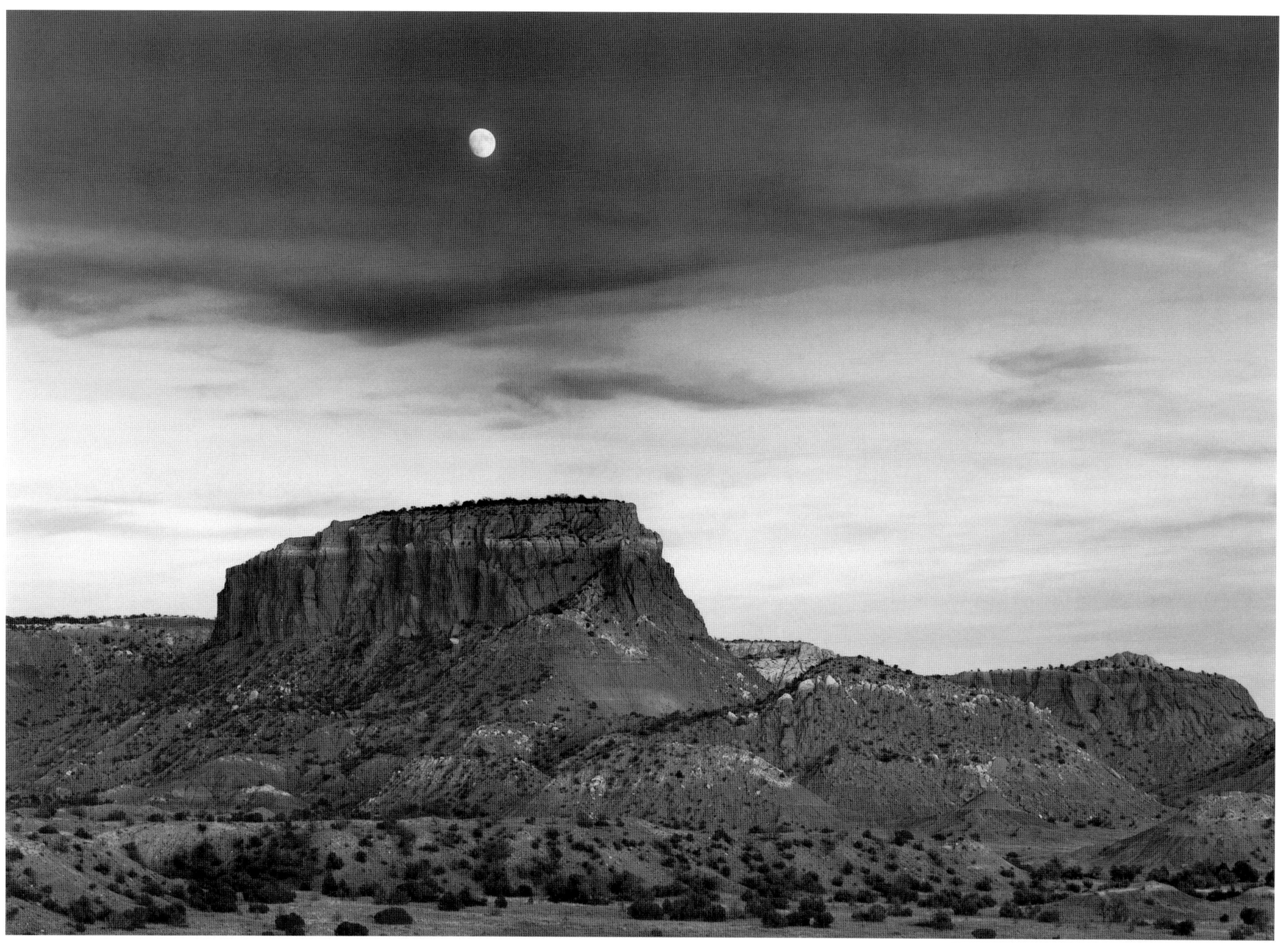

Plate 76: Moon over Orphan Mesa (Island Mesa), Ghost Ranch, New Mexico, 2007

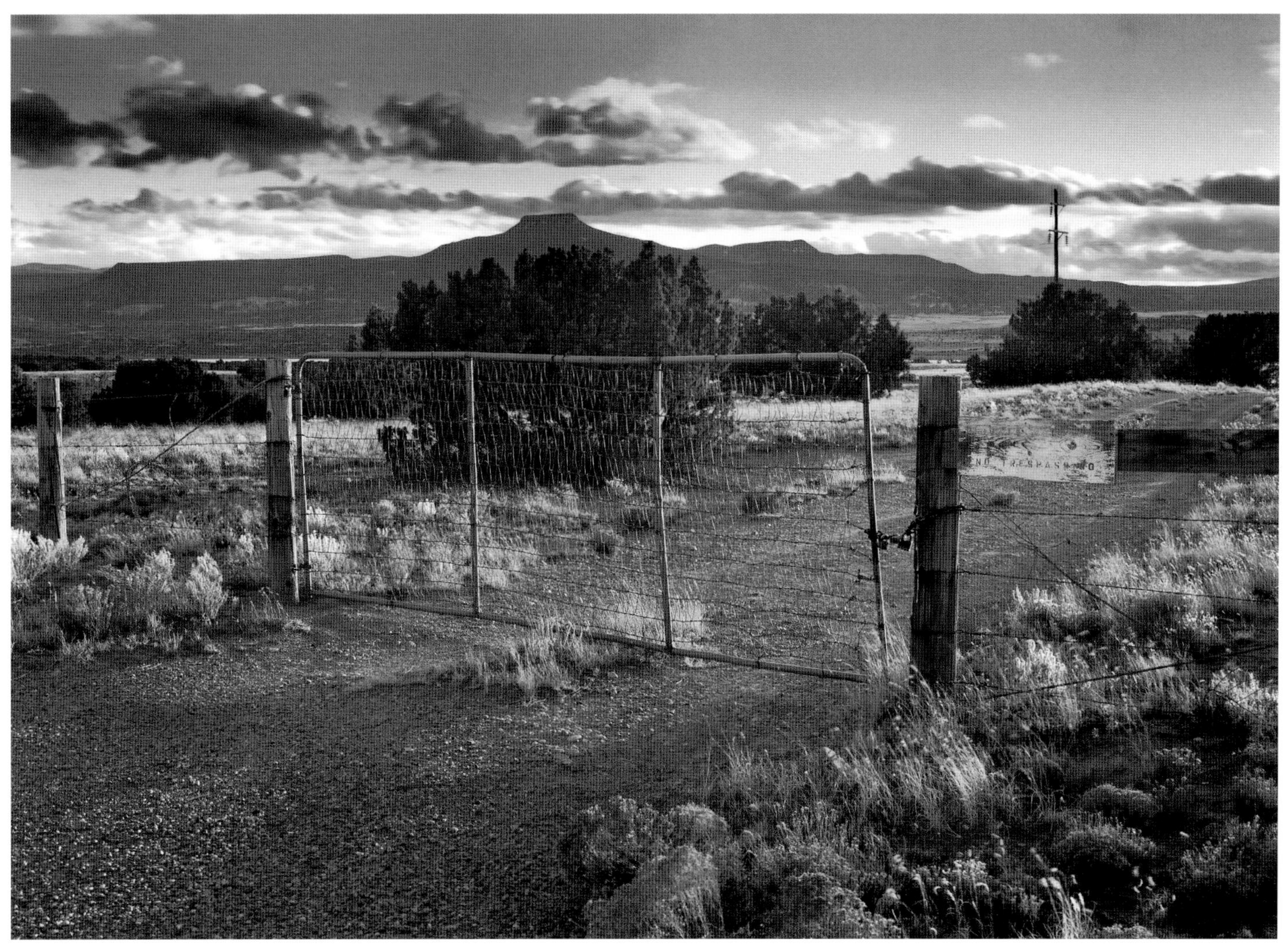

Plate 77: Gate to Civilian Conservation Corps Camp (East Pasture), Ghost Ranch, New Mexico, 2004

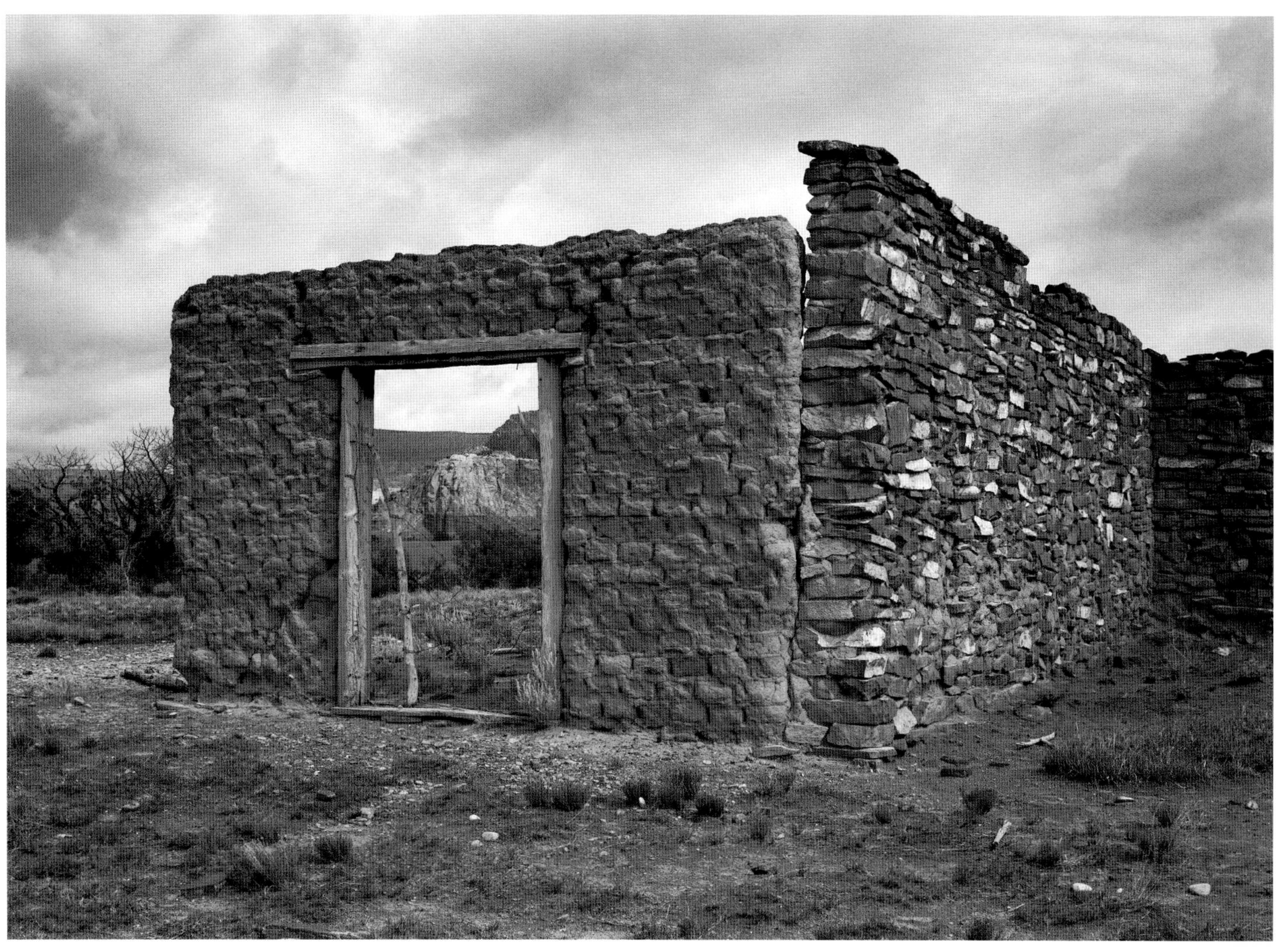

Plate 78: Adobe and Stone Ruin, Civilian Conservation Corps Camp, Ghost Ranch, New Mexiço, 2006

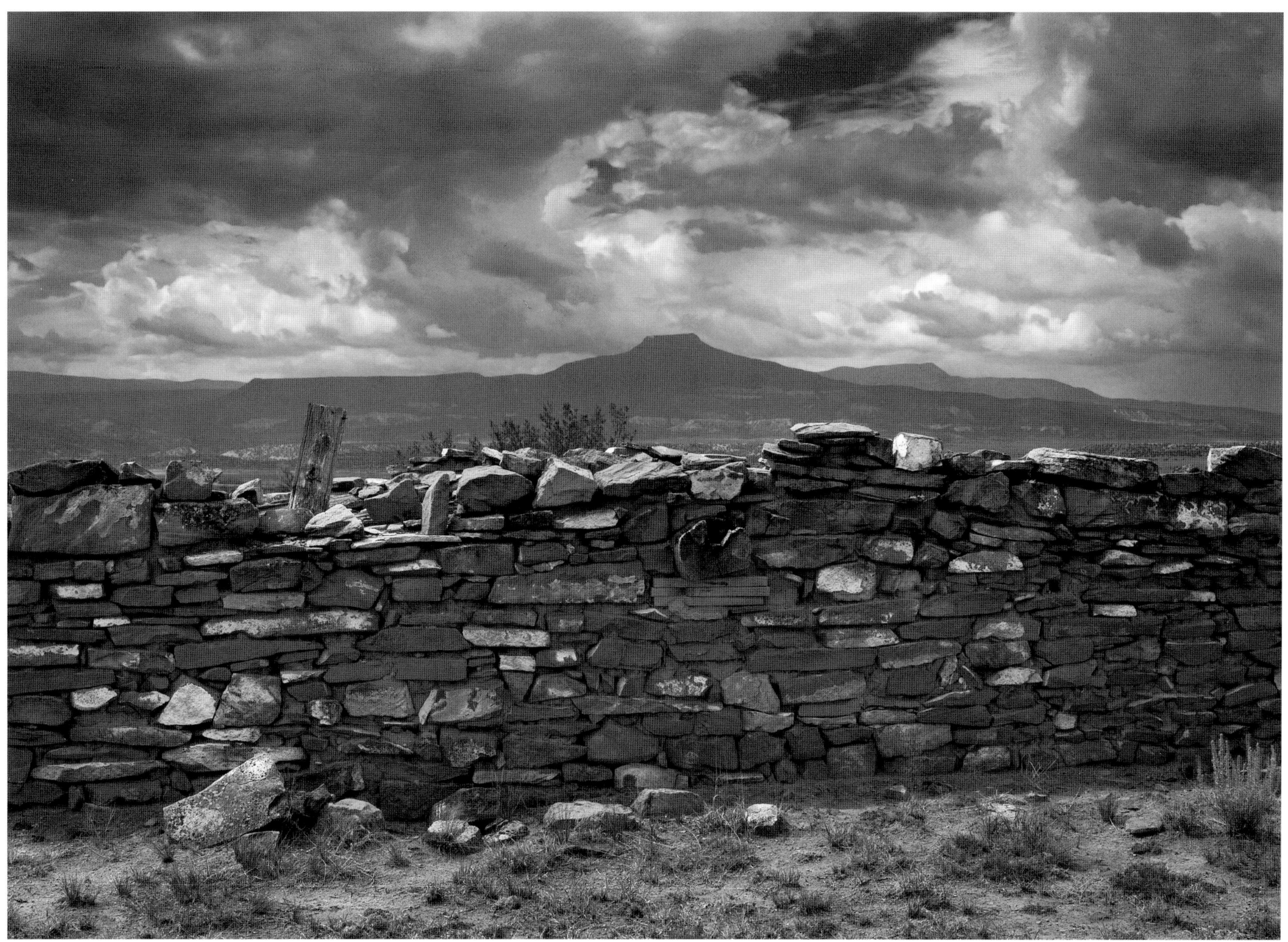

Plate 79: Stone Wall Ruin, Civilian Conservation Corps Camp, Ghost Ranch, New Mexico, 2006

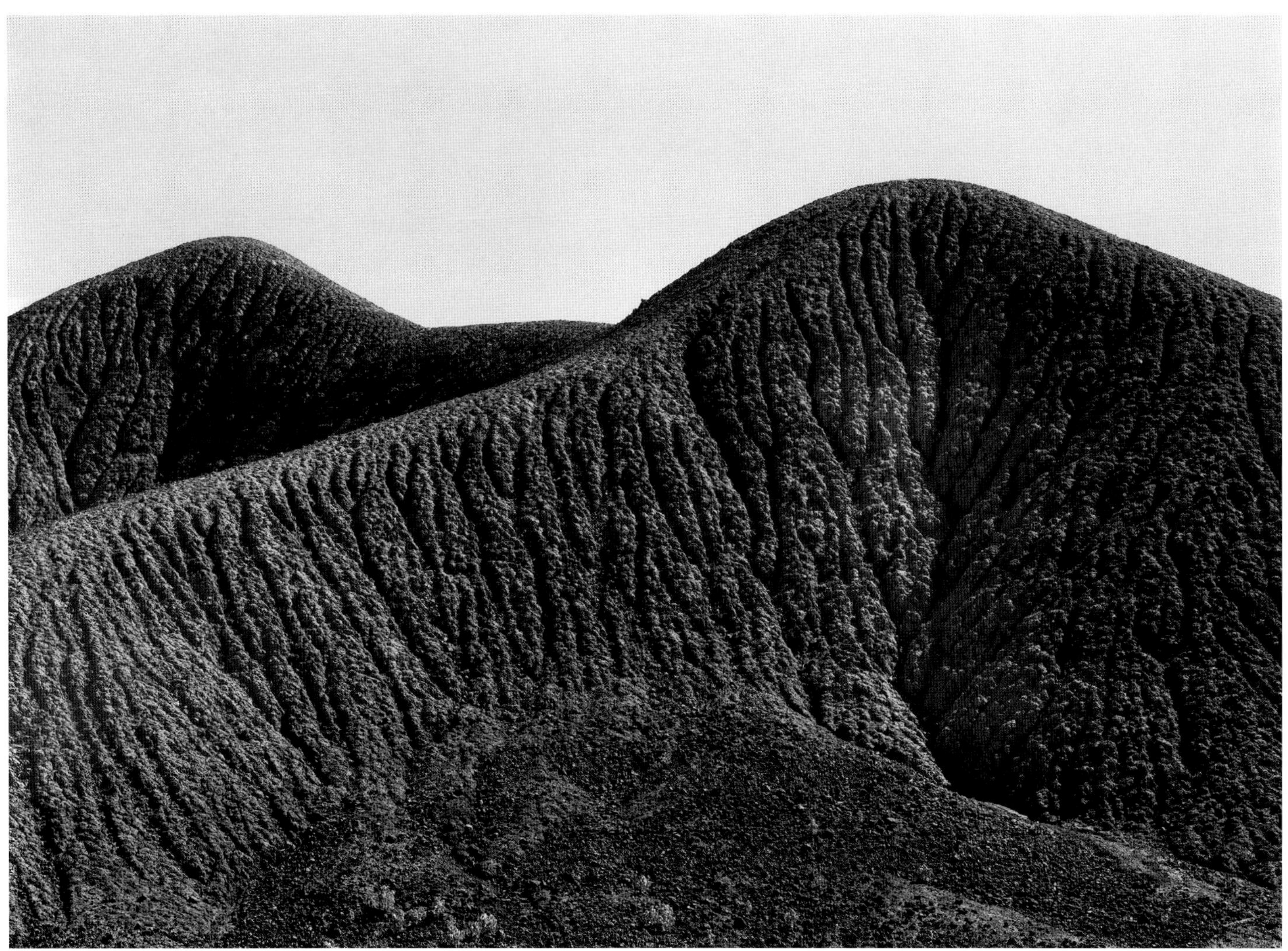

Plate 80: Red Hill Detail, Ghost Ranch, New Mexico, 2007

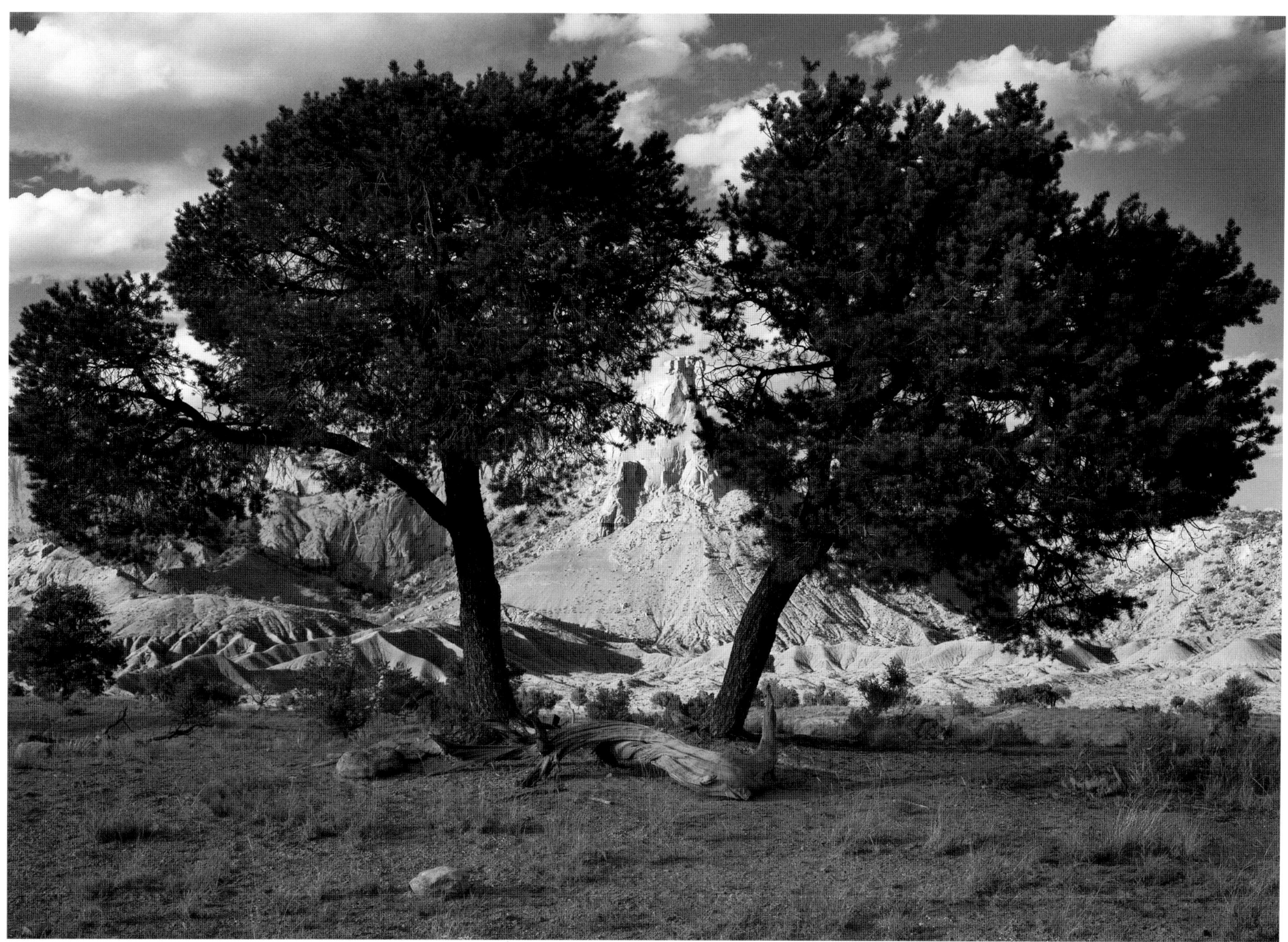

Plate 81: Twin Trees and Chimney Rock, Ghost Ranch, New Mexico, 2005

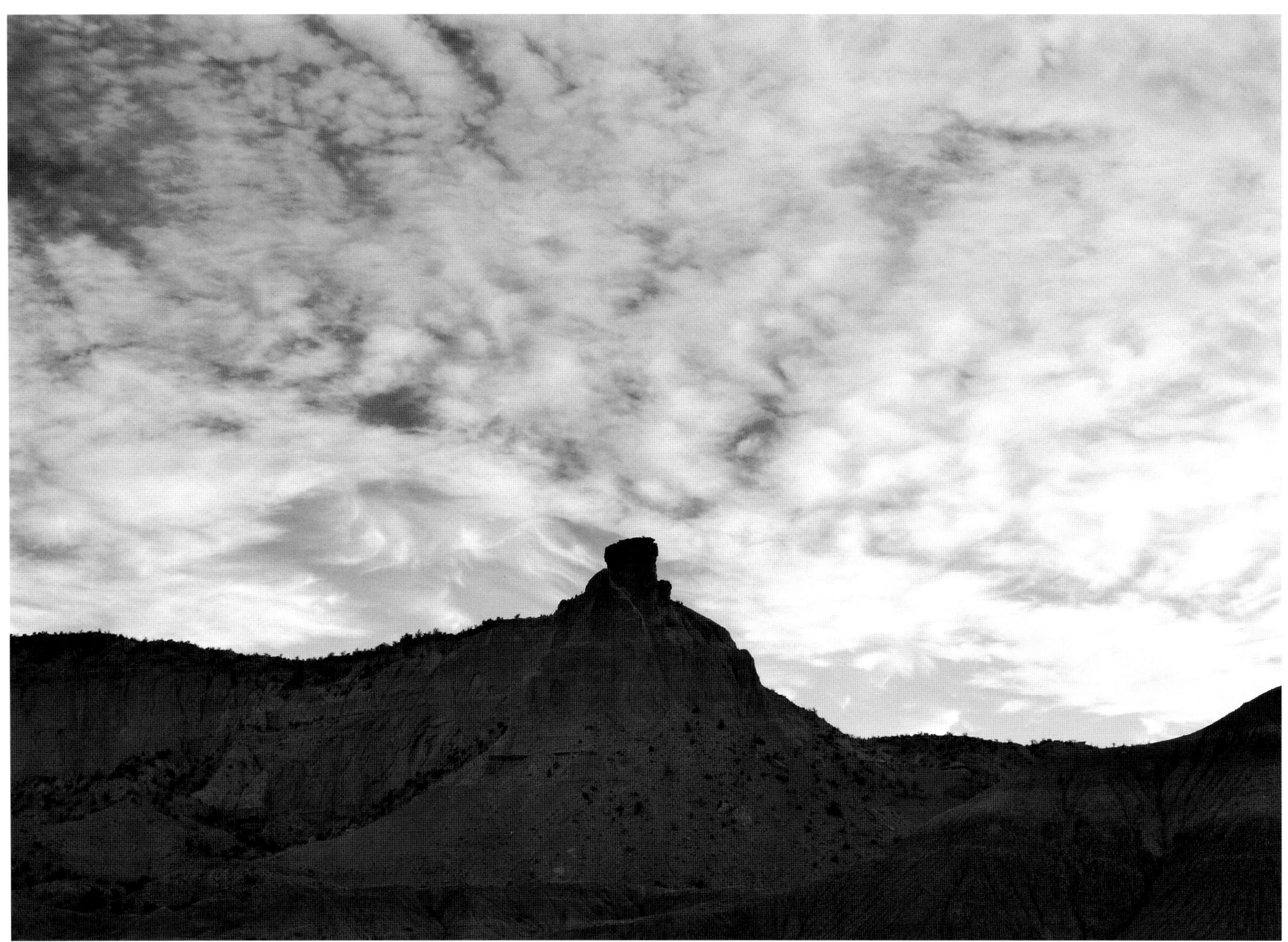

Plate 82: Chimney Rock and Clouds, Sunset, Ghost Ranch, New Mexico, 2007

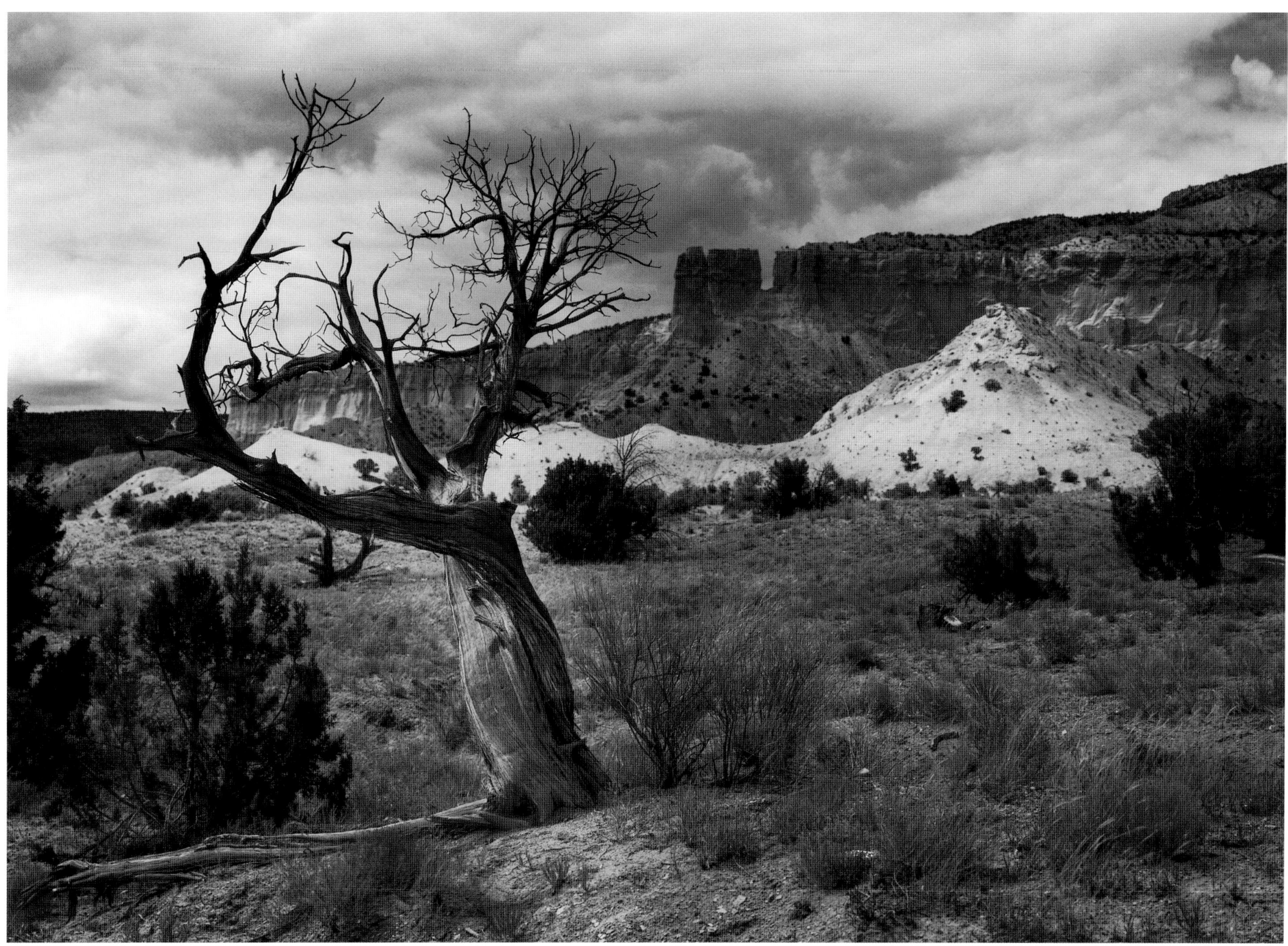

Plate 83: Juniper in Painted Desert, Spring, Ghost Ranch, New Mexico, 2006

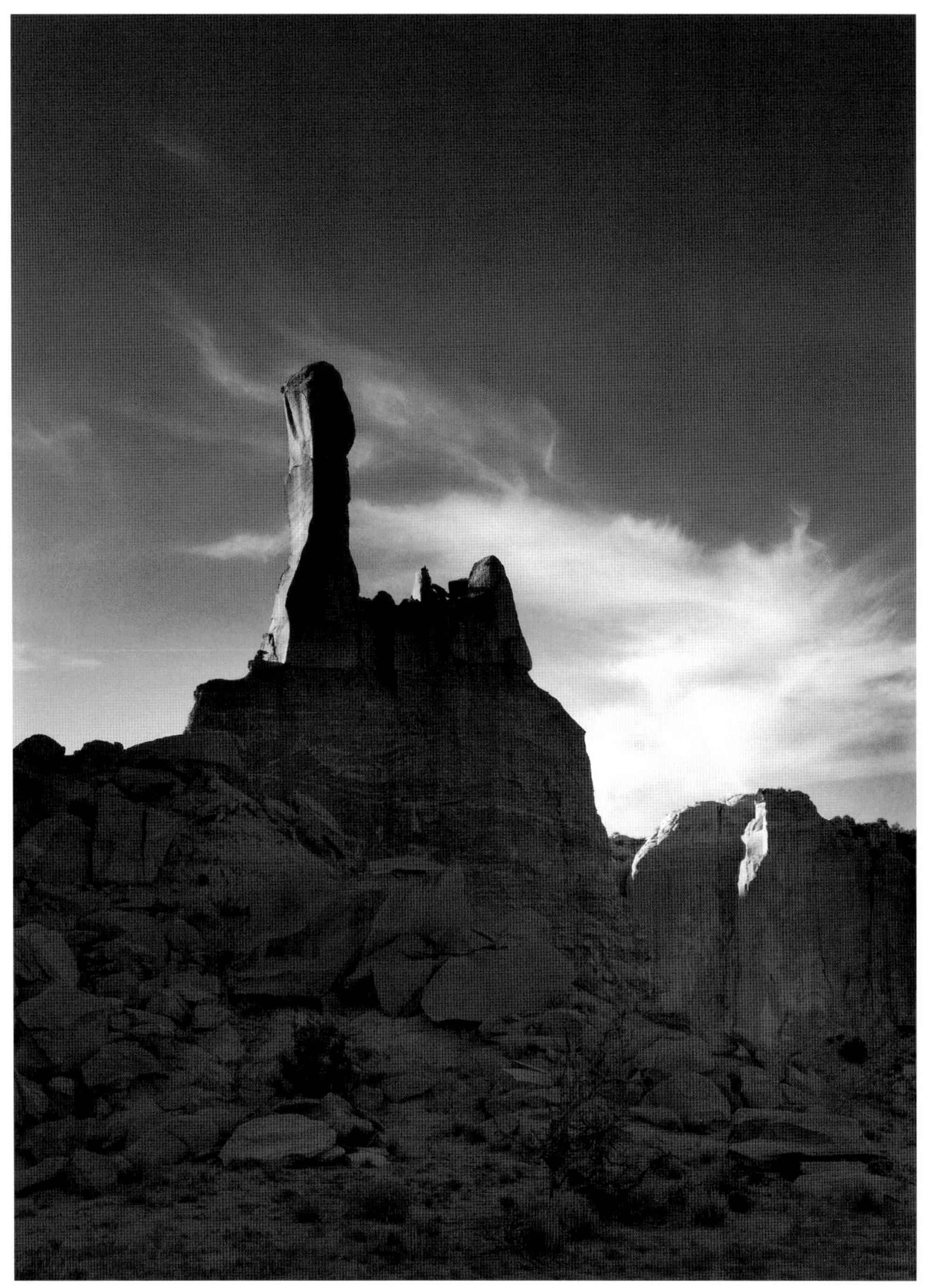

Plate 84: Rock Form, Comanche Canyon (East Pasture), Ghost Ranch, New Mexico, 2007

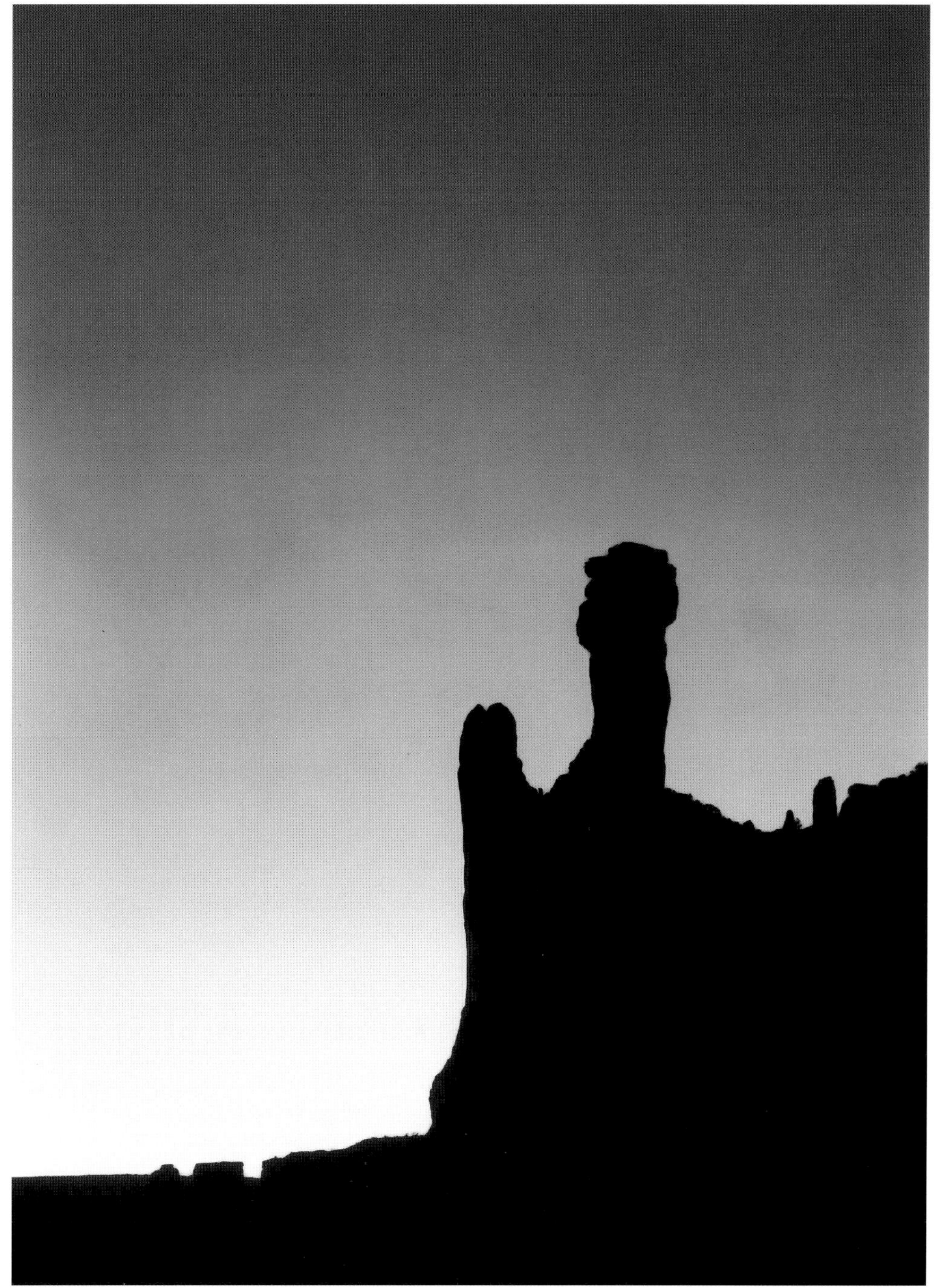

Plate 85: Chimney Rock at Twilight, Abiquiu, New Mexico, 2004

Plate 86: Cerro Pedernal at Twilight, Abiquiu, New Mexico, 2001

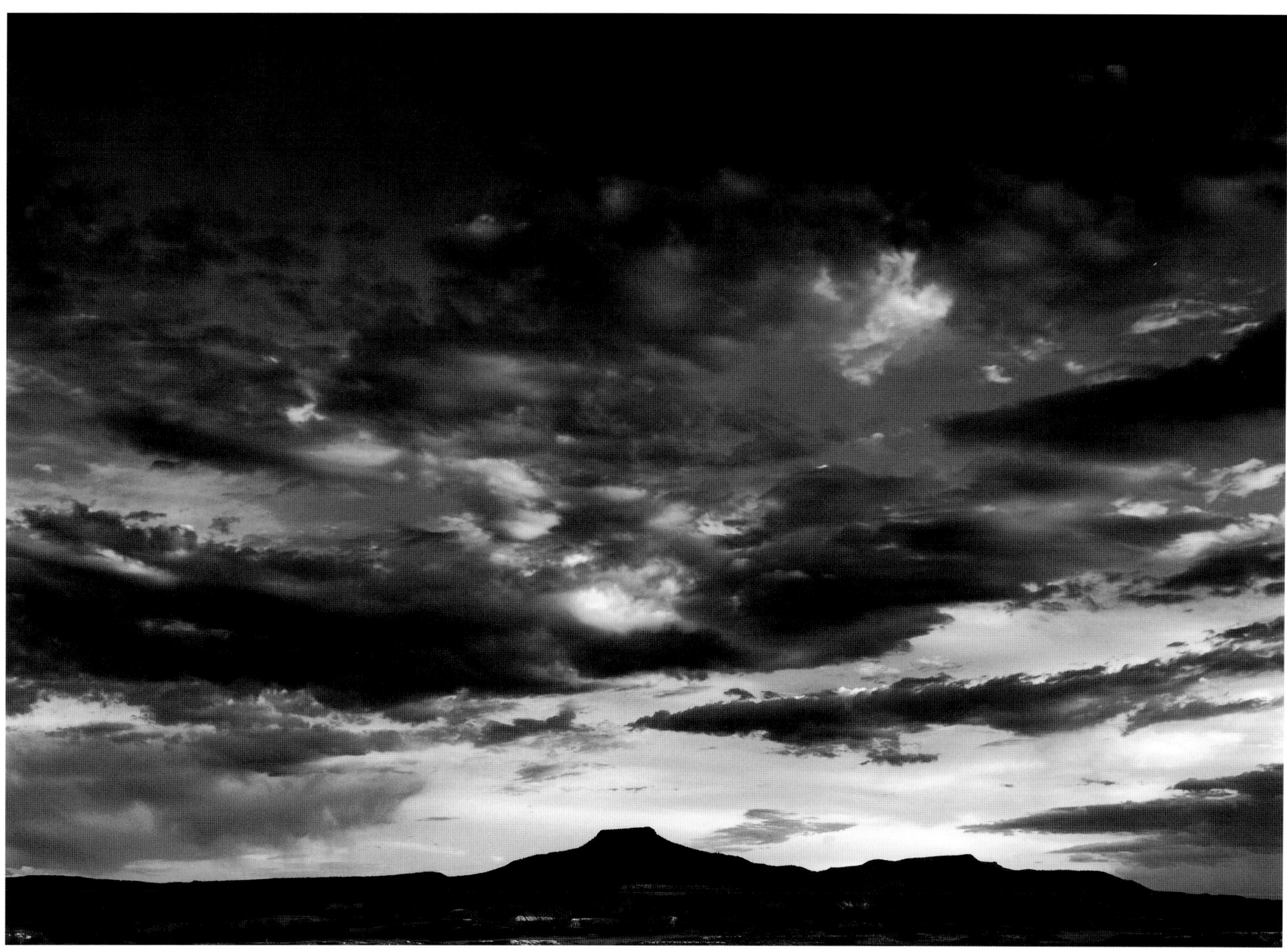

Plate 87: Cerro Pedernal No. 2, Sunset, Abiquiu, New Mexico, 1996

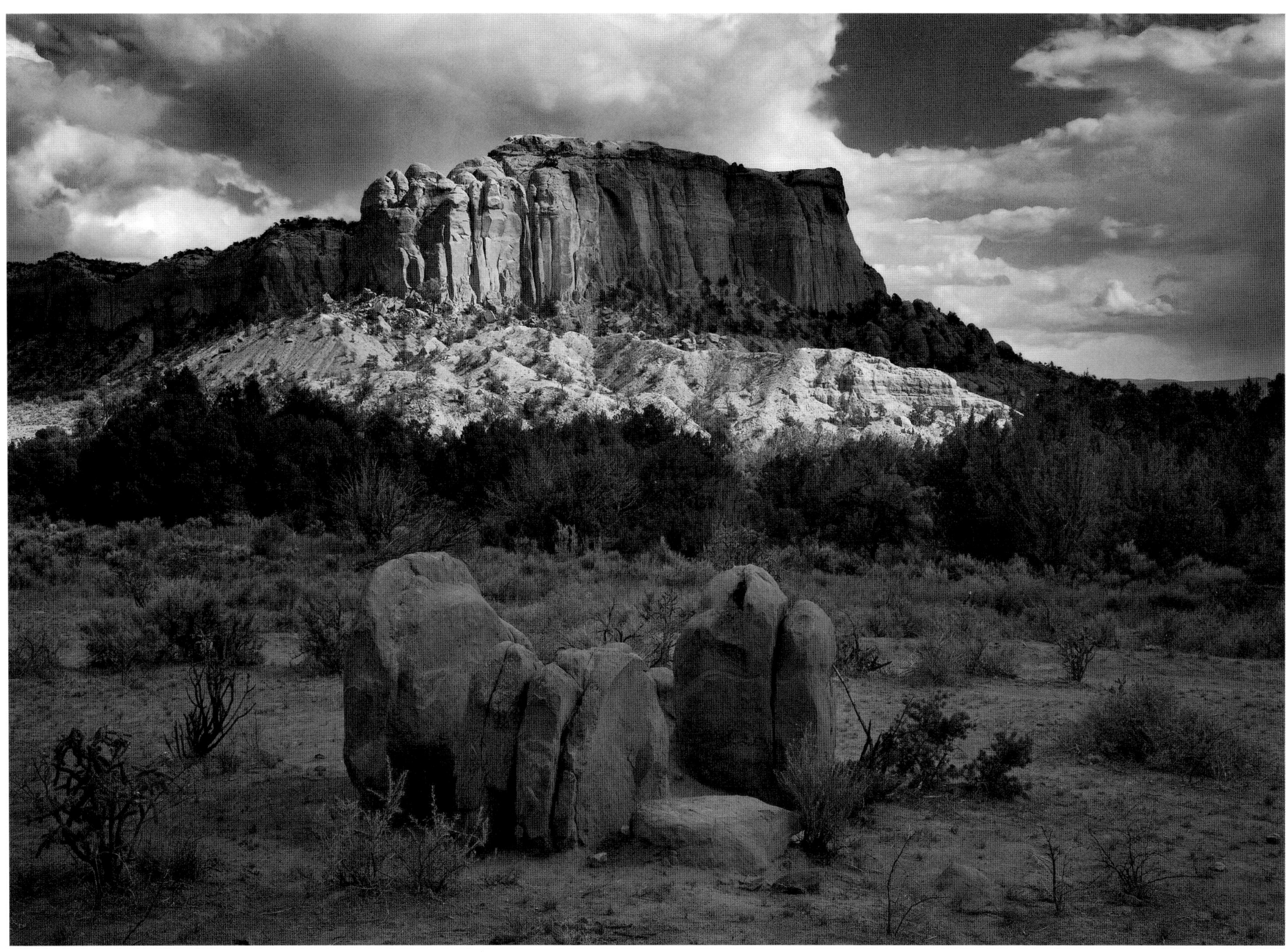

Plate 88: Kitchen Mesa (Ice Cream Rock) and Clearing Storm, Ghost Ranch, New Mexico, 2007

GHOST RANCH

The Sacred Place as Wound and Gift

BELDEN C. LANE

I've lived the first two-thirds of my life on the East Coast and in the Midwest, respectively, and yet in recent years I can't get enough of New Mexico! Especially this place called Ghost Ranch. What is it that draws me here? Spanish philosopher Ortega y Gassat said, "Tell me the place where you live and I'll tell you who you are."[1] He might also have said, "Tell me the place to which you are *drawn* and I'll tell you who you are *becoming.*"

The places to which we are most pulled at times—the "sacred places" in our lives—are often the places where we recognize the wound and the gift to be one. When we find an exterior landscape that mirrors the brokenness (on the one hand) and the deepest longings (on the other hand) of an unexplored *inner* landscape, we suddenly find ourselves in a geography of hope. A place like that demands growth. It says, "Pay attention. What you see around you is an echo of what lies within you." That's how I feel about my experience of New Mexico.

Artist and poet Meinrad Craighead had a similar experience on first coming here years ago. "When I came to New Mexico in 1960," she said, "I found the land which matched my interior landscape. The door separating inside and outside opened. What my eyes saw meshed with images I carried inside my body. Pictures painted on the walls of my womb began to emerge."[2] This stunning sense of déjà vu—finding an exterior landscape that resonates so powerfully with what we suddenly sense to be within us—sharpens our alertness to everything.

Encountering a "sacred place" may be a more common experience than people often recognize. Sacred place, I would argue, is simply an ordinary place ritually set apart to become extraordinary. Storytelling is usually the ritual activity that gives it life. A sacred place, therefore, is preeminently a "storied place." The site occasions the telling of significant tales about tragic and/or healing events that may have happened there. It roots people in a common tradition and points to a sense of transcendent meaning.[3]

Such a place is Ghost Ranch, nestled in the Piedra Lumbre basin of northern New Mexico. Here beauty and suffering meet. This whole "valley of shining stone" is part of a stunning landscape that bleeds.[4] Situated in the red rock country north of Abiquiu, Ghost Ranch offers one of the finest examples of Chinle Formation on the Colorado

Plateau. Wine, rust, crimson, and mauve-colored sandstone from the late Triassic period over 200 million years ago thrusts through the earth's surface here. Every time I drive up from Santa Fe and make that bend in Highway 84 just south of the ranch—where rocks the color of dark red wine suddenly rise like a towering cathedral all around me—I know I'm at home. I recognize Georgia O'Keeffe's passionate paintings of this whole area as having exaggerated nothing.

The surrounding Jemez and Sangre de Cristo mountains glow blood-red at sunset on hazy summer evenings. In springtime, Indian paintbrush appears in the high desert meadows, adding licks of flame to fields of sagebrush and Mormon tea. Even the Chama River along the highway becomes a ribbon of fire after thunderstorms, due to the runoff of flash floods from the hills nearby. Its name comes from the Tewa word (*tzama*) for "red." In short, the terrain surrounding Ghost Ranch forms a ruddied, open wound, shocking and tantalizing in its beauty.

Responses to red rock country are seldom indifferent. It triggers radically different associations in the human imagination. Some find it stark, monotonous, disquieting. Others find it strangely moving and healing. The color red speaks of life and high energy, of heat, fire, and blood. But it also signals danger, passion, anger, and warning. What people perceive in a reddened landscape depends on what they bring to it. Everyone's reading of a place varies, even as the place itself continually changes over time.

My own experience of New Mexico has often focused on its woundedness. It is a place to which I've come at times to deal with death and loss in my life. It is itself a thirsty and wounded land, crying out for water and justice, like much of the Southwest. It is a land marked by a mix of cultures that fight like a dysfunctional family. Its history is full of broken promises and unrealized dreams. Memories of range wars between Spanish settlers and Ute-Comanche raiders, the uneasy spirits of dead cattle rustlers, the plaintive prayers of devout penitentes, and the shouts of land-rights activists (*¡Tierra o Muerte!*, "land or death!") all swirl together in the collective unconscious of the land. These are the wounds of New Mexico. I feel them inside myself. Yet the same terrain is also a place of extraordinary gift—where an unanticipated charm fills a dry land with endless wonders, where all kinds of cultural differences are not just tolerated but celebrated, where I've repeatedly found the experience of wilderness to strip me of everything except what really matters. An intense delight in being alive arises out of a place where a sparse beauty demands simplicity of life.

New Mexican *curanderos*, or shamanic healers, would insist that the wound, by its power, is also gift. One can't have the one without the other. The place where the *new* slips in as unexpected grace is invariably the place where everything at first seems to have fallen apart in our lives. A geographical location that can do both—wound and heal us—will be experienced as sacred.

From the story of Adam and Eve in paradise to the Fisher King in the Grail legend and contemporary insights from the Enneagram, the truth persists that one's deepest wound is the source of one's greatest gift. The losses in our lives, the experiences of failure, the sins we most lament become, strangely, sources of hope in a landscape like the Chama River Valley. Here an ancient, experienced land speaks from its own history to people who have themselves known brokenness. Scars, stretch marks, upheavals of rock, and erosions of land make subtle, unnerving connections between exterior and interior landscapes.

A stubborn grace lies half-hidden in this land of leanness, scarred by a history of geological and social turmoil. It offers a glimpse of the greatest of all human hopes—that our deepest sufferings (even those we cause ourselves) can turn from endless regret to unexpected wholeness. Numerous people, including myself, have encountered the mystery at Ghost Ranch. What follows, then, is admittedly my own skewed interpretation of a place I've learned to love through anguish and struggle. The joy it affords is striking, but never easy.

The Land as Wound

From one way of looking at it, the land on which today's Presbyterian Education and Retreat Center rests is a layered memory of anger and pain, loss and grief. The earth here is a guardian of inherited wounds. The name first given to the small homestead in the late nineteenth century, El Rancho de los Brujos, the ranch of the witches, is an appropriate one. It gives voice to the cries that have long swept over the northern New Mexican landscape. Here the anguished moaning of La Llorona echoes over the mesas, searching for the lost children slain at her own hand. In the folklore accounts, she had avenged the lover who spurned her by killing their children in a burst of uncontrolled anger. Here the shrill night wind uncovers the bones of dead steers, of wild horses shot by government agents, of ancient dinosaurs trapped millions of years ago in a flash flood that buried them alive. Here the blood of the ruthless Archuleta brothers and their victims cries out from unhallowed ground. The two had used the remote homestead as a base for cattle rustling, robbery, and murder in the 1890s. The one brother finally turned against the other in a jealous rage, killing him with an axe. According to legend, the voices of their angry ghosts still haunt the quiet canyons at night.

Half-forgotten *cuentos* of the Genízaros living in the nearby pueblo of Abiquiu in the eighteenth century also resound over the tormented Ghost Ranch landscape. The stories tell of Native people who had been captured in childhood from various nomadic tribes and sold into service to Hispanic households. Gathering them in a single village at Abiquiu, the effort of the early Spanish governor was to "turn these detribalized and transitional Indians into settled pious farmers like their Hispanic neighbors."[5] They were held in suspicion, however, because of their use of magic in hunting. Some were accused of sorcery in causing an infectious disease that took the lives of many in the new community. Tales of witchcraft (of local *brujos* and *brujas*) spread easily in a land of strange rock formations, violent desert thunderstorms, and unavenged injustice.

The wounds of this land include the memory of armed men and angry freedom fighters gathered at Echo Amphitheater just north of the ranch in the fall of 1966. Calling for a justice that hadn't yet been realized, they challenged the right of the U.S. government to possess National Forest lands once guaranteed to Hispanic settlers by earlier land grants. The *Alianza* they formed (an alliance of Hispanic New Mexican activists) went on to occupy the county courthouse in Tierra Amarilla and proclaim a free republic, independent of the State of New Mexico and the United States of America. It took the National Guard and state militia, led by M-42 tanks and jeeps with mounted machine guns, to suppress the rebellion in the following summer.[6] A spirit of proud disobedience springs from the ground here, along with saltbush and snakeweed, wormwood and prickly pear cactus.

Even the whispers of nuclear scientists working on the Los Alamos project in the early 1940s linger in the collective memory of Ghost Ranch soil. World-renowned scientists like Enrico Fermi, Niels Bohr, and J. Robert Oppenheimer came to the ranch for rest and relaxation, amid their work on the deadliest weapon of the modern era. The dawning nightmare of the atomic bomb might well have disturbed the sleep of a man like Oppenheimer, awakening at night to the haunting cries of distant coyotes above Kitchen Mesa.

All these are fractures that engrave the landscape here, as real in their influence as the uplift and erosion of long-term geological forces. Rupture runs deep in the blood-red land. It rises to the surface of consciousness in the fleeting recollections of anger, fear, and unresolved longing that visitors inadvertently experience in such a place. The land's memory elicits a stirring in the soul, the awakening of an inexplicable unsubmissiveness, restlessness, passion.

Imitation, after all, is our most natural human response to landscape. We invariably mimic its cycles, sounds, and strivings. We stand in awe at hummingbirds frozen in space above a magenta cactus bloom. Hiking alone through an unexplored desert canyon, we naturally follow drainage routes toward the irregular slope of a distant ridgeline. Large, unfamiliar tracks in the snow make us wary, like a rabbit listening in winter silence. Like everything else at Ghost Ranch we touch in ourselves the deepest vulnerabilities of life, an echo of the earth's own persistent struggle for survival. We see it mirrored in dying piñon pines that are common in the area today, recent victims of bark beetles and continuing drought. The woundedness of the Piedra Lumbre wilderness is an old and enduring one, preserved through thousands of years by the remains of long-extinct species, intermittent arroyos, eroding canyons, displaced Pueblo dwellers, proud-spirited Chicanos, and crazy gringos alike.

The Land as Gift

Yet the flawed landscape is a healing place as well. It occasions startling gifts, at times unaccountable joy. The Department of Tourism celebrates the whole of New Mexico as a "Land of Enchantment." The mystery happens regularly at Ghost Ranch, as even casual visitors affirm. Moreover, the wonder occurs not *in spite of* the woundedness of the place, but *because* of it. Georgia O'Keeffe asked herself how a land "so poisonous" as New Mexico could also be "so beautiful," so conducive to wholeness. Sites that connect us to the shadows we ordinarily suppress in our consciousness are those we most often identify as holy. The wound and the gift invariably are one. In the mystery of homeopathic medicine we find the curious principle that "likenesses" not only attract; they heal. A desert terrain may bring strange solace to deserted souls. An aggrieved land can oddly lessen grief.

Surrounded by the four sacred mountains of the Navajos, from Mt. Taylor to Wheeler Peak, the whole terrain sings to the music of the Kachina spirits. Surprisingly curative places frequent a landscape that burns in the desert sun. Pilgrims travel to Chimayo to pray for miraculous healing at its *sanctuario*. Others go to Chaco Canyon to seek the lost wisdom of the Anasazi or to Christ in the Desert to pray in its adobe monastery chapel. Still others seek the desert pools under the cliffs at Ojo Caliente to soothe aching bones.

Historically, the region north of Abiquiu has been known as La Tierra de Guerra. Yet the enduring struggles of this land of war have fostered a resolute insistence on hope. The land possesses a beauty at times too painful to bear. Sitting in the shade of a cottonwood tree in front of Corral Block near Ghost Ranch office, I gaze across the llanos to the distant silhouette of Pedernal. I feel its harsh loveliness like a pain in the chest. Yet I know its beauty to be an injury I'd never wish to have mended. This is a broken and redeemed land, powerfully able to bless.

Cerro Pedernal, the anvil-shaped, 10,000-foot peak that dominates the southern horizon, is a wild and enduring presence at the ranch. This is the mountain Georgia O'Keeffe said God had promised to give to her if she painted it enough. Its flint-topped summit harbors mythic tales of Changing Woman and Spider Woman, both sacred to the Navajo people. In the age-old tales, these women were bringers of a change that is always painful, yet offers ever new possibilities for the interwoven connectedness of life.

In Navajo belief, the earth above ground was originally filled with monsters. The land we know as northern New Mexico was a forbidding terrain without hope. Then a baby girl was found atop a sacred mountain at the heart of the Navajo spiritual geography. Some stories identify the place as Cerro Pedernal.[7] The child was Changing Woman, an earth mother continually surprising and renewing the world. As she grew older, she made love to a dazzling young warrior, the sun, and gave birth to Monster Slayer. Her son was a hero destined to rid the world of dread beasts so as to make room for humans and other forms of life.

Changing Woman still remains a powerful presence in the Piedra Lumbre basin. Seen in the turning of the seasons, she is young and beautiful in spring; mature in late summer; gray-haired, wrinkled, and bent in winter. Then she transforms herself once again with blooming phlox and verbena the following spring. Her frequent changes of dress give her various names: White Shell Woman, Turquoise Woman, Abalone Woman. She is the capacity of the land to bless and to be blessed. The ever-changing curves, crevasses, and turns of her body come alive in O'Keeffe's ravishing paintings of Ghost Ranch landscape. Every canyon, butte, ravine, and wash discloses the mother of a once-monstrous terrain who restores life to a wounded land.

Her son Monster Slayer, along with his twin brother Child-of-the-Water, still war against death and drought in their own continued renewing of the land of the Four Corners region. Their virile presence manifests itself in the lightning strikes of July rainstorms and sudden waterfalls that disappear as quickly as they come. This is a land that evokes nurturing life *and* a strength for justice, masculine *and* feminine energies, the work of horse handlers and weavers alike. The two naturally converge in a country where Spider Woman first taught the Navajo people the intertwined mysteries of the loom. Her gift of the thread of life and an eagle feather assisted the brothers in their primeval victory over a monstrous and ill-formed world.

My own chance encounter with Monster Slayer and Changing Woman occurred one summer afternoon several years ago in Ghost Ranch canyons. I had done what you are always told *not* to do when hiking in the desert, especially during the summer thunderstorm season. Don't go alone and keep an eye out for gathering storms so that you can get back in time when you need to. Zen poet and nature writer Gary Snyder once observed that the great thing about wilderness is you don't have to try very hard to make the mistakes that are necessary for really learning something there.[8]

So I found myself caught one afternoon at the end of the Box Canyon trail as a severe thunderstorm suddenly blew up. I scrambled into a small cave, trying to escape hailstones as wild torrents of water swept rocks and debris over the canyon cliff above me. I had never seen a sky so dark, a storm so furious. Every patch of sage, yucca plant, and fir tree was at its mercy. Moreover, the windstorm arrived at a time of death and turmoil in my own life. My mother was dying of cancer with Alzheimer's disease back home, a lingering process that recalled the unresolved death of a long-lost father as well. My dad had taken his life when I was thirteen years old and the shadow of that trauma had followed me ever since. All my life I'd run from death, throwing myself into endless work, nurturing a reputation as a teacher and writer, ever seeking fulfillment in responsibilities outside the home. Escaping the ranch that afternoon in search of the solace of fierce landscapes, I dragged behind me the long-lived wounds of both parents. The tempest sweeping over the New Mexican plains reverberated with an inner storm raging through the canyonlands of the soul.

After the storm's frenzy had passed, I walked out of Box Canyon, the saturated ground pulsing with new life, energies of sky and earth filling the space. As the windstorm waned, the bleeding of the land began. Arroyos from up on Mesa del Yeso emptied into the lower canyon through which I passed. The new waters joining Box Canyon creek were a deep, chocolate red, the runoff of vermilion and rust brown hills in the high country. They formed a menstrual flow, these dark waters, as if the land were cleansing itself of its life-giving blood. Viscous and thick, they poured especially heavy from between two large boulders. I climbed over to the place, cupped my hands, and let the waters fall over my head, rolling down my hair and onto my shoulders. Laughter echoed down through the canyon. I knew myself that day to have been found at a sacred place. The storm's wounding and healing of the land had mirrored a similar process going on inside me, in a way I couldn't fully comprehend. Meeting the Father in lightning and the Mother in blood was a reminder yet again that the place of the wound is inescapably the source of the gift.[9] The wound, indeed, can become the womb of a new life.

But the gift, as I discovered, is rarely what one expects. That's why it so often comes with laughter. The desert has a way of surprising and unsettling people, happily dismissing what they think important, preventing them from taking themselves too seriously. Hilarity at our expense is the desert's favorite way of inviting us outside of ourselves. It laughs at our silly pretensions, our efforts to bolster a fragile reputation, our incessant fears of death. That's often the greatest part of the gift.

In the sayings of the ancient Desert Fathers and Mothers, there is a story of a young man who came for a brief visit to the monastery at Scete, west of the Nile. He approached Abba Macarius, the abbot of the community, saying he had heard people rave about the sanctity of the monks and that he, too, wanted to become a holy man. "But I've only got the weekend," he added. "Can you teach me how to be a holy man in three days?" The abbot smiled, but nodded and told him to spend the rest of the day over at the cemetery nearby, abusing the dead. "Yell at them for all you're worth," he said. "Call them murderers and thieves. Throw rocks at their graves." The man thought this was strange instruction for learning how to be a holy man, but he did as he was told.

When he returned that night, Macarius asked him, "What did the dead people say to you?" "They were dead as door knobs," the man replied. "They didn't say anything." "That's curious," answered the abbot. "Go back again tomorrow and spend the day praising them this time. Call them apostles, saints, and righteous men and women. Think of every compliment you can imagine." Still confused, the young man nonetheless did again as he was told, returning to the cloister at the end of the second day. "What did they say to you this time?" Macarius inquired. "Nothing more than yesterday," answered the would-be novice. "Ah, they must indeed be holy people," replied the abbot. "You insulted them and they did not reply. You praised them and they did not speak. Go and do likewise, my friend, taking no account of either the scorn of men and women or their praises. And you, too, will be a holy man."[10]

Such is the desert's last laugh at our human aspirations to self-importance, our anxious flights from reality. "What do you learn to ignore?" the desert asks. "And what do you learn to love?" These are the two most important gifts the desert offers, coming like Coyote's laughter in very down-to-earth and self-effacing ways.

These are the mysteries of the place called Ghost Ranch. Stories of hope, prophecy, and birth all reside here. Aztlán, the mythical place from which the ancient Aztecs migrated to the central plateau of Mexico a thousand years ago, is sometimes identified with the northern New Mexican landscape. Seven sacred caves once marked the primordial place of emergence, the spiritual source of life for the Aztec people. Rumor also says an unclaimed pot of rustler gold, buried by the Archuleta brothers, still lies hidden somewhere on the ranch's rolling hills. In the imagination of New Mexican novelists like Rudolfo Anaya and Chicano student activists rediscovering the power of their homeland, the promise of Aztlán still pervades the high desert country north of Santa Fe.[11] The land breathes a promise and hope that only Raven is fully able to imagine.[12]

Initiation and Hope

In short, the earth around Ghost Ranch mirrors an important psychological/spiritual journey that people are invited to embrace in their lives. The place lends itself to ritual activity, to an experience of initiation. At its best (and worst) it demands our moving symbolically through excruciating loss to a new wholeness. All true initiation is initiation into loss. The path to new life invariably passes through the desert, not around it. Only in facing our brokenness—"owning our shit," as the ranch horse wrangler might say—do we realize what the apostle Paul meant by a "strength made perfect in weakness." If we flee from what is too painful to bear, we never grow. The cultural and mythic history of the Piedra Lumbre valley shows the danger of men like the Archuleta brothers who never came to terms with their shadow, of women like La Llorona whose denial of loss led to violence and death. Overwhelmed by what they most feared losing, they couldn't conceive the path toward healing as always and only the dark way of the cross.

The landscape itself embodies this truth more powerfully than any text or sermon. Artists and theologians who teach at the ranch are quickly aware that the *place* itself is the best teacher. They simply try to get out of the way so that the land (and the Spirit breathing through it) can do its work. If, as Carl Jung observed, we are transformed more by images than by concepts, then Ghost Ranch terrain reveals itself as a striking vehicle of transformation.

But how does one experience personal change through exposure to a given place? Simply *going* to the desert doesn't guarantee a thing, as early Christian monks readily observed. God is never on call anywhere. Only as we come with intentionality and risk, learning the stories of the place from the community of those who have long dwelt there, and submitting ourselves—often painfully—to its mystery, can the place speak to us out of its power to change. Rituals of entry are necessary if we ever hope to find ourselves "moving through a landscape as one of its details."[13] Deliberately sitting in silence, ritual participation in storytelling, the repetitive movement of liturgy, and mindful walking are all means of making us fully present to place. We grasp concepts through discursive thinking, but we need ritual for the deeper appropriation of images.

My own most recent ritual experience of the Ghost Ranch back country happened last summer at a Men's Rites of Passage event with Franciscan storyteller and teacher Richard Rohr. His emphasis on the need for mid-life initiation in contemporary American society is one that meshes well with what the northern New Mexican landscape has to teach. In the first half of life, Rohr says, men are taught to ascend, striving for success, building a tower that expresses their overwhelming sense of competence. But in the second half, they have to learn the path of descent, letting go of the need to accomplish, jumping off the tower into a new freedom and release. Initiation, for men as well as women, involves a recognition of one's poverty and disrepair, a passage into the labyrinth, the cave, the desert, and dark night. It means getting rid of the calculating mind, abandoning control, meeting (like Parsifal) the wounded king who is helpless to heal himself.[14]

Yet in the midst of that dark night, in the canyons of a beautiful but disturbing landscape, we may happen upon an amazing freedom. The wound we bring into the desert with us reveals an uncanny gift. The worst possible disasters in our lives may occasion an equally implausible salvation. Everything is turned on its head in a land where rough-hewn crosses stand alongside remote penitente chapels or moradas. The earth itself points to the mystery the Penitente Brothers have known so well: "Once the killing of God becomes the redemption of the world, then forevermore the very worst things have the power to become the very best thing."[15] Where loss is finally owned, all is not lost. Joy comes springing out of the crack in the canyon wall, like water from the rock.

Julian of Norwich expressed it this way: "First the fall, and then the recovery from the fall, and *both* are the mercy of God."[16] The fall is indispensably a part of the entire healing process. The wound, the magnificent defeat, the happy sin (*O felix culpa!*) is as crucial to the resulting wholeness as the deliverance itself. Contrary to what we may have learned, authority in the spiritual life does not rest on one's success in triumphing over obstacles. It lies in the compassion and patience one learns in the ache of failure. Arthur Pack, the Harvard-educated publisher and conservationist who gave the ranch to the

Presbyterian Church in 1955, knew the heartbreak of death and a failed marriage through the years he lived here. But he also knew the mending power of the land—as the *mano de Dios*, God's own hand within it, continually works to restore what is broken.[17]

One may carry the wound for a long time, however, before finally discovering it as gift. Coming to the ranch last summer, I brought—as others did—a "father wound" along with me. Like novelist and theological writer Frederick Buechner, I had wrestled all my life with a father who had committed suicide.[18] He had died when I needed him most, before I'd been able to access any of his strength as a policeman or a father. He had struggled through his life with an abusive, alcoholic dad and later a demanding wife. I remember glimpsing a wild freedom in yellowed photographs of him as a young man, but this had long ago been drained out of him. He had learned to seek what value he could find outside the home, in the approval of others. When irredeemable failure came even at the workplace, he had turned his .38 Police Special on himself, taking his life, leaving behind a wife and an only child to make their way in the world as best they could.

Part of the enduring character of the wound was that I had never been able to imagine my father as a strengthening force in my life. I had memories only of his weakness, his ineffectiveness, his final defeat. I'd always longed for a father who could teach me to fly.

The experience of initiation at the ranch reopened all this, as I moved through a process I didn't fully understand. Ritual always appeals to us at a level deeper than the intellect. In the midst of this liminal experience, a truth began to dawn. Not only had pain emerged out of my earliest unfulfilled needs, but also a *vision* of what still might be. What I never received in childhood created a passion for the finest dreams I ever subsequently imagined. All my life, this thirteen-year-old boy had longed for a wild freedom, to commit to family, to act boldly in matters of justice, to work without being self-conscious about how his work is received by others. These lingering desires were what allowed me to exult in the unrestrained freedom I witnessed in the surrounding New Mexican landscape. The nagging memory of the wound (by the grace of God) was finally able to generate its own healing, reawakening the dream. The insight came like a hawk falling from the top of Chimney Rock, then opening into flight: our point of utter vulnerability is where the gift always first appears.

The landscape itself, in sustaining pain and wildly affirming life, made possible the connection. The crumbling cliffs of red mesas trying to hold their own against erosion, the Chama River sweeping its muddy waters toward the Rio Grande, the black profile of Pedernal witnessing to a stubborn, flint-hard endurance—the entire land flaunts an unsuppressed freedom. Fierce in its clarity about matters of unimportance, it nurtures a restless desire to live. It speaks, in a harsh desert accent, of relinquishment and longing.

I asked myself as I walked up into Box Canyon again last August: Can a child who has long grown old know wildness? Can a remote canyon where wilderness thrives connect a son to his lost father's untapped strength and love? Are memories ever really healed? I walked into the desert to let the questions hang in its long silence. I sat through the day in a circle of sticks drawn in the shade of a juniper tree along the canyon wall, waiting for answers.

Nothing came, of course. I should have expected as much. "Nothing" is often the disguise in which the gift first appears. Like Jonah having escaped the belly of the whale—feeling sorry for himself in the desert outside Nineveh—I sat in the ashes of old memories, rigging a T-shirt in the sparse branches overhead, trying to protect myself from the sun. It was a long, hot day.

At first the ants were all over me. I wondered if I had been stupid enough to choose an ant bed for a hermit circle. But when I noticed that they were only curious and not anxious to sting, I finally accepted their butterfly touch with indifference and they were gone as quickly as they had come. I'd gone into the desert looking for "signs"—waiting for arcane messages I could decipher, reading the landscape with all the self-absorption of one who thinks it was put there personally for him. I'm a sucker for that kind of thing.

Ironically, I almost missed the gift that did come. That morning a raven circled low over head. I could hear the haunting sound of its great wings beating the air, like the sound of wind brushing velvet. But it was gone before I even seemed to notice it. The suspicion lingered for the rest of the day that I had lost something significant in not attending to the raven's flight. In craving the holy—looking for a supernatural sign—I had missed the ordinary. That's how the father would have come to me, after all. Not in ghostly splendor, but in the subtlety of half-remembered images. I kept hoping the raven might return. I tried to imagine what it might be like to live in a world where a long-dead father, his strength lost on a son who had never been able to see him fly, could return as a sleek black bird in canyon flight. I had always wanted a father in my life—one able to invite wildness, to demand accountability, to teach his son how to soar.

But the raven never returned that day, just as the father had never come back in my life. Yet in both cases the "not returning" proved to be the best gift of all. In the end, there were no spiritual lessons emblazoned on the land. I'd kept bumping into yucca thorns instead, pushing the edges of my circle to escape the relentless sun. But as evening came and I prepared to leave, I was finally satisfied with what the day had brought (and not brought). I had stayed in one place, remaining attentive, despite all the distractions. I had abandoned illusions of receiving any deep mystical insight from the desert's numinous power. I had been given nothing more than a single image of wildness—a circling bird of prey that had never returned.

I recognized that waiting those many years for something *outside* of myself had simply kept me from realizing what had been within all along. The strength I'd wanted to discover, the commitment to family, the power to resist the culture in which I live, the ability to fly—all these had been inside. All we ever desire most, and fear most, is already within us. The New Mexican landscape itself suggested the contours of a vast and unexplored inner desert, a stunning wilderness stretching for miles within the hidden reaches of the soul. There, within me, the face of the wild Christ beckoned, his own suffering now overwhelmed by resurrection, a flash of untamed joy in his eyes. In the end, I had passed through a ritual of initiation in spite of myself. I had been emptied of excuses for not making changes in my life. If the father were to return, he would have to return in me.

Scattering my circle of sticks and leaving the place as I had found it, I slowly made my way down the canyon rocks and back toward the ranch. A red ochre sunset stretched across the western sky. I realized how little control I had of anything in this place called New Mexico—a crazy place where you first have to lose things if you ever have any hope of finding them. In that moment, Coyote had the last laugh once again. Laughter welled up involuntarily and tears filled my eyes, as I noticed—long after I had ceased to expect it—a single raven on a long straight flight high overhead, moving west toward home. This time the raven wasn't the long-lost father, or the mother who had also died, but my own flight into a new life that I was just beginning.

Spiritual insights, at least in my own experience, usually arrive on the wings of inconsequence. "The things that ignore us save us in the end," says Buddhist teacher Andrew Harvey.[19] At a place like Ghost Ranch the inconsequential and indifferent, as well as the beautiful and monumental, have a way of regularly disclosing the sacred. That's why the place is so amazing. Here the wound is revealed as unaccountable gift. The place of brokenness occasions its own healing. That's why I love it as I do.

Belden C. Lane is a retired professor of theological studies at Saint Louis University.

Notes

1. Quoted in Kathleen Norris, *Dakota: A Spiritual Geography* (New York: Ticknor and Fields, 1993), 156.
2. Meinrad Craighead, *The Mother's Songs: Images of God the Mother* (New York: Paulist Press, 1986), 67.
3. For a discussion of the nature of sacred place, see Belden C. Lane, *Landscapes of the Sacred: Geography and Narrative in American Spirituality* (Baltimore: Johns Hopkins University Press, 2001). See also Keith H. Basso, *Wisdom Sits in Places: Landscape and Language among the Western Apache* (Albuquerque: University of New Mexico Press, 1996).
4. For a history of the region see Lesley Poling-Kempes, *Valley of Shining Stone: The Story of Abiquiu* (Tucson: University of Arizona Press, 1997).
5. Frances Leon Quintana, "Abiquiu in New Mexico History," *Ghost Ranch Journal* 4:3 (Fall 1989): 12.
6. See Peter Nabokov, *Tijerina and the Courthouse Raid* (Albuquerque: University of New Mexico Press, 1969).
7. See Gladys A. Reichard, *Navaho Religion* (Princeton: Princeton University Press, 1970), 21, 452–53. Identifying the geographical location of mythic mountains is a difficult task in the analysis of Navajo sacred places.
8. Gary Snyder, *The Practice of the Wild* (San Francisco: North Point Press, 1990), 23.
9. See Belden C. Lane, *The Solace of Fierce Landscapes: Exploring Desert and Mountain Spirituality* (New York: Oxford University Press, 1998), 115–23.
10. Adapted from *The Sayings of the Desert Fathers*, trans., Benedicta Ward (Kalamazoo, MI: Cistercian Publications, 1975), 132.
11. See Rudolfo A. Anaya and Francisco A. Lomelí, eds., *Aztlán: Essays on the Chicano Homeland* (Albuquerque: University of New Mexico Press, 1989).
12. In Native American mythology Raven is a bringer of knowledge, symbol of transformation, and trickster. His keen sight allows him to issue warnings to the living and to lead the dead on their final journey. See Catherine Feher-Elston, *Ravensong: A Natural and Fabulous History of Ravens and Crows* (New York: Tarcher/Penguin, 2005).
13. The phrase is from Wendell Berry's *Recollected Essays, 1965–1980* (San Francisco: North Point Press, 1981), 241.
14. See Richard Rohr, *Quest for the Grail* (New York: Crossroad, 2004).
15. Richard Rohr, *Adam's Return: The Five Promises of Male Initiation* (New York: Crossroad, 2004), 46.
16. "Sin is necessary," said Julian, a tragedy that becomes joyous, evoking God's matchless forgiveness. See *Julian of Norwich: Showings*, trans., Edmund Colledge and James Walsh (New York: Paulist Press, 1978), 148f.
17. See Arthur Newton Pack, *We Called it Ghost Ranch* (Abiquiu, NM: Ghost Ranch Conference Center, 1965).
18. Frederick Buechner speaks of his father's suicide in the *Sacred Journey: A Memoir of Early Days* (San Francisco: Harper, 1991) and *Telling Secrets* (San Francisco: Harper, 1992).
19. Andrew Harvey, *A Journey in Ladakh* (Boston: Houghton Mifflin, 1983), 93.

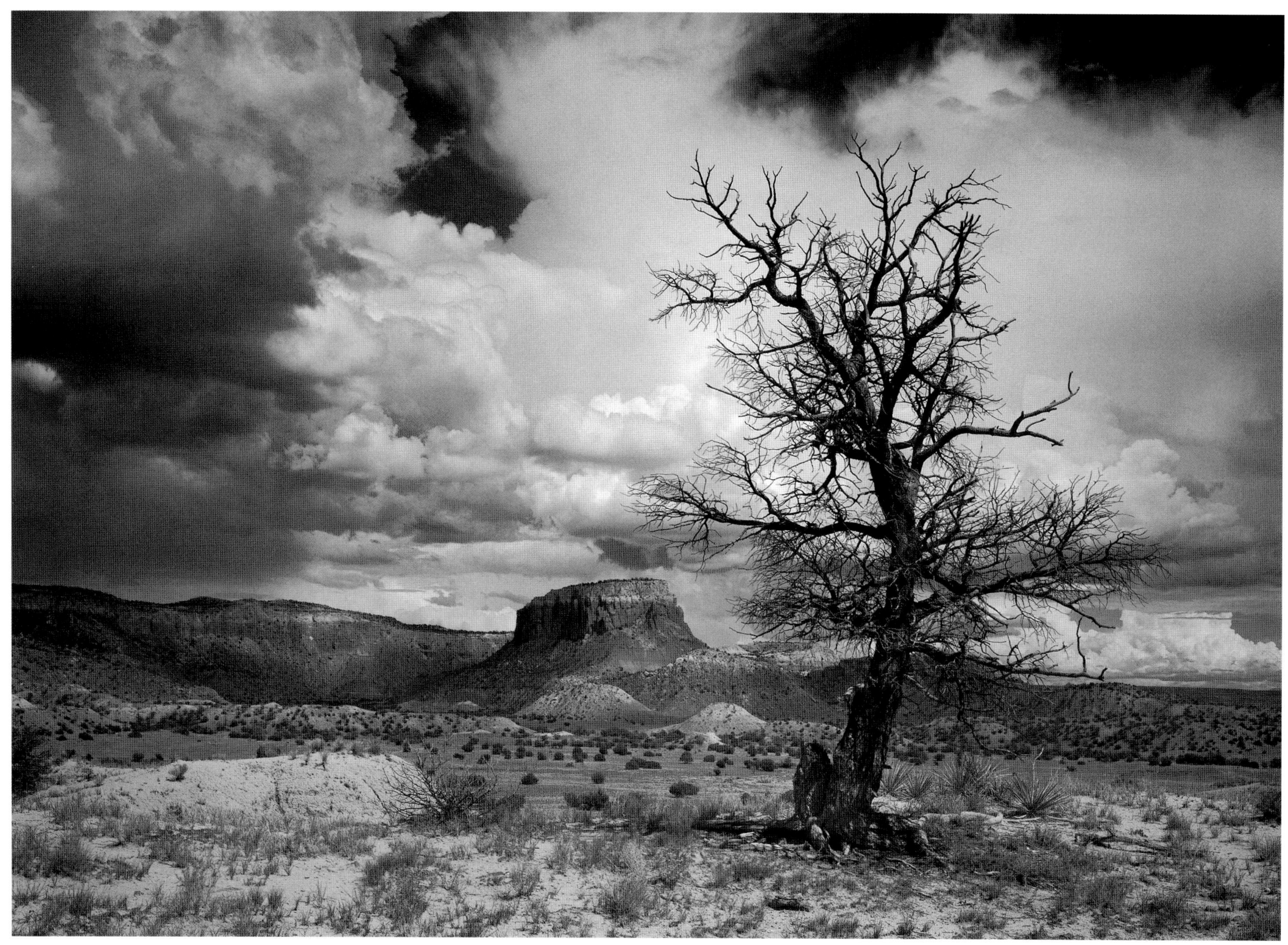

Plate 89: Black Tree and Orphan Mesa (Island Mesa), Ghost Ranch, New Mexico, 2005

According to Henry McKinley, who grew up at Ghost Ranch during the 1930s and 40s, Orphan Mesa was also known as Island Mesa.

SEEKING GRACE

The Aesthetic of Craig Varjabedian

DOUGLAS A. FAIRFIELD

> *I always honor and obey the shock of a moment of revelation; the creative part of which is summed up in a quick 'Yes' to a subject.*
>
> MINOR WHITE, PHOTOGRAPHER[1]

When Minor White wrote those words in 1964 he was arguably the most captivating photographer in the United States. He was, in all seriousness, photography's contemporary guru. Ansel Adams, photographer and colleague of White's, acknowledged in his autobiography that "Minor, through his teaching, exhibitions, lecturing, and consulting, achieved remarkable and fully justified fame. His portfolios and books place him among the most important figures in twentieth-century photography."[2]

White's progressive explorations into the mysticism of creativity forged new ground for the art of photography, both through imagery and in discussion. In so doing, he served as spokesperson for a distinctive group of fine art photographers whose work transcended the mere image to various levels of contemplation. At the same time, White left photographers too literal in their thinking (and seeing) puzzled by his verbiage and written transcriptions of his metaphysical mindset. Indeed, Adams referred to his teaching method as "intense 'verbalization'—the talking out of creative intentions, concepts, and directions."[3] But as photographer and professor Jonathan Green points out: "Words do not produce photographs."[4] To everyone's satisfaction, then and now, White's images speak, in the quietest of ways, louder than words.

White's heightened consciousness of the natural world manifested itself through the medium of photography and led him to experience moments of revelation. In split seconds of time, like that of shutter speeds, White posited: "During those rare moments something overtakes the man and he becomes the tool of a greater Force; the servant of, willing or unwilling depending on his degree of awakeness [*sic*]. The photograph, then, is a message more than a mirror, and the man a messenger who happens to be a photographer."[5]

Catch a wave and you'll be sittin' on top of the world.

BRIAN WILSON, MUSICIAN/SONGWRITER[6]

Fleeting moments of intrinsic clarity are experienced in many ways, and not just in the visual arts. Musicians, writers, performers in various guises, athletes, and even kids on a roller coaster have all, at one time or another, seized upon moments of increased sensation. Some call it a "rush," others see it as a moment of perfection; surfers get "stoked." When big-wave riders slice down the face of thirty-foot swells and suddenly find themselves enveloped within a cylinder of rushing, circulating water—the tube, the pipeline, or the "green room"—they are in a moment of extreme revelation. For that brief interval of time they are one with Nature; the forces of which are in complete control. Seconds later the surfer is spat out from the collapsing liquid vortex and transcends back into the everyday world only to discover that the wave has collapsed unto itself and the revelatory moment is gone in the wink of an eye. By all accounts, times like these occur when constituent elements come together to create something beyond an individual's capacity to fully control the moment, but the individual is by his or her own choosing an integral part of it. In fact, it is exactly that moment of transcendence where seekers of heightened reality hope to be taken.

Such experiences in a photographer's life—and, for that matter, a surfer's life—are understood as gifts, gifts that come from unexpected circumstances that culminate into a moment in which a greater reality occurs. That greater reality may be understood as beauty, symmetry, transcendence, oneness with all things great and small, or any number of unanticipated transfigurations of Nature that are difficult to describe but unmistakably felt. Craig Varjabedian understands these experiences as moments of grace. And within these moments of grace Varjabedian finds beauty. One look at his photographs tells you he's been stoked.

Photography is the means by which Varjabedian seeks and, in turn, shares such transitory moments of grace. Found in a multitude of subjects in places far and near, Varjabedian transcribes in photographic imagery those gifts of visual beauty that have graciously revealed themselves; but not without the critical sight that a photographer must possess. In writing about photographic beauty, Edward Weston declared:

> Photographic beauty as a term is only applicable to a finished print. But the photographer who would achieve it must remember that it is his seeing that creates the picture; exposure records it, developing and printing execute it—but its origin, in his way of seeing, determines its final value. His seeing must discover before his technique can record.[7]

Varjabedian's pictures exhibit more than an idle glance or a passing thought. His images are the result of time long spent in the field gathering data taken in by the five senses, as well as a few notes now and again. He looks for formal beauty in solitary objects and in existing landscapes that display unique personae fashioned by light, shadow, color, and the effects of weather. Rather than impose an artificial expression upon his subject matter, Varjabedian allows for circumfluent components to converge in bringing forth that 'Yes' moment of knowing. In short, it's that moment when one is obliged to click the shutter and be forever grateful. But indeed, that is easier said than done.

In reflecting upon his own experiences, Ansel Adams stated: "My private glimpses of some ideal reality create a lasting mood that has often been recalled in some of my photographs . . . Deep resonances of spirit exist, giving us glimpses of a reality far beyond our general appreciation and knowledge."[8]

Varjabedian's aesthetic spirit, like that of Adams, is built upon patience, persistence, and fortitude, coupled with a sensibility for beauty. As a result, his photographs take us to realms both literal and conceptual to which we normally would not venture. We find ourselves contemplating those places and things that the photographer has singled out by way of happenstance or deliberation. Varjabedian's photographs are not only beautiful documents in and of themselves but, in addition, they serve as conduits that lead us to another plane of thought. They are visual touchstones whereupon we imagine ourselves in the photographer's shoes at the right place at the right time. Lucky for us Varjabedian does the footwork and the looking. From his extensive travels—by plane, truck, and hiking boot—we are the recipients of his discerning eye.

It is noteworthy that Varjabedian was in his mid-teens when he met Ansel Adams. The master photographer was attending a reception for an exhibition of his photographs in Michigan at the time. And thanks to Adams, Craig, being of Armenian ancestry, had unwittingly contracted *loosankarchakan tend* or, to put it in plain English, "photographic fever."[9] But what was truly transmitted that day was most accurately described in 1887 by writer Alexander Black as "the curious contagion of the camera."[10] This unanticipated experience of wonderment about the power of photography, not to mention the beauty conveyed in Adams's prints, was life changing for Varjabedian. By the close of the reception he knew he would become a photographer. Craig recalls: "My life's purpose truly began with this moment of realization."[11] A few years later he completed a photographic workshop with Adams. Since then, Varjabedian has not wavered in his quest to express himself through the art of photography, holding to a high standard set by his mentor.

The photography of Craig Varjabedian has been informed not only by Adams, but by a select group of photographers, living and deceased, who sought greater significances beyond the descriptive powers of the camera. Alongside the imagery of Adams, White, and Edward Weston, Varjabedian acknowledges the work of Brett Weston, Eliot Porter, William Clift, Wynn Bullock, and Paul Caponigro as influential.[12] Indeed, the majority of these photographers are known for their panoramic landscapes as well as segmented views of the land. Each has been closely associated with landscape photography, particularly conveying Nature in black and white and, to a lesser extent, in color. Varjabedian is no exception. Although he is best known for black-and-white imagery, his work in color is simply part of his photographic journey in seeking grace.

Considering the physical world from a modernist point of view, Varjabedian, in part, aspires to what Caponigro has called "the landscape behind the landscape."[13] Photo historian Naomi Rosenblum elaborates that Caponigro's examination of the physical world, big and small, in fragments and whole, proceeds to go "beyond perception to evoke the mystic divinity in all of Nature."[14] Varjabedian's examination of the divine is translated, again, as beauty; that is, moments of grace in which life forces coalesce to produce a preternatural reality. Put in another way, it is the unexpected jog of Nature or the subtle cadence in things that Varjabedian strives to capture in a photograph.

An aesthetic of ideal reality was alluded to in the work of nineteenth-century West Coast photographers Carleton E. Watkins (1829–1916) and Eadweard Muybridge (1830–1904). Both were earnest in their endeavors to photograph Yosemite Valley in all its unsullied glory, but did so primarily for profit rather than self-discovery. Undoubtedly, both were emotionally moved by what they photographed, but it is highly unlikely either photographer considered the landscape behind the landscape. The majesty of their pictures is found in their descriptive qualities of the best general views of a land yet to be inundated by weekend campers. Divinity in their pictures was there by popular culture: the prevailing Emersonian aesthetic that God is Nature and Nature is God. Adams knew this quite well and took the mantle for Yosemite—and of Emerson—to new heights. His photographs of Yosemite display a beauty that can only be described as surreal. Given the abstract qualities of black-and-white photography, Adams's photos of natural phenomena transcend the mere descriptive to levels of visual poetry.

Such poeticism distinguishes Varjabedian's photography. In both his landscapes and his close-up work one can detect the poetics in the smallest of details, not unlike the detailing one sees in the best of Paul Strand's work (and Adams's and Weston's and White's) where a singular object is symbolic for all that is vital in the universe. James Enyeart, photographer, scholar, and former director of the Friends of Photography as well as the George Eastman House, is instructive:

> By abstracting fragments of reality and presenting them as symbols for what was desired from the past and for what could be seen as inspirational in the present, a new breed of photographer contributed to the continuum of images drawn from the spirit of the landscape.[15]

Indeed, beauty comes in packages large and small. In addition, beauty can be understood as a spiritual value capable of sustaining the human spirit. In so many ways, Varjabedian's discerning eye freeze-frames that spirit via the convergence of light, shadow, and texture that culminates into pictures that invite contemplation. In other words, moments of spirituality are quiet affairs, be they with the dissolution of a cloud formation, the graceful bowing of a horse, or at the peak of a passing thunderstorm.

In describing Alfred Stieglitz's concept of the equivalent, photographer and professor Gary Metz points out that, "In the equivalent, subject matter and photographic form combine to produce pictorial configurations which conceptually correspond with felt states . . . Work on these extended terms has been realized in the West by Minor White, Paul Caponigro and William Clift."[16] One must include Adams and Weston in this select group. Needless to say, Varjabedian has been well informed by the work of these photographers.

Spending time with Varjabedian's photographs informs the visual acuity of the viewer. And that is what makes his work so appealing. Conceptually, his imagery may be considered on many levels. If we regard landscape photography, as put forth by professors Estelle Jussim and Elizabeth Lindquist-Cock, as constructs of the real world and as artifacts communicating ideologies about it, one may consider Varjabedian's images from a variety of subsets within the genre. Citing the chapters in Jussim's and Lindquist-Cock's book *Landscape as Photograph* is appropriate to assigning multiple meanings to Varjabedian's photographs.

Landscape as Artistic Genre	Landscape as God
Landscape as Fact	Landscape as Symbol
Landscape as Pure Form	Landscape as Popular Culture
Landscape as Concept	Landscape as Politics and Propaganda[17]

Not all of the above apply, of course, but one could make a case that Varjabedian's work segues from one subset to another as best befits how a viewer experiences his work. A full analysis of each subset is not called for here, but it is clear that Varjabedian's landscape imagery allows for a variety of contexts.

However one considers Varjabedian's photographs, he remains true to the dictates of straight photography, unfettered by manipulation. It is simply not in his makeup to alter his images. To do so would negate the alterations already produced by eons of natural manipulation. He believes that as Nature unfolds before us, it is the challenge of the photographer to choreograph vision and camera in capturing a moment signified as relevant. It is that instance of becoming one with his subject that manifests Varjabedian's aesthetic into a singular image or a body of work that conveys his raison d'être. According to the photographer, "[When making a photograph,] the one thing that never changes is that moment of recognition when I feel the play of light, shadow, and texture resolve itself into something wonderful."[18] In short, Varjabedian has set his course as a photographer. He seeks meaningful moments of beauty in the physical world. This is clearly the case for *Ghost Ranch and the Faraway Nearby.*

The body of work that comprises *Ghost Ranch and the Faraway Nearby* is a testament to the photographer's spirit of sharing. Such a dedicated exploration of a particular place seems, at first, not open to public scrutiny. Indeed, one is reminded of Adams's reference to the privacy of glimpses to an ideal reality. But Varjabedian is willing to expose his intimate and ongoing relationship with Ghost Ranch to a broad audience. For those not having experienced Ghost Ranch, or the environs of northern New Mexico, one appreciates Varjabedian's time and devotion to this specific region of the United States. To some, Ghost Ranch, let alone New Mexico, may seem very faraway, even remote; but that does not preclude the beauty nor the allure of place that Varjabedian depicts.

The enthusiasm to look at photographs depicting distant locales dates back to the infancy of the medium. For instance, British photographer Francis Frith (1822–1898) trekked to foreign destinations in the 1850s seeking places that would captivate viewers back home, not to mention providing for a lucrative source of income. Frith's so-called "topographical" images of Egypt, for example, were an immediate sensation and viewed with delight and fascination throughout Europe. As photo historian Ian Jeffrey points out, "Above all, [Frith] set out to show his audience what it felt like to be in these remote and exotic regions."[19]

Varjabedian's photographs of Ghost Ranch may not be as exotic as the Great Pyramids of Giza, nor would we want them to be; that's not what they're about. Yet they portray a unique place equally enduring. His individual pilgrimage to Ghost Ranch began more than twenty years ago and may never have closure. This speaks directly to the power of place. As conveyed by Varjabedian, Ansel Adams once wrote: "It is all very beautiful and magical [at Ghost Ranch] . . . You have to live it and breathe it . . . you [become] isolated in a glowing world between the macro- and the micro-, where every [single] thing is sidewise under you and over you, and the clocks stopped long ago."[20]

It is well known that the landscape of northern New Mexico has drawn artists to it for more than a hundred years. The light, the changing colors, distant spaces, and the cultural diversity make for an alluring combination. In 1937 Georgia O'Keeffe, arguably the most famous artist to ever reside at Ghost Ranch, entitled one of her paintings *From the Faraway Nearby*. Consequently, this connotation has become emblematic of Ghost Ranch and the surrounding area.[21] In fact, the migration of artists, photographers, and writers to northern New Mexico continues to this day.

The apotheosis of Ghost Ranch to near-sacred significance has long been implemented, most decisively through the paintings of O'Keeffe and the photographs of Adams. And continuing over the years, countless painters and photographers have graced the land that comprises Ghost Ranch, from snap-shooters to the ranks of the professional, from novices to know-it-alls. Consequently, one can imagine all kinds of pictures of Ghost Ranch, from the most amateurish to the most accomplished, that have been taken, processed, and printed as mementos of that special place. But special it remains despite a myriad of image makers from year to year.

Undeniably, Varjabedian is one among legions of picture takers that have set their apertures at Ghost Ranch. But his extended relationship with the place has instilled within him a reverent approach to the landscape that few others can begin to realize. Seemingly, Varjabedian took to heart that part of the "vision" statement for Ghost Ranch that promotes it as "a place to wonder, to challenge, to create, to explore; [and as] a touchstone for light and leaven in an uncertain world."[22] Varjabedian confesses that, "When I was first photographing [Ghost Ranch], I was overwhelmed by its vastness . . . I got a sense of it by watching clouds move across the sky and the light change throughout the day . . . [and] after nearly twenty years, I finally felt I knew Ghost Ranch well enough to photograph it successfully."[23] In short, he made it his own. Again, James Enyeart:

> It can be demonstrated that artists who have sensed the power of the places in which they work also allow and cultivate the spiritual character of such places in their work.[24]

Without question, Varjabedian's photographs of Ghost Ranch are much more than visual transcriptions. This dedicated portfolio of work goes far beyond the point-and-shoot mentality. His personal sensibility toward Ghost Ranch has been realized only after decades of self-discovery within the parameters of an aesthetic composed of highly critical demands. To his credit, very few photographers possess such perseverance in achieving goals and the absolute dedication to craft that Varjabedian accepts as matter of course. His images display spiritual characteristics revealed to him only after considerable study on site. Indeed, one cannot help but see in Varjabedian's imagery his own keen sense of place.

Today, swaths of pristine land are few and far between. They are, indeed, faraway places rather than nearby settings. Understandably so, John Szarkowski, former curator of photography for the Museum of Modern Art in New York, put forth that for photographers the true American frontier lasted only a generation, from the Civil War to the turn of the century.[25] From that point on photographers had to broaden their search for isolated pockets of landscape seemingly untouched by civilization. Footpaths became roadways, horizon lines became rooflines, and the magnificent quietude of Nature was—and is still—put upon by our fellow neighbors relating to the Great Outdoors in the most engaging ways. Thus, contemporary photographers are hard-pressed in seeking out just the right vantage points to convey ideal realities within the scope of the Southwestern landscape.

Ghost Ranch is far from pristine in the classic sense. Not surprisingly, it has been put upon by human contrivances: Adirondack chairs encircling like covered wagons, signage that directs you here and there, and the occasional power cable that crisscrosses what was once an unobstructed mountain view. Despite such interventions, Ghost Ranch retains a mystique that draws people to it for a variety of reasons, including Varjabedian. He fully understands that Ghost Ranch endures as a place of respite removed from the demands of everyday society and the landscape is cherished for its beauty and serenity.

If one is willing to venture to the outer limits of Ghost Ranch, moments of grace await you. Varjabedian takes us there and then some. His photographic portrait of Ghost Ranch defines it in the best possible way. As well, his photographs reaffirm our understanding of his commitment to seeking beauty in the physical world.

Photographer and writer Peter Turner once stated: "A photograph is (simply) an equation of light, time, and space."[26] Basically speaking that's true; but, of course, there's more to it than that. A much more complex set of variables has to be in place to produce a successful and meaningful photograph. To quote photographer Nicholas Nixon:

> Each successful photograph balances content with form and truth with aspect, using a solution unique to itself. While describing something that matters with clarity, economy, and force seems to be photography's perennial esthetic, how this comes about remains for most a private and, for the most part, intuitive matter. The best photographs are transparent, sensual, intelligent, fulfilled, freshly arrived, enduring and, in the deepest sense, are of the world.[27]

Such distinctions are clearly seen in the photographs of Craig Varjabedian. Moreover, the interconnectedness of his body of work conveys an overriding aesthetic of beauty found in a particular place. But as he continues to seek moments of grace, whether in a return to Ghost Ranch or stepping into his own backyard, he is truly seeking beauty in terms of a deeper sense of self discovery. Minor White concluded that, "Conscious camerawork is . . . when either by Grace or plan [the] camera unites me with the Creative Principle [and] the desirable working state: heightened awareness of my Self."[28]

Douglas A. Fairfield is an arts writer for Pasatiempo, *the arts, entertainment, and culture magazine of the* Santa Fe New Mexican.

Notes

1. Minor White, *Mirrors, Messages, Manifestations*, 2nd ed. (New York: Aperture, 1982), 194. Minor White (1908–1976) was a photographer, educator, writer, poet, and mystic. In 1952 he cofounded *Aperture*, a quarterly on photography, with Ansel Adams (1902–1984), Melton Ferris, Dorothea Lange (1895–1965), Ernest Louie, Barbara Morgan (1900–1992), Beaumont (1908–1993) and Nancy (1908–1974) Newhall, and Dody Warren Thompson. In 1962, White was a founding member of the Society for Photographic Education (SPE).
2. Ansel Adams, *Ansel Adams: An Autobiography* (Boston: New York Graphic Society, 1985), 321.
3. Adams, *Ansel Adams: An Autobiography*, 318. Adams did not agree with Minor's compulsion to continually analyze the inner message of a photograph.
4. Jonathan Green, *American Photography: A Critical History 1945 to the Present* (New York: Abrams, 1984), 55.
5. Minor White, "Consciousness in Photography: The Creative Audience" (unpublished manuscript), Volume I, Preface, 9. Cited by Michael Hoffman in "Preface to the Second Edition" for White, *Mirrors, Messages, Manifestations*, unpaginated.
6. "Catch a Wave" by Brian Wilson and Mike Love. © 1963 Irving Music, Inc. (BMI). Copyright Renewed. Used by Permission. All Rights Reserved.
7. Edward Weston, "What is Photographic Beauty?" in *American Photography*, 45:12 (December 1951): 743.
8. Adams, *Ansel Adams: An Autobiography*, 385.
9. My thanks to Craig Varjabedian for the translation.
10. Sarah Greenough, Joel Snyder, David Travis, and Colin Westerbeck, *On the Art of Fixing a Shadow: One Hundred and Fifty Years of Photography* (Washington, D.C.: National Gallery of Art, 1989), 130. Original reference is from "The Amateur Photographer," *The Century* 34 (September 1887): 722.
11. Craig Varjabedian and Robin Jones, *Four and Twenty Photographs: Stories from Behind the Lens* (Albuquerque: University of New Mexico Press, 2007), xv.
12. Varjabedian met Caponigro (b. 1932) in 1984 and served as his darkroom assistant in 1991.
13. Robert Hirsch, *Seizing the Light: A History of Photography* (New York: McGraw-Hill, 2000), 366.
14. Naomi Rosenblum, *A World History of Photography* (New York: Abbeville Press, 1984), 516.
15. James Enyeart, *Land, Sky, and All that is Within: Visionary Photographers in the Southwest* (Santa Fe: Museum of New Mexico Press, 1998), 80–81.
16. From "The Sense of Place" by Gary Metz in Sandy Hume, Ellen Manchester, and Gary Metz, editors, *The Great West: Real/Ideal* (Boulder: University of Colorado, 1977), 41–42.
17. Estelle Jussim and Elizabeth Lindquist-Cock, *Landscape as Photograph* (New Haven: Yale University Press, 1985), v.
18. Varjabedian and Jones, *Four and Twenty Photographs*, 4.
19. Ian Jeffrey, *Photography: A Concise History* (London: Thames and Hudson, 1981), 34. Between 1856 and 1859, Frith traveled to Egypt and the Far East no less than five times to make photographs that were published in various formats and multiple volumes.
20. Varjabedian and Jones, *Four and Twenty Photographs*, 97. Adams wrote this in a letter to photographer and New York gallery owner Alfred Stieglitz (1864–1946) while visiting Georgia O'Keeffe (1887–1986) at Ghost Ranch.
21. O'Keeffe used the term "the far away" in conversation and letters to differentiate New Mexico from New York and later qualified her use of the term to designate her locale in Abiquiu. See Jack Cowart and Juan Hamilton, *Georgia O'Keeffe: Art and Letters* (Washington D.C.: National Gallery of Art, 1987), 230, 286n80. She lived at Ghost Ranch from 1934 to 1945 before moving permanently to Abiquiu.
22. "Mission and Vision Statement" for Ghost Ranch Education and Retreat Center at http://www.ghostranch.org (accessed March 20, 2008).
23. Varjabedian and Jones, *Four and Twenty Photographs*, 96.
24. Enyeart, *Land, Sky, and All that is Within*, 83.
25. John Szarkowski, *American Landscapes* (New York: Museum of Modern Art, 1981), 10.
26. Peter Turner, essay in *Reading Photographs: Understanding the Aesthetics of Photography* (New York: Pantheon Press, 1977), 83–86. Turner was editor of the influential British magazine *Creative Camera* from 1970 to 1978 and again from 1986 to 1991.
27. Cited in William Jenkins, "Introduction to The New Topographics" in *Reading into Photography: Selected Essays, 1959–1980*, Thomas Barrow, Shelley Armitage, and William Tydeman, editors (Albuquerque: University of New Mexico, 1982), 53.
28. White, *Mirrors, Messages, Manifestations*, 182.

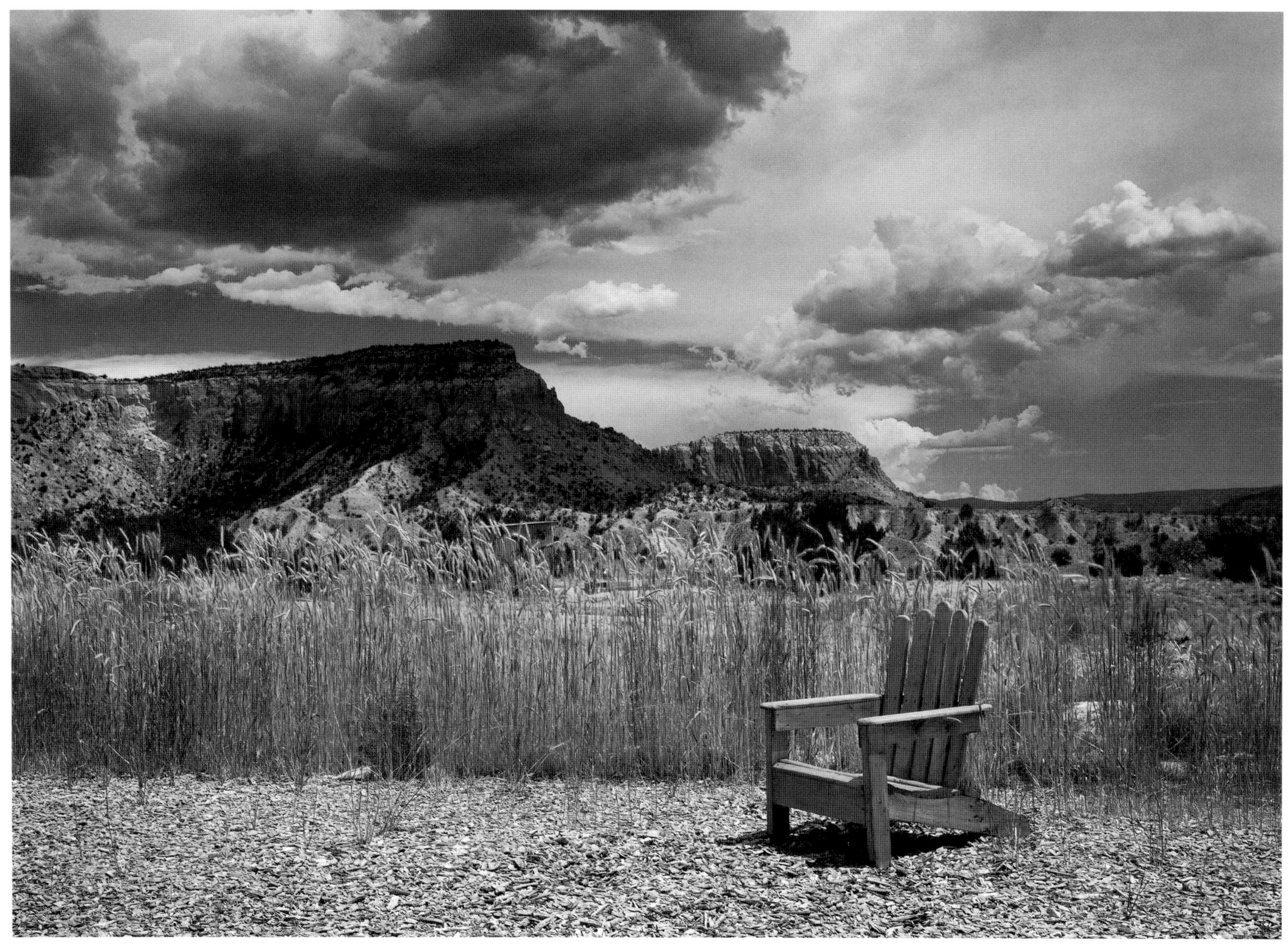

Plate 90: Pack's Point and Orphan Mesa (Island Mesa), Ghost Ranch, New Mexico, 2007

NEARBY

Let Our World Change Your World

ROB CRAIG

Each day I have spent at Ghost Ranch has been a day of beauty and gratitude. Being able to read and see that same response in *Ghost Ranch and the Faraway Nearby* has been inspiring. The essays have broadened my appreciation of this awesome place. The grace and wonder of Ghost Ranch is now at my fingertips, thanks to Craig's luminous photographs. Lingering over the images, I can smell the juniper, feel the wind, and see the light.

While operated by the Presbyterian Church, U.S.A., Ghost Ranch demonstrates that our foundational faith value is hospitality for all people. Not everyone comes here seeking answers to questions about faith. Nor do we expect the content of everything offered to be faith-based. While much of the experience here is spiritual, we are not demanding that everyone be the same or think the same. Instead we believe that all those who experience this awesome and transforming landscape deserve a demonstration of God's hospitality.

Many people come here and wish to "adopt" Ghost Ranch or claim it, in a very positive way. I like to think that by coming here, by giving up the noise and confusion of the everyday world for a while, people are making themselves available to be claimed or adopted by God. My Christian understanding of God is that God claims us. We are not merely seekers finding God through our own efforts. Instead, if we make ourselves available, we discover God working in our lives. When people experience the vast and revealing awesomeness of Ghost Ranch, many are opened to all sorts of spiritual revelations and transformations.

I experienced this type of revelation and transformation at Ghost Ranch in my own life. I had been at the ranch much earlier, as a younger man with my family. I had been diagnosed with cancer and was in the middle of treatment. It was a rough time in which I was physically tired, mentally sore, and fearful. But here at Ghost Ranch, I received hope because I was nurtured to be a normal person again and have something normal people often forget about—fun. It was a life-giving experience for me. Ghost Ranch served as a bulwark for forward movement and helped to transition me beyond cancer. I am grateful for my experience during that time of turmoil and for all the years since with their rewards of beauty, new friends, and lessons learned. There is a special tie here for me, as there is for thousands of people who have come here and who have returned.

I returned to Ghost Ranch to begin my tenure as the executive director in 2000. Coming back here was not an immediate or easy decision, however. When I was asked to consider the position, I was unsure if I should leave the pastoral work in which I was engaged in Washington, D.C. I had put so much care and effort into my ministry with the terrific people of the New York Avenue Presbyterian Church. But I was given a series of signs that revealed to me that I was being called from the Church to go to this new land and this new challenge.

The first sign came during a 1999 summer visit as a guest. During the week, the committee seeking a new executive director spoke with me. I was interested, but was not taking the conversation very seriously until Sunday morning. As I sat in outdoor worship and experienced God's presence, the joy of the leaders, and the spectacular landscape, I began to weep. For me it was an unusual and vulnerable moment. The weeping continued throughout worship. I realize now that God was working within me. God was claiming my attention and taking charge, reminding me to be available to God and to the moment.

A few days later, after receiving some encouragement from the search committee, I was driving home in downtown Washington when I came upon a red traffic signal. On the spur of the moment I hung my head and said, "God, if you've got a message for me about all of this, let me have it!" I laughed at my request, raised my eyes, and randomly focused on the license plate on the car in front of me. It was from New Mexico. How many New Mexico cars do you think there are in downtown D.C.?

Days later, after more support from the search committee, I was still considering my vocational direction. What was God calling on me to do? Was I done with my work here in D.C.? Could I take on a new and different ministry? My wife, Sharon, and I met for lunch on a park bench. I carefully outlined all the reasons—pro and con—I should stay. I finished ticking them off my fingers and said firmly, "So I think the best decision is to stay here." As the word "here" left my mouth, a bird flew overhead and left a large deposit on my head. When Sharon had finished laughing, she said, wiping her eyes, "Rob, now you know what God thinks of *that* idea."

Then, as I was getting close to answering the call, I did some planning. I generally preach from the Bible lectionary, a three-year cycle of scriptures that many Christians follow. Once in a while I vary from that list as a sermon situation demands. It occurred to me that if I were to announce my departure from the congregation, I would likely select some text other than the usual flow. I looked at my calendar, determined the Sunday I might resign, and looked at the assigned text. The story was Paul's farewell to the Church at Philippi.

I was catching on to what God already knew: I was heading to Ghost Ranch. I may be a little dull. It took some diligence on God's part with tears, license plates, birds, and logic. Thank God I stayed open and available to the message. I was free enough not to listen at all or miss this message entirely, you know.

So I arrived at Ghost Ranch to take on this joyful task. From my seminary education and the wonderful ministry situations to which I had been previously called, I pretty well understood the dynamic relationship between Church institutions and their environments. It is very important to understand how the community environment influences a place and how a healthy institution can help to shape that community environment for the better.

A new chapter of that understanding unfolded as I learned more about the Spanish land grant history in New Mexico. In the law of the Indies, which guided the King of Spain in 1766, a land grant provided plots for families. In addition there might be a plaza for common buildings like a church, a school, or a meeting place. Then there was the *ejido*, the vast common land for grazing, hunting, wood and water gathering, and enjoyment. At Ghost Ranch, I feel we have inherited an ejido, vast acreage belonging to us all together and to no one in particular. It is an environment that positively shapes us and we must be good stewards influencing others. Our environment and our community go beyond the boundaries of Ghost Ranch because what happens outside the ranch affects our natural and social world.

In the past, Ghost Ranch funds were allocated to support a medical center and other community causes and the ranch traded land so that 111 titles were returned to New Mexico residents by the Forest Service. Ghost Ranch assists our ranching neighbors by offering winter grazing on our land, when cattle are moved from the summer pastures on private land or in the national forests. In addition, hundreds of acre feet of Ghost Ranch water in Abiquiu Lake are donated annually to our downstream acequia neighbors.

That sense of community, where we all work together, can be seen everywhere at Ghost Ranch. The playing fields are leveled here. It is fun and remarkable watching people who are very high powered, now in T-shirts and jeans, just talking to other folks who, if they knew to whom they were talking, would probably have a change of attitude (and vice versa). Identity is not geared toward possessions and positions, but toward healthy relationships.

Many different types of people come here for safe community. Some need sanctuary and rest. Some need adventure. Single people come and meet new friends. Families and friends have reunions. Single parents are thrilled to find a place where their needs and the needs of their children are being met. Interracial and interfaith families and people in partnerships have found a home at Ghost Ranch. With all its safety, our programming is intended to challenge people to learn and grow. We try to put provocative subjects among our offerings, choosing faculty who are skilled in dealing with diversity in the population so we don't become completely one-sided. People will find what they seek here, if they are open to the unexpected and open to change.

As has been true for many others over the years, my very first instinct was to try somehow to possess the uniqueness of Ghost Ranch. Instead, the environment called me to be to be spiritually available. I did not adopt Ghost Ranch, the ranch adopted me. It kicked me out of the driver's seat and taught me about the land, the peoples, and new phases of service. I am convinced that God is at work in special ways at Ghost Ranch, positively transforming individuals and groups. I hope these photographs and essays have done well at introducing you to this place of awesome delight. Please come to see us. Let our world change your world.

Epilogue

A good year has gone by since I was called away from Ghost Ranch to be pastor of First Presbyterian Church of Columbus, Indiana. I love being a pastor and First Church is a wonderful congregation in which to complete my ministry.

Early in 2007 it had become clear to me that I had successfully accomplished my initial Ghost Ranch goals, but changes in the Presbyterian Church were producing the need for operational shifts. The landscape that had adopted me as a young adult visitor, and a middle-aged worker, had further shaped me and was letting me be called away. I knew, deep down, that a different set of leadership skills would be advantageous for Ghost Ranch. And I was needed more in a new place. Making room for alternative Ghost Ranch direction was the way to love her best.

I received a number of kind messages as I departed. One of the most meaningful was from a colleague who sometimes pressed me about the depth of my passion for Ghost Ranch. As he watched me depart, he indicated that he then understood how very deeply I care.

Reverend Rob Craig is currently pastor of First Presbyterian Church in Columbus, Indiana. From 2000 to 2007 Rob served as executive director of Ghost Ranch and continues to serve on the National Ghost Ranch Foundation.

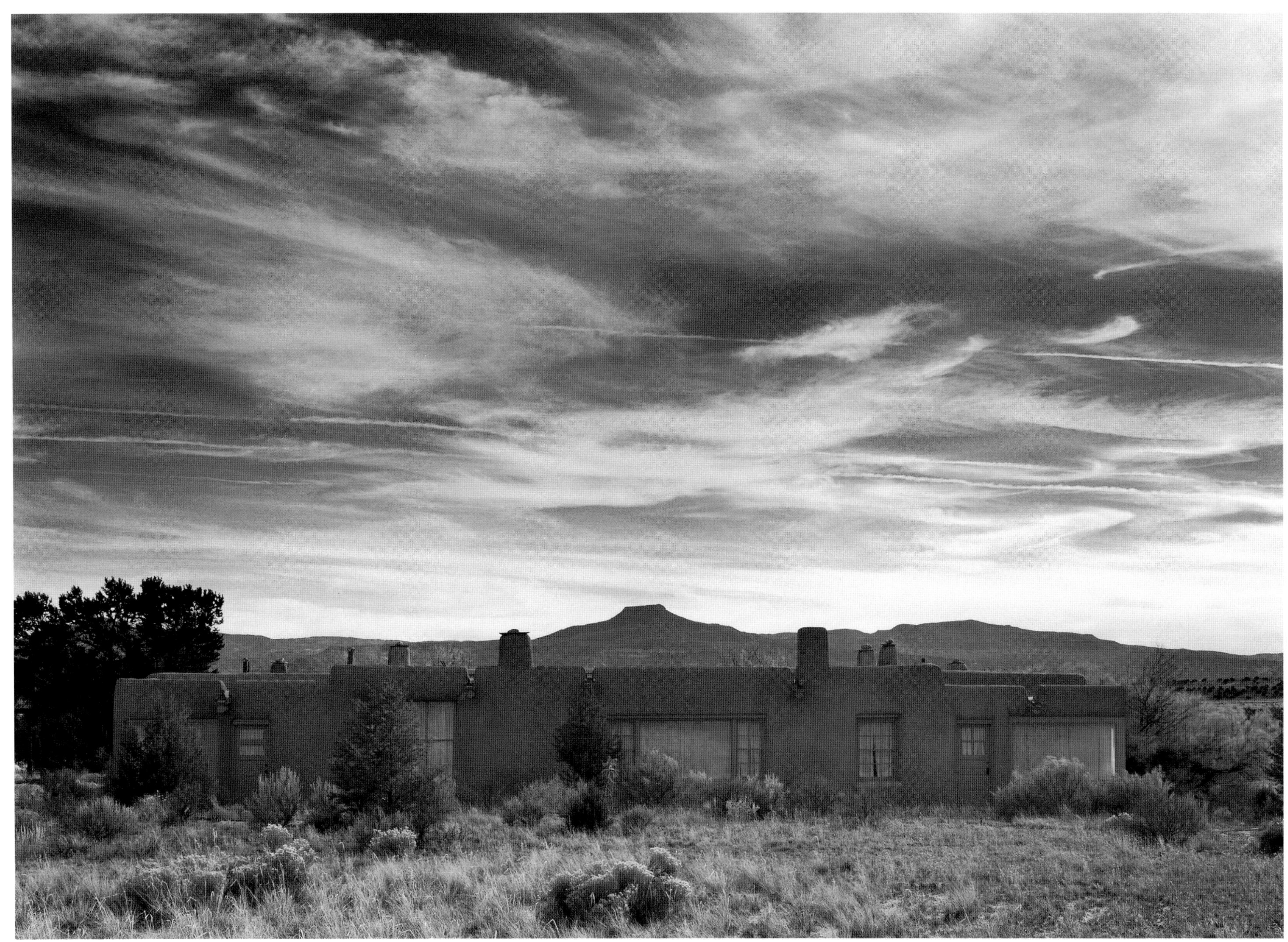

Plate 91: Georgia O'Keeffe's Home, Ghost Ranch, New Mexico, 2005

AFTERWORD

Ghost Ranch: An Appreciation

GEORGIA O'KEEFFE

In 1980 Jim Hall, then director of Ghost Ranch, wrote in a letter to Georgia O'Keeffe:

> It has been 25 years since the gift of the ranch to the church was made by Arthur and Phoebe Pack, and in thinking of this 25th anniversary it seems appropriate to us to plan for a small booklet which would gather together a few appraisals of the impact of the ranch over these 25 years. . . . Would you be willing to write 150–200 words or so for us? You are our nearest neighbor, and share many of our concerns for the well-being of other of our neighbors. I know it's much to ask, but on the other hand couldn't see doing this booklet without at least inviting you to share in it. A few reflections, or since the anniversary looks to the future as well as the past, any thoughts you have for the future would be most welcome.

The following was Miss O'Keeffe's response.

When I first saw the Ghost Ranch, the road went along the high hills above the spectacular part of it. A wide red valley with a long row of high red and yellow cliffs with red hills below them reaching far.—This was my world immediately—big and wide—with no one living in it.

In time, it became a dude ranch—and I came in the summers to paint. Later, it was bought by Arthur Pack, and I began living in the first house he had built. For me it was good because I like a quiet place by myself to work. When the Presbyterians moved in, the best thing they did for me was not to tell anyone where I lived.

I started painting the purple hills immediately—the country looked like something already painted with its dry colorful cliffs—hills—and sparse trees.

One day, I was looking for a place in the shade to paint the cliffs—I turned—and saw Mr. Hall on horseback right behind me. I suppose we spoke—I don't remember. In time we became acquainted and he did many things to make my living there easier.

The last 25 years have gone very fast and a good deal has been done with the far and wide world that I first saw from the hill tops.—The road has moved into the valley and many many people have come and gone. It is one of the most beautiful spots in the country. It's another world that you can ride over—walk—or climb.*

---

* *Ghost Ranch: The First 25 Years* (Ghost Ranch Conference Center, Abiquiu, NM: The National Ghost Ranch Foundation, 1980).

ACKNOWLEDGMENTS

In the early days of the theatre, actor/songwriter George M. Cohan would step through the curtain at the end of a performance, along with his family, to express his sincere appreciation to the audience. The members of his family would clasp hands and bow, and then George would take a step forward and say, "Ladies and gentlemen, my mother thanks you, my father thanks you, my sister thanks you, and, I assure you, I thank you!" Books and accompanying exhibitions are seldom the products of a single hand, and these works are no exception. I wish to express my sincere appreciation to the many individuals and organizations who made the work and its completion a little easier:

To a place called Ghost Ranch. I thank the ranch for the lessons it has taught me. Words fail me to describe the beauty of the evanescent moments that passed far too quickly to be remembered on film. While my time of attendance at the ranch is over and I am not there every day, photographing in the cool mornings among the red hills below Chimney Rock, I am forever changed by my experiences there.

To the late Reverend David Rogge (1940–1994), a gentle man of big feeling whose life of fifty-four years was far too short. I thank him for planting the seeds of the idea that became this volume. Thanks also to his wife Chris, who continues to work at Ghost Ranch and offered many helpful comments on the manuscript.

To the writers who provided essays for this book: Jay Packer, photographer, writer, and physician; Marin Sardy, writer and editor-in-chief of *Santa Fean* magazine; Belden Lane, retired professor of theological studies and American studies at Saint Louis University; and Rob Craig, former executive director of Ghost Ranch and current pastor of First Presbyterian Church in Columbus, Indiana. I thank each of them for sharing so eloquently in words the sense of awe they have experienced at Ghost Ranch. I also wish to thank Doug Fairfield, arts writer at the *Santa Fe New Mexican*, for his essay providing a thoughtful frame of reference for my photographic work.

To Debra Hepler, executive director of Ghost Ranch, for so wonderfully embracing this project, and for the words in her insightful foreword. I am grateful for the generosity of her spirit and the thoughtfulness of her counsel. I like that we don't communicate using paper napkins.

To the Albuquerque Museum of Art and History, particularly Cathy Wright, director, for curating and presenting the inaugural exhibition of these Ghost Ranch images and for the thoughtful words of her foreword. If the alchemy of curating an exhibition, as arts writer Jerry Saltz points out, is the placement of objects in such a way that a cascade of thoughts and reactions take place so you learn things you didn't know you needed to know and can't imagine ever not knowing again—she is indeed the master. I thank her sincerely for her guidance and enthusiasm for this project, and for her ever-present good humor. Tom Antresian, curator of exhibits; Elizabeth Becker, associate curator of education; Andrew Connors, curator of art; Robin McClannahan, graphic artist; T. Connor O'Laughlin, assistant director; Robert Prichard, curator of collections; and Leah Persons, gallery store manager, also deserve special mention.

To Jay Packer, a fine photographer in his own right, for his insightful commentary on the essays in this book. His valued friendship and constancy is appreciated more than he may know.

To Floyd Trujillo and the late Virginia Trujillo, for allowing me to enjoy the hospitality of their home during an intense five-year period of making photographs at the ranch. It has been a pleasure to be a part of their family for so many years. I am deeply saddened by Virginia's passing, as I will miss the sharpness of her wit and the gentleness of her humor. I am grateful to Floyd for allowing me to plumb the depths of his knowledge of Ghost Ranch, drawn from thirty-five years of working there.

To dear friends Henry and Peggy Pack McKinley, both of whom spent their early years on the ranch some seventy years ago—my connection to Arthur Pack and Ghost Ranch of the past. I thank them for sharing their stories and family photographs, and for their abiding friendship. When I grow up, I want to sit tall in the saddle like Henry.

To Reverend Mark David Hostetter, whose inspired words on the plaque at Ghost Ranch's new Agape Center gave voice to my own feelings about how to dedicate this book.

To Rob Craig, whose insightful observations on the centering value of clerical vestments increased the significance of my trusty bandana.

To everyone at the University of New Mexico Press, especially my publisher Luther Wilson, whose exceptional patience, and appreciation for and dedication to quality, did much to inspire this book. My appreciation also goes to Melissa Tandysh for her design of this book, which creates an elegant synergy between its words and photographs. Maya Allen-Gallegos, managing editor; Glenda Madden, marketing manager, and Amanda Sutton, publicist, also deserve mention here.

To the New Mexico Humanities Council and the National Ghost Ranch Foundation for their financial support of the exhibition. I want to thank Craig Newbill, executive director of the New Mexico Humanities Council, for his wise counsel and passion for the humanities of our enchanted land. I also wish to thank the members of the NGRF for their faith in my work and in this project.

To the Georgia O'Keeffe Museum, especially director George King, a true gentleman, who was unstinting in his helpfulness; to curator Barbara Buhler Lynes, for graciously sharing her expert knowledge of Georgia O'Keeffe and for reviewing the section of the book that relates to the artist; and to collections manager Judy Chiba Smith, who made the journey to Abiquiu from Santa Fe several times to provide access to the Georgia O'Keeffe house at Ghost Ranch, for photographic purposes. Jackie M., director of education and public programs also deserves special mention.

Other friends and colleagues who reviewed and provided valuable comments on the essays include Paul Cousins, retired Presbyterian minister and photographer; Rob Craig, former executive director of Ghost Ranch, and his wife, Sharon; Edgar Davy, retired Ghost Ranch librarian; Alex Downs, curator at the Ruth Hall Museum of Paleontology, Ghost Ranch; Kay Peters Johnson, current Ghost Ranch librarian; and Barbara Schmidtzinsky, Ghost Ranch archivist.

To my wife and daughter, Kathryn and Rebekkah, for allowing me the space to complete such a enormous and time-consuming body of work. I lack the words to explain how much I missed them both when the light called me away to make these pictures.

To my assistant and dear friend Cindy Lane, who kept all the details of this project in order and assisted with the enormous task of making all of the book and exhibition prints. If angels exist on earth, she is indeed one of them.

To my parents, Suren and Hazel Varjabedian, who encouraged

in me, from an early age, the independence of my actions and perseverance of my dreams. My folks are remarkable people.

To my wife's parents, Richard and Ruth Strickland. I thank them for their generosity, which has over the years allowed for my family and me to experience a life that is better and richer than it might have been otherwise.

To Howard and Ellen Lowery, dear friends who give so much to Ghost Ranch and make everyone better by knowing them.

To my editor Joy Waltemath, for helping me find clarity in my ideas and poetry in my words. She is the best.

To Brian Crockett, museum consultant, whose enthusiasm for our work is only exceeded by his good humor and generous spirit. I thank him for working with us to share the beauty and history of Ghost Ranch through a traveling exhibition.

To Charles Wright for graciously allowing us to quote from his poem "Appalachia." I too want to know the names things call themselves when no one's listening.

To Mark Meloy for allowing us to use an excerpt from his late wife Ellen's exquisitely written book, *The Anthropology of Turquoise.* I am saddened by her passing, yet touched that Ghost Ranch was the last place she spent on vacation with Mark.

To my dealers: the Gerald Peters Gallery in Santa Fe and the incomparable Catherine Whitney; the Afterimage Gallery in Dallas, especially Ben Breard; and the Joseph Bellows Gallery in La Jolla, especially Joseph Bellows and Carol Lee Brosseau. I am grateful for their support of my work.

Over the years, many people have contributed in a variety of ways to my photographic work and this project. The late Phil Davis set the bar for photographic excellence and provided me a shining example to which I have always aspired. I would also like to thank Brian Brigham, printer; John Berkenfield, director of planning, El Ranchos de las Golondrinas; Paul Caponigro, photographer; Bob Carney, Elevator Professional Lab, Toronto; Mark Cox, photographer and Richard David, entrepreneur; Harold Lee Jones, photographer and former assistant; Bob MacDougall, photographer; Dorothy Massey and Mary Massey Wolf of Collected Works Bookstore, Santa Fe; Donna Packer, artist; and Michael David Sherwood, musician/composer.

The continuing support of several individuals from the photographic world has been extremely valuable. I would like to thank Kriss Brunngraber and Donna Narkiewicz at Bogen Imaging; Amy Kawadler of Canon USA's Professional Products Group; Robert Farber of Photoworkshop.com; Lynne Eodice of Double Exposure e.magazine and the esteemed Mr. Hiromi Sakanashi, president of the Ebony Camera Company, Ltd.

My students at the Eloquent Light Photography Workshops and previously, the New Mexico Photography Field School, deserve more than a casual nod. Many of them are good photographers fighting lonely battles with a medium that is seemingly impossible to tame—not for fame or financial reward, but because they would rather be making pictures than anything else in the world. I admire them greatly.

And finally, no acknowledgment would be complete without some mention of my dog, Dektol, sometimes a muse, always a best friend. My life would be one of complete overwork without the daily whack of his large billy-club paw on my leg, beckoning me and reminding me to play.

SELECTED BIBLIOGRAPHY

Ghost Ranch and Northern New Mexico

Borne, Lawrence. *Dude Ranching: Complete History*. Albuquerque: University of New Mexico Press, 1983.

Colbert, Edwin H. *The Little Dinosaurs of Ghost Ranch*. New York: Columbia University Press, 1995.

Hanna, Jane, "Ghost Ranch's Ghost Town" in *Ghost Ranch Journal*, vol. 6, no. 2, spring 1991.

Pack, Arthur Newton. *We Called it Ghost Ranch*. Abiquiu, NM: Ghost Ranch Conference Center, 1966.

Poling-Kempes, Lesley. *Ghost Ranch*. Tucson: University of Arizona Press, 2005.

———. *Valley of Shining Stone: The Story of Abiquiu*. Tucson: University of Arizona Press, 1997.

Craig Varjabedian

Varjabedian, Craig. *As the Spirit Stands Still*. Photographs by Craig Varjabedian with essay by Gussie Fauntleroy. Limited edition. Santa Fe, NM: Cirrus Editions Limited, 1998.

———. *By the Grace of Light: Images of Faith from Catholic New Mexico*. Photographs by Craig Varjabedian with essays by the Most Reverend Michael J. Sheehan, Archbishop of Santa Fe; Mag Dimond; and Cathy Wright. Colorado Springs: Colorado Springs Fine Arts Center, 1998.

———. *En Divina Luz: The Penitente Moradas of New Mexico*. Photographs by Craig Varjabedian with essay by Michael Wallis. Albuquerque: University of New Mexico Press, 1994.

———. *Four and Twenty Photographs: Stories from Behind the Lens*. Photographs by Craig Varjabedian with text by Robin Jones; afterword by Jay Packer. Albuquerque: University of New Mexico Press, 2007.

———. *This Enchanted Land*. Exhibition catalog of photographs by Craig Varjabedian with essay by Marc Simmons. Seguin: Texas Lutheran University, 2001.

Georgia O'Keeffe

Cowart, Jack, Juan Hamilton, and Sarah Greenough. *Georgia O'Keeffe: Art and Letters*. Washington, D.C.: National Gallery of Art, 1987.

Lisle, Laurie. *Portrait of an Artist: A Biography of Georgia O'Keeffe*. New York: Seaview Press, 1980. Reprint, New York: Washington Square Press, 1986.

Lynes, Barbara Buhler, Lesley Poling-Kempes, and Frederick W. Turner. *Georgia O'Keeffe and New Mexico: A Sense of Place*. Princeton, NJ: Princeton University Press; Santa Fe, NM: Georgia O'Keeffe Museum, 2004.

Lynes, Barbara Buhler and Ann Paden, editors. *Maria Chabot—Georgia O'Keeffe, Correspondence, 1941–1949*, Albuquerque: University of New Mexico Press, 2003.

Merrill, Christopher and Ellen Bradbury. *From the Faraway Nearby: Georgia O'Keeffe as Icon*. Reading, MA: Addison-Wesley Pub. Co., 1992.

O'Keeffe, Georgia. *Georgia O'Keeffe*. New York: Viking Press, 1976.

Robinson, Roxana. *Georgia O'Keeffe: A Life*. New York: Harper and Row, 1989.

Turner, Elizabeth Hutton. *Georgia O'Keeffe: The Poetry of Things*. New Haven: Yale University Press, 1999.

Art and Landscape

Alinder, Mary Street and Andrea Gray Stillman, eds. *Ansel Adams: Letters and Images, 1916–1984*. Boston: Little Brown, 1988.

Kant, Immanuel, "The Sense of the Beautiful and Sublime," 1764, in Friedrich, Carl J. (ed.), *The Philosophy of Kant: Immanuel Kant's Moral and Political Writings*. Modern Library, New York, 1949.

Lane, Belden C. *Landscapes of the Sacred: Geography and Narrative in American Spirituality*. Expanded ed. Baltimore, MD: Johns Hopkins University Press, 2002.

———. *The Solace of Fierce Landscapes: Exploring Desert and Mountain Spirituality*. New York: Oxford University Press, 1998.

Rodriguez, Richard. "The God of the Desert," *Harper's Magazine*, January 2008, 35–46.